T0313831

Floating-Rate Securities

Frank J. Fabozzi, Ph.D., CFA

Steven V. Mann, Ph.D.

Published by Frank J. Fabozzi Associates

FJF

To my wife Donna and my children,
Francesco, Patricia, and Karly

SVM

To my wife Mary and our daughters,
Meredith and Morgan

Acknowledgments

We appreciate the efforts of Andrew J. Kalotay and Michael Dorigan of Andrew J. Kalotay Associates and George O. Williams of Lehman Brothers for helping us write Chapter 4, "Valuing Floaters with Embedded Options." The following individuals offered us various forms of assistance: Joe Camp (Fleet Mortgage), Arthur Chu (Lehman Brothers), Laurie Goodman (PaineWebber), Robin Grieves (HSBC Securities), Satish Mansukhani (Bear, Stearns), Tim Ryan (Fidelity Investments), and Don Solberg (Freddie Mac).

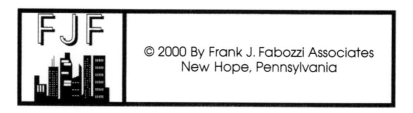

© 2000 By Frank J. Fabozzi Associates
New Hope, Pennsylvania

This publication is designed to provide accurate and authoritative information in regard to the subject matter covered. It is sold with the understanding that the publisher is not engaged in rendering legal, accounting, or other professional services.

ISBN: 1-883249-65-1

Table of Contents

About the Authors

Frank J. Fabozzi is editor of the *Journal of Portfolio Management* and an Adjunct Professor of Finance at Yale University's School of Management. He is a Chartered Financial Analyst and Certified Public Accountant. Dr. Fabozzi is on the board of directors of the Guardian Life family of funds and the BlackRock complex of funds. He earned a doctorate in economics from the City University of New York in 1972 and in 1994 received an honorary doctorate of Humane Letters from Nova Southeastern University. Dr. Fabozzi is a Fellow of the International Center for Finance at Yale University.

Steven V. Mann is an Associate Professor of Finance at the Darla Moore School of Business, University of South Carolina. He earned a doctorate in finance from the University of Nebraska in 1987. His research interests are in the area of investments, particularly fixed-income securities and derivatives. He has published over 35 articles in finance journals and books. Dr. Mann is an accomplished teacher, winning 16 awards for excellence in teaching. He is a consultant to investment/commercial banks and has conducted more than 60 training programs for financial institutions throughout the United States.

Chapter 1

Features and Investment Characteristics of Floaters

T he term "floating-rate security" covers several different types of securities with one common feature: the interest rate will vary over the life of the instrument. The rate may be based on some market or constructed interest rate, a non-interest rate financial benchmark or price, or it can be determined at the issuer's discretion. Typically, floating-rate securities have coupons based on a short-term money market rate or index that reset more than once a year, such as weekly, monthly, quarterly or semiannually. Usually the term "adjustable-rate" or "variable-rate" security refers to those issues with coupons based mostly on a longer-term interest rate or index and reset not more than annually. In this book we will refer to both floating-rate securities and adjustable-rate securities as floating-rate securities or simply *floaters*.

Typically the opening chapter of a book dedicated to a particular investment product begins by extolling the virtues of the product. That is not necessary in the case of floaters. Floating-rate securities are the investment of choice for financial institutions or other entities whose funding costs are based on a short-term floating rate. Depository institutions are the best examples. Other entities include money managers whose strategy is to create leverage by borrowing short-term via the repurchase (repo) market. Other entities invest in floaters as a substitute for money market instruments in order to reduce the transaction costs associated with rolling over a maturing investment. Money market funds are examples

Despite the key role of floating-rate securities in the strategies of institutional investors, much of the focus in the fixed income area has been on fixed-rate securities.[1] The purpose of this book is to provide comprehensive coverage of floating-rate securities. Our coverage includes the following:

- features of floaters (including mortgage-backed and asset-backed products) and their investment characteristics
- models for valuing floaters (both simple floaters and floaters with embedded options)
- measures of relative value for floaters (that is, spread for life, adjusted simple margin, adjusted total margin, discount margin, and option-adjusted spread) and the limitations of these measures

---

[1] While there have been a good number of articles on the subject of floating-rate securities, the only book devoted to the topic appeared in 1986, Frank J. Fabozzi (ed.), *Floating Rate Instruments* (Probus Publishing, Chicago, IL, 1986).

• measures to quantify the exposure of a floater to changes in interest rates (i.e., effective duration, spread duration, and index duration)

In this chapter, we will discuss the features of floaters and their investment characteristics. We will defer discussion of floater products in the mortgage-backed securities and asset-backed securities markets until Chapters 7, 8, and 9 because of the nuances associated with these products. We then discuss several popular strategies employing floaters. At the end of this chapter, we provide an overview of the book.

GENERAL FEATURES OF FLOATERS

At one time it was fairly simple to describe the structure of a floater. The coupon rate was specified in terms of a simple coupon formula and there was typically a cap, and possibly a floor. In today's capital market there is a wide range of floating-rate structures. These structures have been created for issuers by financial engineers using certain derivative instruments (typically, swaps and options) combined with medium-term notes. The resulting floaters are referred to as *structured notes*. Also, financial engineers have created floaters in the mortgage-backed securities and asset-backed securities markets by slicing up cash flows from a pool of loans or receivables. Not surprisingly, floaters are created from a pool of loans or receivables that pay a floating rate. What is surprising is how financial engineers have created (without the use of derivatives) floaters when the underlying loans pay a fixed rate.

In this section we will describe the general features of floaters: the various coupon structures, caps and floors, principal repayment features, and early redemption features.

Coupon Structures

A floater is an instrument whose coupon rate is reset at designated dates based on the value of some reference rate. The coupon rate can be determined by a coupon formula, by a schedule, or at the discretion of the issuer.

Coupon Formula

The typical formula that expresses the coupon rate in terms of the reference rate is:

Reference rate + Quoted margin

The *quoted margin* is the adjustment that the issuer agrees to make to the reference rate. For example, suppose that the reference rate is the 1-month London interbank offered rate (LIBOR) and that the quoted margin is 100 basis points. Then the coupon formula is:

1-month LIBOR + 100 basis points

So, if 1-month LIBOR on the coupon reset date is 5%, the coupon rate is reset for that period at 6% (5% plus 100 basis points).

The quoted margin need not be a positive value. The quoted margin could be subtracted from the reference rate. For example, the reference rate could be the yield on a 5-year Treasury security and the coupon rate could reset every six months based on the following coupon formula:

5-year Treasury yield − 90 basis points

The quoted margin is −90 basis points. So, if the 5-year Treasury yield is 7% on the coupon reset date, the coupon rate is 6.1% (7% minus 90 basis points).

Mismatched Floaters There is no requirement that the frequency at which the coupon is reset be equal to the frequency of the coupon payment. For example, consider the Wells Fargo & Company's Floating Rate Subordinated Capital Notes that matured in August 1, 1996.[2] The coupon rate for this floater reset weekly at $\frac{1}{16}$ of 1% over 3-month LIBOR and payable quarterly. That is, the coupon rate reset a number of times during the period based on the reference rate applicable to the whole period. The reference rate was based on 3-month LIBOR, not 1-week LIBOR. Floaters with this characteristic are called *mismatched floaters*.[3]

Inverse Floaters Typically, the coupon formula on floaters is such that the coupon rate increases when the reference rate increases, and decreases when the reference rate decreases. There are issues whose coupon rate moves in the opposite direction from the change in the reference rate. Such issues are called *inverse floaters* or *reverse floaters*.[4]

In the agency, corporate, and municipal markets inverse floaters are created as structured notes. Inverse floaters in the mortgage-backed securities market are common and are created without the use of derivatives, as we will see in Chapter 8.

---

[2] Another example is the floater issued by Republic New York Corp. due in December 2002 that delivered coupon payments semiannually with a coupon formula equal to the 7-year swap (i.e., LIBOR) rate minus 43 basis points. The entire issue was called in March 1996.

[3] Mismatched Eurodollar floating-rate notes were first issued in 1984 at a time when the yield curve was steep in the 1-month to 6-month portion of the yield curve. They provided an opportunity for investors to enhance return by buying mismatched floaters with funds borrowed at the 1-month rate and earning the higher coupon rate offered on the basis of the 6-month rate determined monthly. This is in fact what occurred in the first quarter of 1985, which explains why the issuance of mismatched Eurodollar floating-rate notes exceeded that of other Eurodollar floating-rate notes in that period. Recognizing that the risk investors face with such a strategy is that the yield curve may become inverted in the short-term sector, issuers included protection for investors by having the coupon rate reset at the maximum of a short-term and long-term money market rate.

[4] These issues were also referred to as *yield curve notes*. For example, the General Motors Acceptance Corporation's Yield Curve Notes that were due April 15, 1993 were based on 15.25% minus 6-month LIBOR.

The coupon formula for an inverse floater is:

$K - L \times$ (Reference rate)

When L is greater than 1, the security is referred to as a *leveraged inverse floater.* For example, suppose that for a particular inverse floater K is 12% and L is 1. Then the coupon reset formula would be:

12% – Reference rate

Suppose that the reference rate is 1-month LIBOR, then the coupon formula would be

12% – 1-month LIBOR

If in some month 1-month LIBOR at the coupon reset date is 5%, the coupon rate for the period is 7%. If in the next month 1-month LIBOR declines to 4.5%, the coupon rate increases to 7.5%.

Notice that if 1-month LIBOR exceeded 12%, then the coupon formula would produce a negative coupon rate. To prevent this, there is a floor imposed on the coupon rate. Typically, the floor is zero. There is a cap on the inverse floater. This occurs if 1-month LIBOR is zero. In that unlikely event, the maximum coupon rate is 12% for our hypothetical inverse floater. In general, it will be the value of K in the coupon formula for an inverse floater.

Suppose instead that the coupon formula for an inverse floater whose reference rate is 1-month LIBOR is as follows:

28% – 3 × (1-month LIBOR)

If 1-month LIBOR at a reset date is 5%, then the coupon rate for that month is 13%. If in the next month 1-month LIBOR declines to 4%, the coupon rate increases to 16%. Thus, a decline in 1-month LIBOR of 100 basis points increases the coupon rate by 300 basis points. This is because the value for L in the coupon reset formula is 3. Assuming neither the cap nor the floor is reached, for each one basis point change in 1-month LIBOR the coupon rate changes by 3 basis points.

As an example, consider an inverse floater issued by the Federal Home Loan Bank in April 1999. This issue matures in April 2002 and delivers quarterly payments according to the following formula:

18% – 2.5 × (3-month LIBOR)

This inverse floater has a floor of 3% and a cap of 15.5%. Beginning July 29, 1999, this issue is callable at par with five business days notice.

Deleveraged Floaters The coupon rate for a deleveraged floater is computed as a fraction of the reference rate plus a fixed percentage. For example, Banker's

Trust issued such a floater in April 1992 that matures in March 2003. This issue delivers quarterly coupon payments according to the following formula: 2.65% + 0.40 × (10-year Constant Maturity Treasury rate) with a floor of 6%.

Dual-Indexed Floaters The coupon rate for a dual-indexed floater is typically a fixed percentage plus the difference between two reference rates. For example, the Federal Home Loan Bank System issued a floater in July 1993 (matured in July 1996) whose coupon rate was the difference between the 10-year Constant Maturity Treasury rate and 3-month LIBOR plus 160 basis points. This issue reset and paid quarterly.

Range Notes A special type of floater is a *range note*. For this instrument, the coupon rate is equal to the reference rate as long as the reference rate is within a certain range at the reset date. If the reference rate is outside of the range, the coupon rate is zero for that period. The range note is a structured note.

For example, a 3-year range note might specify that the reference rate is 1-year LIBOR and that the coupon rate resets every year. The coupon rate for the year will be 1-year LIBOR as long as 1-year LIBOR at the coupon reset date falls within the range as specified below:

	Year 1	Year 2	Year 3
Lower limit of range	4.5%	5.25%	6.00%
Upper limit of range	5.5%	6.75%	7.50%

If 1-year LIBOR is outside of the range, the coupon rate is zero. For example, if in Year 1 1-year LIBOR is 5% at the coupon reset date, the coupon rate for the year is 5%. However, if 1-year LIBOR is 6%, the coupon rate for the year is zero since 1-year LIBOR is greater than the upper limit for Year 1 of 5.5%.

Consider a range note issued by Sallie Mae in August 1996 that matures in August 2003. This issue makes coupon payments quarterly. The investor earns 3-month LIBOR plus 155 basis points for every day during the quarter that 3-month LIBOR is between 3% and 9%. Interest will accrue at 0% for each day that 3-month LIBOR is outside this range. As a result, this range note has a floor of 0%.

Ratchet Bonds In 1998 a new adjustable-rate structure was brought to market by the Tennessee Valley Authority. This structure, referred to as a *ratchet bond*, has a coupon rate that adjusts periodically at a fixed spread over a non-money market reference rate such as the 10-year constant maturity Treasury. However, it can only adjust downward based on a coupon formula. Once the coupon rate is adjusted down, it cannot be readjusted up if the reference rate increases. Basically, a ratchet bond is designed to replicate the cash flow pattern generated by a series of conventional callable bonds.[5]

Floaters with a Changing Quoted Margin

Some issues provide for a change in the quoted margin at certain intervals over a floater's life. These issues are often referred to as *stepped spread floaters* because the quoted margin could either step to a higher or lower level over the security's life. For example, consider Standard Chartered Bank's floater that matures in December 2006. From issuance until December 2001, the coupon formula is 3-month LIBOR plus 40 basis points. From December 2001 until maturity, the quoted margin "steps up" to 90 basis points.

Some issues are on an "either or" basis. One such example is Barclays-American Corporation Floating Rate Subordinated Notes that were due November 1, 1990. Interest was payable quarterly and calculated monthly at the higher of (1) the prime rate minus 125 basis points or (2) the 30-day commercial paper rate plus 25 basis points. Other issues have their coupon rates determined through a Dutch auction procedure or remarketing process, with the applicable interest rate the one at which all sell orders and all buy orders are satisfied.

Reset Margin Determined at Issuer Discretion

There are floaters which require that the issuer reset the coupon rate so that the issue will trade at a predetermined price (typically above par). These issues are called *extendible reset bonds*. The coupon rate at the reset date may be the average of rates suggested by two investment banking firms. The new rate will then reflect: (1) the level of interest rates at the reset date, and (2) the margin required by market at the reset date. Notice the difference between an extendible reset bond and a typical floater that resets based on a coupon formula. For the latter, the coupon rate resets based on a known margin over some reference rate (i.e., the quoted margin). In contrast, the coupon rate on an extendible reset issue is reset based on the margin required by the market at the reset date as determined by the issuer or suggested by several investment banking firms.

For example, consider the Primerica Corporation's Extendible Notes that were due August 1, 1996. This issue was scheduled for an interest rate change on August 1, 1987. The coupon rate was 13.25%, but as market rates were considerably lower, the issuer set the rate from August 1, 1987 through July 31, 1992 at 8.40%, about 105% of the then 5-year constant maturity Treasury of 8.00%. The minimum percentage under the indenture was 102.5%. Apparently this rate was not satisfactory to the holders and many notes were either put back to the issuer during the first two weeks of July 1987 or the holders threatened to do so. In any event, several days prior to the commencement of the new rate and interest period a notice appeared in the newspaper of record announcing that the company "... is exercising its option under the terms of the Extendible Notes due 1996 to establish an interest rate higher than the rate previously announced..." The rate was increased to 8.875%, equal to 110.9% of the constant maturity Treasury.

---

[5] For a discussion of the motivation of the issuance of ratchet bonds by issuers and the benefits to investors, see Andrew Kalotay and Leslie Abreo, "Ratchet Bonds: Maximum Refunding Efficiency at Minimum Transaction Cost," *Journal of Applied Corporate Finance* (Spring 1999), pp. 40-47. The TVA ratchet bond is described in the article.

Non-Interest Rate Indexes

While the reference rate for most floaters is an interest rate or an interest rate index, a wide variety of reference rates appear in coupon formulas. This is particularly true for structured notes. The coupon for a floater could be indexed to movements in foreign exchange rates, the price of a commodity (e.g., crude oil), movements in an equity index (e.g., the S&P 500), or movements in a bond index (e.g., the Merrill Lynch Corporate Bond Index). In fact, through financial engineering, issuers have been able to structure floaters with almost any reference rate. As an example, Merrill Lynch issued in April 1983 Stock Market Annual Reset Term Notes which mature in December 1999. These notes pay interest semiannually. The formula for the coupon rate is 0.65 multiplied by the annual return of the S&P MidCap 400 during the calendar year. These notes have a floor of 3% and a cap of 10%.

In several countries, there are government bonds whose coupon formula is tied to an inflation index. The U.S. Treasury in January 1997 began auctioning 10-year Treasury notes whose semiannual coupon interest depends on the rate of inflation as measured by the Consumer Price Index for All Urban Consumers (i.e., CPI-U). In the market, these issues are referred to as *Treasury Inflation-Protection Securities* (TIPS). The first such issue matures on January 15, 2007 and carries a coupon rate of 3.375%. The initial value of the CPI-U was 158.43548. On January 1, 1998, the CPI-U was 161.55484. Accordingly, the semiannual coupon payment (per $100 of par value) was computed as follows:

$$\$1.72027 = (0.03375/2) \times (161.55484/158.43548) \times \$100$$

For a conventional 10-year U.S. Treasury note with a fixed coupon rate the semiannual coupon payment would have been $1.68875 (per $100 of par value).

In 1997 corporations and agencies in the United States began issuing inflation-linked (or inflation-indexed) bonds. For example, in February 1997, J.P. Morgan & Company issued a 15-year bond that pays the CPI plus 400 basis points & Co. In the same month, the Federal Home Loan Bank issued a 5-year bond with a coupon rate equal to the CPI plus 315 basis point and a 10-year bond with a coupon rate equal to the CPI plus 337 basis points.[6]

Caps and Floors

A floater may have a restriction on the maximum coupon rate that will be paid at any reset date. The maximum coupon rate is called a *cap*.[7] For example, suppose for our hypothetical floater whose coupon formula is 1-month LIBOR plus 100

---

[6] For examples of these issues see Andrew Rosen, Michael Schumacher, and John Cassaudoumecq, "Corporate and Agency Inflation-Linked Securities," Chapter 18 in John Brynjolfsson and Frank J. Fabozzi (eds.), *Handbook of Inflation Indexed Bonds* (New Hope, PA: Frank J. Fabozzi Associates, 1999).

[7] Many issues state that the maximum rate is 25% due to New York State's usury law but holders of $2.5 million or more of an issue are exempt from this.

basis points, there is a cap of 11%. If 1-month LIBOR is 10.5% at a coupon reset date, then the coupon formula would give a value of 11.5%. However, the cap restricts the coupon rate to 11%. Thus, for our hypothetical security, once 1-month LIBOR exceeds 10%, the coupon rate is capped at 11%.

Because a cap restricts the coupon rate from increasing, a cap is an unattractive feature for the investor. In contrast, there could be a minimum coupon rate specified for a floater. The minimum coupon rate is called a *floor*. If the coupon formula produces a coupon rate that is below the floor, the floor is paid instead. Thus, a floor is an attractive feature for the investor. For example, First Chicago (now 1st Chicago NBD Corp.) issued a floored floating-rate note in July 1993 that matures in July 2003. This issue delivers quarterly coupon payments and the coupon formula is 3-month LIBOR + 12.5 basis points with a minimum coupon rate of 4.25%.

Some issues have declining floors. For example, for a Citicorp floater issue that was due September 1, 1998, the minimum rate was 7.50% through August 31, 1983, then 7.00% through August 31, 1988, and then 6.50% to maturity.

A floater can have both a cap and floor. This feature is referred to as a *collar*. For example, the Economic Development Corporation issued a collared floater in February 1993 that makes semiannual coupon payments and matures in February 2003. The coupon formula is 6-month LIBOR with a minimum coupon rate of 5% and a maximum coupon rate of 8%. There are some issues that grant the issuer the right to convert the floater into a fixed coupon rate at some time. There are also some issues referred to as *drop-lock bonds*, which automatically change the floating coupon rate into a fixed coupon rate under certain circumstances.

Principal Repayment Features

A floater will either have a stated maturity date, or it may be a *perpetual*, also called *undated*, issue (i.e., it has no stated maturity date).[8] For floaters that do mature, the issuer agrees to repay the principal by the stated maturity date. The issuer can agree to repay the entire amount borrowed in one lump sum payment at the maturity date.

Amortizing Securities Fixed-income securities backed by pools of loans (mortgage-backed securities and asset-backed securities) often have a schedule of principal repayments. Such securities are said to be *amortizing securities*. For many loans, the payments are structured so that when the last loan payment is made, the entire amount owed is fully paid off. We discuss the features of these securities in Chapter 7, 8, and 9.

Indexed Amortizing Notes Thus far in our description of floaters, we have explained how the coupon rate depends on the reference rate. There are notes where the coupon rate is fixed but the principal repayments are made prior to the

---

[8] For example, in April 1997, Sakura Capital Funding issued a perpetual floating-rate note with a coupon formula of 3-month LIBOR plus 90 basis points. The issue is callable in September 2002. However, if the issuer does not call the issue, the coupon rate steps up to 240 basis points over 3-month LIBOR.

stated maturity date based on the prevailing value for the reference rate. The principal payments are structured to accelerate when the reference rate is low. These structures are referred to as *indexed amortizing notes*. So, technically, while these instruments are not floaters in the sense that their coupon rate changes with a reference rate, they can be viewed as "principal floaters" in that the principal repayment floats with a reference rate.

Early Redemption Features

Early redemption features grant the issuer and/or the investor an option to retire all or a portion of the outstanding principal prior to the stated maturity date. Below we describe these features.

Call and Prepayment Provisions

As with fixed-rate issues, a floater may be callable. The call option gives the issuer of the floater the right to retire the issue prior to the stated maturity date. The advantage of the call option to the issuer is that at some time in the future either (1) the general level of interest rates may fall so that the issuer can call the issue and replace it with a fixed-rate issue or (2) the required margin decreases so that the issuer can call the issue and replace it with a floater with a lower quoted margin. This right is a disadvantage to the investor in floaters since proceeds received must be reinvested at a lower interest rate or a lower margin. As a result, an issuer who wants to include this right as part of a floater offering must compensate investors by offering a higher quoted margin.

Unlike conventional fixed-rate issues, many have call features permit the issuer to redeem the bonds only on specific dates, often the date on which the holder may put the bond. Others have fairly standard call features. Only a few of the issues have sinking funds requiring the periodic retirement of a portion of the issue.

For amortizing securities that are backed by loans and have a schedule of principal repayments, individual borrowers typically have the option to pay off all or part of their loan prior to the scheduled date. Any principal repayment prior to the scheduled date is called a *prepayment*. The right of borrowers to prepay is called the *prepayment option*. Basically, the prepayment option is the same as a call option. However, unlike a call option, there is not a call price that depends on when the borrower pays off the issue. Typically, the price at which a loan is prepaid is at par value. We will discuss this feature of floaters when we cover mortgage-backed and asset-backed securities.

Put Provision

An issue with a *put provision* included in the indenture grants the security holder the right to sell the issue back to the issuer at a specified price on designated dates. The specified price is called the *put price*. The put feature in floaters varies. Some issues permit the holder to require the issuer to redeem the issue on any interest payment date. Others allow the put to be exercised only when the coupon is reset. In cases of extendible notes where the new terms, including the coupon and the interest period are reset only every few years, the put may be exercised only on those dates. The time required for prior notification to the issuer or its agent varies from as little as four days to as much as a couple of months.

The advantage of the put provision to the holder of the floater is that if after the issue date the margin required by the market for the issue to trade at par rises above the issue's quoted margin, the investor can force the issuer to redeem the floater at the put price and then reinvest the proceeds in a floater with a higher quoted margin.

INVESTMENT CHARACTERISTICS OF FLOATERS

Floaters expose investors to the same types of risk as faced by investors in fixed-rate securities. There is credit risk, interest rate risk, call risk, and liquidity risk. Credit risk is gauged by the rating assigned by the nationally recognized statistical rating organizations (Moody's Investors Service, Standard & Poor's Corporation, Fitch IBCA, and Duff & Phelps Credit Rating Company). There are unique credit risk issues that are considered by rating companies in evaluating floaters in the mortgage-backed and asset-backed securities markets and these credit risks are discussed in Chapters 8 and 9. One such risk for asset-backed securities is the difference between the reference rate for the underlying pool of loans or receivables and the reference rate for the floater issued.

With the new structures introduced into the floater market, investors must be concerned with liquidity risk. A particular structured note may have such a unique structure — customized for a particular investor — that there is very limited liquidity. However, often such floaters are purchased by investors with the intent of holding them to maturity. Nevertheless, mark-to-market investors who plan to hold a structured note to maturity must be concerned with obtaining pricing marks and therefore are concerned with liquidity. Moreover, investors who finance such floaters in the repo market are concerned with the impact of liquidity on the prices used by the financing dealer to mark a repoed floater to market.

When investing in a security, a key investment characteristic of a security is how its price might change over time. Even if an investor plans to hold the security until the maturity date, adverse price changes for the security will adversely affect the security's return performance. Moreover, for securities financed via repo agreements, adverse price changes may trigger margin requirements calling for the investor to provide additional cash or collateral. Consequently, it is important to understand the price volatility characteristics of floaters.

Price Volatility

The change in the price of a fixed-rate security when market rates change is due to the fact that the security's coupon rate differs from the prevailing market rate.

So, an investor in a 10-year 7% coupon bond purchased at par, for example, will find that the price of this bond will decline below par value if the market requires a yield greater than 7%. By contrast, for a floater, the coupon is reset periodically, reducing a floater's price sensitivity to changes in rates. For this reason, floaters are said to more "defensive" securities. However, this does not mean that a floater's price will not change.

A floater's price will change depending on the following factors:

1. time remaining to the next coupon reset date
2. whether or not the market's required margin changes
3. whether the cap or floor is reached

We will describe how to quantify these factors in later chapters. For now, we provide a description of the impact of each of these factors.

Time Remaining to the Next Coupon Reset Date

The longer the time to the next coupon reset date, the greater a floater's potential price fluctuation. Conversely, the less time to the next coupon reset date, the smaller the floater's potential price fluctuation.

To understand why, consider a floater with five years remaining to maturity whose coupon formula is the 1-year Treasury bill rate plus 50 basis points and the coupon is reset today when the 1-year Treasury bill rate is 5.5%. The coupon rate will then be set at 6% for the year. One month from now, the investor in this floater would effectively own an 11-month instrument with a 6% coupon. Suppose that at that time, the market wants a 6.2% yield on comparable issues with 11 months remaining to maturity. Then, our floater would be offering a below market rate (6% versus 6.2%). The floater's price must decline below par to compensate for the sub-market yield. Similarly, if the yield that the market requires on a comparable instrument with a maturity of 11 months is less than 6%, the price of a floater will trade above par. For a floater in which the cap is not reached and for which the market does not demand a margin different from the quoted margin, a floater that resets daily will trade at par value.

Whether or Not the Market's Required Margin Changes

At the initial offering of a floater, the issuer will set the quoted margin based on market conditions so that the security will trade near par. If after the initial offering the market requires a higher margin, the floater's price will decline to reflect the higher spread. We shall refer to the margin that is demanded by the market as the *required margin*. So, for example, consider a floater whose coupon formula is 1-month LIBOR plus 40 basis points. If market conditions change such that the required margin increases to 50 basis points, this floater would be offering a below market quoted margin. As a result, the floater's price will decline below par value. The price can trade above par value if the required margin is less than the quoted margin — less than 40 basis points in our example.

The required margin for a specific issue depends on: (1) margin available in competitive funding markets, (2) the credit quality of the issue, (3) the presence of the embedded call or put options, and (4) the liquidity of the issue. In the case of floaters, an alternative funding source is a syndicated loan. Consequently, the required margin will be affected by margins available in the syndicated loan market.

The portion of the required margin attributable to credit quality is referred to as the *credit spread*. The risk that there will be an increase in the credit spread required by the market is called *credit spread risk*. The concern for credit spread risk applies not only to an individual issue, but to a sector and economy as a whole. For example, the credit spread of an individual issuer may change not due to that issuer but to the sector or the economy as a whole.

A portion of the required margin will reflect the call risk associated with the floater. Because the call feature is a disadvantage to the investor, the greater the call risk, the higher the quoted margin at issuance. After issuance, depending on how rates and margins change in the market, the perceived call risk and the margin attributable to this risk will change accordingly. In contrast to call risk due to the presence of the call provision, a put provision is an advantage to the investor. If a floater is putable at par, all other factors constant, its price should trade at par near the put date.

Finally, a portion of the quoted margin at issuance will reflect the perceived liquidity of the issue. The risk that the required margin attributable to liquidity will increase due to market participants' perception of a deterioration in the issue's liquidity is called *liquidity risk*. Investors in new and innovative floater products are particularly concerned with liquidity risk.

Whether the Cap or Floor Is Reached

For a floater with a cap, once the coupon rate as specified by the coupon formula rises above the cap, the floater then offers a below market coupon rate, and its price will decline below par. The floater will trade more and more like a fixed-rate security the further the capped rate is below the prevailing market rate. This risk that the value of the floater will decline because the cap is reached is referred to as *cap risk*.

On the other side of the coin, if the floater has a floor, once the floor is reached, all other factors constant, the floater will trade at par value or at a premium to par if the coupon rate is above the prevailing rate for comparable issues.

Duration of Floaters

We have just described how a floater's price will react to a change in the required margin, holding all other factors constant. The measure used by managers to quantify the sensitivity of the price of any security to changes in interest rates is called *duration*. Basically, the duration of a security is the approximate percentage change in its price for a 100 basis point change in rates. We will explain how to compute the duration of a security, specifically the effective duration, when we discuss how to value floaters in Chapter 4.

Two measures have been developed to estimate the sensitivity of a floater to each component of the coupon formula. *Index duration* is a measure of the price sensitivity of a floater to changes in the reference rate holding the quoted margin constant. *Spread duration* measures a floater's price sensitivity to a change in the "spread" assuming that the reference rate is unchanged. Since there are many measures of spread for a floater that we will describe in Chapter 5, we will discuss spread duration in that chapter.

PORTFOLIO STRATEGIES

Now that we know the features of floaters and their investment characteristics, let's look at some portfolio strategies using these instruments. Our discussion is not intended to be an exhaustive list of applications, but just what we believe the key strategies are and what the associated risks are.

Basic Asset/Liability Management Strategies

Financial institutions can borrow funds on a fixed-rate or floating-rate basis. The investment objective is to earn a spread over the cost of funding the portfolio. That spread has to be adequate to compensate for the risks associated with the strategy and to provide a fair to investors. Typically, the strategy involves leveraging (i.e., borrowing funds) in order to generate an adequate return.

The most obvious use of floaters is in strategies for depository institutions. These institutions typically borrow short-term and can invest the funds raised in a maturity of any length with a fixed or floating rate. The objective is to lock in a spread over the short-term funding costs. The risk of investing in a long-term fixed-rate security is that at the time of acquisition even though the spread above the funding cost is positive, a rise in market interest rates will reduce the spread. This is because the institution will have to pay a higher funding cost in the future. If rates rise enough, the spread can become negative.

The U.S. savings and loan association debacle is the classic example of the problem with a "borrowing short and lending long" strategy. Historically, S&Ls borrowed short via deposits and invested those funds in long-term fixed-rate residential mortgage loans — being encouraged to do so through government regulation and tax incentives seeking to foster the development of the housing finance market. The strategy worked well when the federal government imposed ceilings on deposit rates and investors had no competitive market alternatives to deposits. In the early 1980s, the federal government abandoned rate ceilings, money market funds were introduced, and historically high rates were reached. The mismatching of the maturity of the assets and liabilities by S&Ls proved a financial disaster.

The use of floaters to better match short-term funding costs does not come without risks. For example, the short-term funding rate is uncapped — unless the depository institution purchases an interest rate cap. However, the floater will typically have a cap. This means that in a rising interest rate environment the spread between assets and liabilities will decline when rates rise above the cap. We mentioned that this risk for an individual floater is called cap risk. We can see that cap risk also applies to an asset/liability strategy that includes capped floaters. Moreover, while we have not discussed mortgage-backed products at this time, we will see that products such as adjustable-rate mortgages include complicated caps that increase cap risk.

Another risk in asset/liability strategies has to do with differences between the reference rate for the floater and the reference rate for funding. For example, if the floater's reference rate is the 6-month Treasury rate plus a quoted margin and the funding cost is 6-month LIBOR plus a quoted margin, then for the first six months, assuming that the issuer does not default, the spread that will be earned is known. However, in subsequent periods the relationship between 6-month LIBOR and the 6-month Treasury rate may change. Thus, the institution does not know what spread will be earned in the future and it is possible for that spread to be inadequate. This risk is referred to as *basis risk*. (The relationships between common reference rates are examined in Chapter 2.) Moreover, it not only how the relationship between these reference rates will change that is important but also how the institution's funding spread (i.e., the spread above 6-month LIBOR in our illustration) will change.

Another risk is the one associated with callable and prepayable floaters. The risk here is that the issue will be called or prepaid when the issuer can refund at a lower required margin to the reference rate. This means that the institution must reinvest the proceeds in another floater that has a smaller margin.

"Risk Arbitrage" Strategies

In the low interest rate environment of the 1990s, some money managers attracted clients by *offering* the potential for extremely high returns relative to prevailing rates while still investing in "safe investments." Basically, these money managers used leverage and certain types of floaters in the mortgage-backed securities market to implement the strategy.

Some money managers and dealers have referred to these strategies as "risk arbitrage strategies." The term "arbitrage" in its purest sense means that there is no risk in a strategy but that the strategy offers the opportunity to earn a positive return without investing any funds. Unfortunately, some money managers and dealers use the term arbitrage in a more cavalier way. Even if there is risk in a strategy, so long as that risk is perceived to be small — small being a quantity defined by the user of the term — the term arbitrage is used. Some market participants will qualify the term by using the adjective "risk" — that is, risk arbitrage. In such a context, arbitrage with no risk is then referred to as "riskless arbitrage."

Let's look at a so-called risk arbitrage strategy that was has been used by some money managers. Suppose that a manager buys an adjustable-rate mortgage passthrough security backed by Freddie Mae or Fannie Mae, two government sponsored enterprises. (We will describe this product in Chapter 7.) Suppose that the coupon rate is reset monthly based on the following coupon formula:

1-month LIBOR + 80 basis points

with a cap of 9%.

Suppose that the manager can use these securities in a repo transaction in which: (1) a repo margin of 5% is required, (2) the term of the repo is one month, and (3) the repo rate is 1-month LIBOR plus 10 basis points. Also assume that $1 million in funds is provided by clients. With the $1 million, this manager can purchase $20 million in par value of these securities since only $1 million of equity is required (i.e., 5% of $20 million). The amount borrowed would be $19 million. Thus, the manager realizes a spread of 70 basis points on the $19 million borrowed since LIBOR plus 80 basis points is earned in interest each month (coupon rate) and LIBOR plus 10 basis point is paid each month (repo rate).

This strategy is sometimes referred to as an *arbitrage*. However, it has two risks. First, the price of the security may decline because the required margin for the floater may widen to more than 80 basis points. Thus, there is price risk if the floaters that have been financed must be sold prior to maturity. Second, there is cap risk because the cost of funds may exceed the cap. For example, if 1-month LIBOR is 9.9% in some month, the coupon rate on the floater would be capped at 9%. However, the cost of funds would be 10% (1-month LIBOR plus 10 basis points), the borrowing cost not being capped. Thus, the dollar return and percent return for the month would be:

9% coupon on $20 million par value	$1,800,000
10% borrowing cost on $19 million	$1,900,000
Dollar return for month	–$100,000
Return on equity for month	–10%

In our illustration, we assumed that the reference rate for the floater and the funding cost are the same. Some managers when implementing this strategy were funded at LIBOR but purchased certain types of mortgage-backed securities whose reference rate was the Eleventh District Cost of Funds Index, an index we discuss in the next chapter. The mismatch of the reference rate then introduces basis risk into the strategy.

Moreover, there were other problems associated with such strategies. Some managers seeking to maximize return, fully invested client proceeds without consideration of the possibility that there would be a margin call on the repo agreement should the floater's price decline. When prices did decline, cash could not be obtained to satisfy a margin call, resulting in the repoed floaters being sold by the dealer.

Consequently, these risk arbitrage strategies were far from risk free, as investors subsequently discovered.

Betting on Changes in the Required Margin

Earlier we explained why the a floater's required margin may change. There are investors who bet on changes in the required margin for individual issues or sectors. For example, if the investor believes that a required margin will narrow for a particular issue, he or she can purchase the issue (typically on a leveraged basis). If the investor's expectations are realized such that the required margin does narrow, then there will be an enhanced return. The bet may not involve just one issue. Some investors bet on the changes in the relative required margins between two issues.

Investors pursuing a strategy based on changes in the required margin will rely on statistical analysis of historical margins. In the case of betting on the change in the required margin for a single issue or sector, credit analysis is performed to determine if in the investor's view the market is properly assessing the issue's credit risk.

Creating an Enhanced Synthetic Fixed-Rate Spread

There are some managers in the fixed-rate market who have sought to enhance returns via the purchase of a floater and converting the floater's cash flows into a fixed-rate security via the interest rate swap market. (We will discuss the swap market in Chapter 6.) For example, suppose that an investor can purchase a 5-year 6% coupon bond at par or a floater. If the floater can be purchased and 5-year interest rate swap terms are such that the manager can swap the cash flows from the floater to create an effective 5-year 6.2% fixed-rate bond at par value, then the manager would find it beneficial — assuming he or she is entitled to use swaps — to create a synthetic fixed-rate security.

Today, however, the interest rate swap market has done a great job of integrating the fixed-rate and floating-rate markets. It is doubtful whether such opportunities to enhance return exist. When there is some incremental spread on a synthetic fixed-rate security, it is usually due to the presence of another risk that is inherent in the transaction. For example, there is counterparty risk in a swap. Also, the floater's cash flows may not match the floating-rate payments precisely due to cap risk, call risk, or prepayment risk.

OVERVIEW OF BOOK

Now let's look at what is ahead in this book. In Chapter 2, the various reference rates used for floaters are described. In addition, economic and empirical relationships between the reference rates are provided.

In Chapters 3 and 4 we provide a framework for the valuation of floaters. The valuation of floaters without embedded options is provided in Chapter 3. In Chapter 4 we describe a framework for valuing floaters with embedded options. The valuation model described is the arbitrage-free binomial model. There we will see how to value range notes, capped floaters, and capped callable floaters.

We will also show how to value indexed amortizing notes. At the end of Chapter 4, we will see how to compute the effective duration of a floater.

Most market participants use some "spread" measure to assess the relative value of a floater. These measures include spread for life, adjusted simple margin, adjusted total margin, discount margin, and option-adjusted spread. In Chapter 5 we explain and illustrate these measures, highlighting their limitations. We also define spread duration and explain how it is computed. In Chapter 6, we show how the interest rate swap market can be used to assess the relative value of a floater.

In Chapters 7, 8, and 9 we look at floaters available in the mortgage-backed and asset-backed securities market. Chapter 7 focuses on adjustable-rate mortgage passthrough securities. Floaters available in the CMO market are the subject of Chapter 8 and floaters in the asset-backed securities market are covered in Chapter 9. The analysis of mortgage-backed and asset-backed floaters is provided in Chapter 10 where the Monte Carlo simulation model is introduced.

Finally, Chapter 11 discusses inverse floaters, how to value them, and their price volatility characteristics.

Chapter 2

The Choice of a Floater's Reference Rate

The relationships among the reference rates that determine a floater's coupon payment are constantly changing. For example, the spread between 3-month LIBOR and 3-month Treasury is positive but the size of the spread exhibits considerable variability. This is not surprising since LIBOR is a risky rate and bills rates are considered to be risk-free. One would suspect the yield differential for bearing this additional risk to be time-varying. Moreover, any yield differential due to differences in liquidity would also vary with market conditions. Therefore, the reference rate contained in a floater's coupon formula will be an essential determinant of how it performs over time.

To illustrate this relationship, suppose in the first week of January 1987, an investor has a choice between two pure floaters (i.e., without embedded options) with a 3-year maturity whose coupon payments are paid/reset quarterly. Floater A's coupon formula is 3-month LIBOR plus 37 basis points. Floater B's coupon formula is the 3-month U.S. Treasury bill rate plus 100 basis points. At the time the spreads for A and B were determined, these two floaters had identical coupons. If the spread remained more or less constant, the two securities should generate approximately the same cash flows over the next three years. Such performance did not materialize. After one year, the difference between the coupon rates was 125 basis points. This dramatic difference in coupons occurred because the October 1987 stock market crash caused spreads between 3-month LIBOR and 3-month bills to widen significantly, reflecting a dramatic increase in investors' risk aversion in the crash's wake.

As illustrated by this example, the choice of reference rate has, quite understandably, a considerable impact on a floater's performance. In fact, some issues give the investor a choice between reference rates. For example, the Student Loan Marketing Association ("Sallie Mae") issued in June 1999 some student loan-backed floating-rate securities (discussed in Chapter 9). In this issuance, the class A-1, A-2, and A-3 notes are broken into two tranches each: A-1T and A-1L, A-2T and A-2L, and A-3T and A-3L The A-1T, A-2T, and A-3T notes are indexed off of the 91-day U.S. Treasury bill rate and reset weekly/pay quarterly. For instance, the coupon formula for A-1T (due in April 2008) is the 3-month Treasury bill rate plus 87 basis points. Correspondingly, the A-1L, A-2L, and A-3L notes are indexed off of 3-month LIBOR and reset/pay quarterly. The coupon formula for A-1L (due in April 2008) is 3-month LIBOR plus 8 basis points. Thus, Sallie Mae issued two sets of floaters backed by the same student loan portfolio (SLM Student Loan Trust 1999-2) whose coupon formulas are based on different reference rates. The relative performance of the T-bill floaters versus the LIBOR floater will depend to a large degree on the relationship between these two rates over time.

Active investors view floaters with different reference rates and different reset periods as a means for betting on the spread between two rates or on the direction of rates. For example, the availability of floaters indexed off LIBOR and Treasury bills rate give investors a vehicle to take a position on spread between these two rates. Moreover, bullish (bearish) investors prefer, all else equal, coupon formulas with less frequent (more frequent) reset periods. For these reasons and others soon to be discussed, the choice of a floater's reference rate is a critical one. This chapter examines the relationships among some common reference rates and how these relationships change over time.

REFERENCE RATES

This section presents a brief description of the most popular reference rates for floaters. As noted, the reference rate is interest rate or index that appears in a floater's coupon formula and is used to determine the coupon payment on each reset date within the boundaries designated by embedded caps and/or floors. The first four reference rates described (LIBOR, Treasury bills yields, prime rate, domestic CD rates) appear in the coupon formulas of a wide variety of floating-rate products. We will also describe the reference rates utilized in more specialized markets, namely mortgage-related floaters and floaters in the municipal market.

If the reference rate is the yield on an interest-bearing security, a critical part of the description is the security's day-count convention. A day-count convention is a rule used by the market to determine how interest accrues on interest-bearing security during the coupon period. A day-count convention specifies how to count the number of days between any two dates and how much interest an investor earns over this period.

LIBOR

The *London interbank offer rate* (LIBOR) is the interest rate which major international banks offer each other on Eurodollar certificates of deposit (CD) with given maturities. The maturities range from overnight to five years. So, references to "3-month LIBOR" indicate the interest rate that major international banks are offering to pay to other such banks on a CD that matures in three months.

Eurodollar CDs pay simple interest at maturity on an "ACT/360 basis." Under an ACT/360 day count, the numerator is the actual number of days between two dates and the denominator is always 360 days. Thus, if an investor holds a security for 50 days during a coupon period and chooses to sell the security, he/she is entitled to 50/360 of the interest payment in accrued interest on the settlement date. The ACT/360 day-count convention is used for most money market instruments in markets worldwide.

During the 1990s, LIBOR has increasingly become the reference rate of choice for floaters. There are several reasons for the dominance. Chief among them, LIBOR is the most important cost of funds for financial institutions. LIBOR rates are available on Bloomberg's money markets page.

In addition to LIBOR, some floaters employ LIBID and LIMEAN as their reference rates. LIBID is simply the *London interbank bid rate*. For example, Manufacturers Hanover Trust Co. issued a Eurodollar floater in March 1985 (that matured in 1997) whose coupon formula was 6-month LIBID flat. LIMEAN is the *London interbank mean rate* (i.e., the average of LIBID and LIBOR). As an example, Banque Indosuez (France) issued a Eurodollar floater in June 1985 (matured in 1997) with a coupon formula of 3-month LIMEAN plus 37.5 basis points and a cap of 13.0625%.

Treasury Bill Rates

U.S. Treasury bills are discount instruments, meaning they bear no interest. An investor purchases the bills at a discount from their face value and they are redeemed for their full face value at maturity. The day-count convention is ACT/360. The U.S Treasury routinely issues bills with 3-month (91 days), 6-month (182 days), and 1-year (364 days) maturities. Treasury bills have two obvious attractions as a reference rate for floaters. One is a huge, highly liquid secondary market and the other is virtually zero credit risk. U.S. Treasury bill rates are available on Bloomberg's Money Markets page.

Prime Rate

While 3-month LIBOR represents an important determinant of the cost of a financial institution's source of funds, the prime rate plus a spread is a rate banks charge on loans. Traditionally, the *prime rate without a spread* was considered to be the best available rate available to corporate customers. Beginning in the early 1980s, a spate of litigation forced banks away from this definition and from prime rate pricing of their loans. Today, there are many prime rates or "base rates" quoted by banks that may or may not be the lowest rates charged on loans. The prime rate that garners most of the attention is the *national prime rate* quoted by money center banks.

The prime rate is an administered rate as opposed to a market determined rate. Prime is available on Bloomberg's Index page in the money market section under "Central Bank and Prime Rates."

Domestic CD Rates

Eurodollar CDs and domestic CDs are two important funding sources for financial institutions such as commercial banks and thrifts. Domestic CDs pay simple interest at maturity on an ACT/360 basis. Not surprisingly, domestic CD rates are common reference rates for floaters just like their Eurodollar counterparts. This information is available from the Federal Reserve Statistical Release H. 15 which is available on Bloomberg Index menu with a ticker symbol NDX.

REFERENCE RATES FOR MORTGAGE-RELATED FLOATERS

Some the most common references for adjustable-rate mortgages (ARMs) or CMO floaters (or inverse floaters) include: (1) the weekly average yield of constant 1-year maturity Treasury (i.e., 1-year CMT); (2) the Eleventh District Cost of Funds; (3) 6-month LIBOR; and (4) the National Monthly Median Cost of Funds Index. We described LIBOR above. Below we describe the other three reference rates.

1-Year Constant Maturity Treasury

At the end of each trading day, primary U.S. Treasury securities dealers report closing prices of the most actively traded bills, notes, and bonds to the Federal Reserve Bank of New York. CMT indexes are computed from yields on these securities. For various maturities, four indexes are computed: (1) daily, (2) weekly (an average of the past week's daily rates), (3) monthly (an average of the past month's daily rates), and (4) annually (an average of the past year's daily rates). The weekly 1-year CMT is a common reference rate for mortgage-related floaters and the index used is the weekly average of actively traded securities with a constant maturity of one year.

The Federal Reserve publishes the 1-year CMT in its weekly statistical H.15 release. This report is released each Monday at approximately 3:30 p.m. (Eastern time) with data from the previous Monday-Friday period. The statistical release H.15 is available on Bloomberg from the Index page with the ticker symbol NDX under Government indices and from Telerate page 7052.

Note that the 1-year CMT is not the yield on the on-the-run 1-year bill. However, the two rates are highly correlated.

Eleventh District Cost of Funds Index

A common reference rate for floating-rate mortgage-backed securities is the Eleventh District Cost of Funds Index. The index, popularly referred to as COFI, is a weighted average of the borrowing costs of member bank institutions of the Federal Home Loan Bank of San Francisco (the Eleventh District). The index is reported monthly, generally with a two month lag. For example, the January index is reported in March.

COFI is not a market rate because member savings institutions most commonly borrow in the form of fixed-rate CDs of varying terms (several days to several years). The interest rates paid are determined at the time of the deposit. As a result, COFI is relatively stable and will typically lag movements in other market interest rates by six to nine months. COFI is available on Telerate page 7058 and on Bloomberg's Index page with the ticker symbol COF 11.

One final point about COFI should be noted. During the 1990s, there has been continued consolidation among the member institutions in the Federal Home Loan Bank's Eleventh District. As a result, a few large institutions now account for most of the liability composition of COFI. Specifically, as of December 1997, seven institutions controlled 85% of the $248.9 billion in average liabilities used to calculate COFI.[1] This increasing concentration will likely impact the future direction of COFI in two ways. First, a change in the liability composition in a large institution will have a measurable impact on the index. Second, an increase in COFI's volatility due to the loss of institution diversification within the index.

National Monthly Median Cost of Funds

Depository institutions insured by the Saving Institutions Insurance Fund (i.e., SAIF, formerly the FSLIC) report their monthly cost of funds data to their regulator, the Office of Thrift Supervision (OTS). The OTS determines and reports a cost of funds index by ranking all the institutions by their cost of funds and then determining the median of these data. The National Median COFI differs from the more popular Eleventh District COFI in two respects. First, the National Median COFI is a median (as the name implies) while the Eleventh District COFI is a weighted average. Second, the National Median COFI uses the current month's liabilities while the Eleventh District COFI uses the average liabilities of the current and prior month.

The National Median COFI is available on Telerate page 7058 and on Bloomberg's Index Menu under the ticker symbol COF NA.

REFERENCE RATES FOR MUNICIPAL FLOATERS

The reference rate for municipal floaters can be either a Treasury rate, the prime rate, or a municipal index. Three popular municipal indexes are described below.

J.J. Kenney Index

The reference rate for many municipal securities is the *J.J. Kenney Index*. This index, established in 1981, is calculated weekly and is released on Tuesdays. Prices of at least five "high grade" issuers are established each week via a poll of active brokers/dealers. The index is calculated by Kenney-S&P Evaluation Services. The index is available on Bloomberg on the Municipal page with the ticker symbol JJ.

Bond Buyer 40 Bond Index

Another popular reference rate is derived from the *Bond Buyer 40 Bond Index*. This is a "rules-based" index which means that in order for a bond to be included

---

[1] Satish M. Mansukhani, "Eleventh District Cost of Funds Index: An Investor Bulletin," *Mortgage Research*, Bear, Stearns & Co., Inc. (May 11, 1998), p.1.

in the index it must satisfy a well-defined list of criteria. The index includes 40 recently issued bonds with a fixed coupon rate paid semiannually that meet the following criteria: (1) each bond must have an A– or better rating from Standard & Poor's or an A or better rating from Moody's; (2) the issue size must be at least $50 million; (3) each bond must have at least 19 years until maturity; (4) the bond must be callable with a first call date between 7 and 16 years at the time it is included in the index; and (5) each bond must have a market price within the range of 95 to 105, must have been reoffered and be out of syndication. These bonds are priced twice a day by six leading municipal bond brokers. The bond prices are averaged and the average is divided by a conversion factor that equates the bond's price to an 8% coupon bond. Finally, the average is multiplied by a coefficient that determines the index value. A futures contract on this index is traded on the Chicago Board of Trade.

This index is available on Bloomberg's Index page under Municipals with the ticker symbol BBMI.

Merrill Lynch Municipal Securities Index

The *Merrill Lynch Municipal Securities Index* measures the performance of over $100 billion of U.S. tax-exempt bonds. The index is rebalanced on the last calendar day of the month and it is published at the end of each business day. Criteria for a bond's inclusion in the index are as follows: (1) U.S. pay, tax-exempt bond with a remaining maturity of one year or greater; (2) original issue size of at least $50 million; (3) 5 years or less since the original issue date; (4) a fixed coupon schedule; (5) credit rating must be investment grade (Baa3 or above) based on Moody's rating; and (6) private placements are excluded. The bonds in the index are priced daily based on price information provided by J.J. Kenney Inc.

This index is available on Bloomberg's Index page under Merrill Lynch indices in the municipals section.

RELATIONSHIPS AMONG VARIOUS REFERENCE RATES

The reference rate for most floaters is an interest rate or an interest rate index. The majority of floaters are indexed to benchmark money market interest rates (e.g., Treasury bills, certificates of deposit (CDs), LIBOR, etc.), administered rates (e.g., prime) or a computed rates (e.g., COFI). From the investor's perspective, the reference rate embedded in the floater's coupon formula is an important determinant of the security's price performance. Floaters will outperform/underperform otherwise comparable securities because of (in large part) movements in the spreads between these securities' reference rates. Accordingly, an analysis of the spreads between the prevalent reference rates and the primary factors that cause the spreads to change is necessary to understanding floaters. In this section, we examine the relationships among some common reference rates.

Exhibit 1: 3-Month LIBOR versus 3-Month Bills Spread

3-Month LIBOR Versus 3-Month U.S. Treasury Bills

We first examine the relationship between 3-month LIBOR and 3-month U.S. Treasury bills. Treasury-bill-based floaters have lost popularity since the early 1990s. There are several reasons for this. First, the correlation between the 3-month bill rate and the Federal Funds rate has diminished considerably since 1990.[2]

To see this, we examined weekly observations of the Federal Funds rate and the 3-month bill rate for the period of January 1, 1987 to December 31, 1998.[3] During the first nine years of this period, the correlation coefficient between the Federal Funds and 3-month bills was 0.99. However, during the period 1996-1998, the correlation dropped to 0.52. Second, a study by Duffee suggests that the U.S. Treasury bill market is becoming increasingly segmented and there is a measurable increase in the idiosyncratic variability of the bill yield since the mid-1980s.[4] One possible reason is that when foreign central banks intervene in currency markets to manage the exchange rate between the dollar and other currencies, they normally buy/sell U.S. Treasury bills.[5] As a result, the yield on bills may move away from the yield on other money market instruments.

To understand the relationship between LIBOR and Treasury bill yields, we examine the period of January 1, 1987 to December 31, 1998. We focus on the spread (in basis points) between 3-month LIBOR and 3-month Treasury yields each week (Friday) for this time period. Exhibit 1 depicts a time series plot of weekly spreads. There are two striking features of the data. First, there are three

---

[2] The Federal Funds rate is a bank's cost of borrowing immediately available funds from another institution, primarily overnight.

[3] Source: Federal Reserve Statistical Release H.15

[4] Gregory R. Duffee, "Idiosyncratic Variation of Treasury Bill Yields," *Journal of Finance* (June 1996), pp. 527-551.

[5] See, Timothy Q. Cook, "Treasury Bills," in *Instruments of the Money Market,* Seventh Edition, (Richmond: Federal Reserve Bank of Richmond, 1993), pp. 75-88.

prominent spikes in the data that reflect financial/global crises. Second, spreads trend downward over the time period. We will consider each feature in turn.

U.S. Treasury securities and the U.S. dollar are considered "safe havens" in times of crisis, regardless of their underlying causes. During times of turmoil, the resulting "flight to quality" widens the spread between LIBOR rates and Treasury-bill rates. For instance, the first spike in the data occurs in October 1987. At the end of October 1987, the spread between 3-month LIBOR and 3-month bills was 252 basis points. Five weeks earlier, the spread was 106 basis points. The catalyst, of course, for this huge increase in the spread was the collapse of the world's equity markets. On October 19, 1987, the Dow Jones Industrial Average fell 22.6% while equity markets tumbled around the world. The total worldwide decline in stock values exceeded $1 trillion.[6]

The next spike occurred in the fall of 1990. The precipitant was the invasion of Kuwait by military forces from Iraq on August 2, 1990. During the next several weeks, the combination of rising oil prices and slowing U.S. economy caused a severe drop in U.S. stocks. By the middle of October, U.S. stocks had fallen 18%. Once again, investors around the world fled to the safety of U.S. Treasuries and the spread widened to 159 basis points at the end of December 1990 (just prior to the January 15, 1991 United Nations imposed deadline for Iraq to withdraw from Kuwait).

The remaining spike in the spread is in the fall of 1998. On August 17, Russia devalued its currency, the ruble, and halted payments on its debt obligations. As a result, bond prices fell across-the-board in markets around the world. In the ensuing weeks, reports surfaced indicating that a very large hedge fund, Long-Term Capital Management, had sustained multi-billion dollar losses. On September 23, the hedge fund received an infusion of $3.65 billion in capital from a consortium of investment banks. The rescue was brokered by the Federal Reserve. During this time, investors fled emerging markets' equity and debt, liquidity in corporate bonds dried up, and money poured into Treasuries. The spread between 3-month LIBOR and 3-month bills was 132 basis points on October 20, 1998. The spread returned to more normal levels as the Federal Reserve cut the Federal Funds rate three times in the following two months to avert a credit crunch.

Another pattern evident in these data is the downward trend in the spread between 3-month LIBOR and 3-month Treasury bills. To see this, we computed the following summary statistics for each calendar year: mean, standard deviation, minimum, and maximum. These results are presented in Exhibit 2. Two trends are evident: (1) the mean spreads fell over the 1987-1998 period and (2) save for the uptick in volatility in 1998, volatility trended downward as well.[7] The explanation is simple. Over this period, LIBOR became the benchmark interest rate. Currently, the majority of funding for financial institutions is LIBOR-based. As this trend continues, spreads should continue to tighten.

---

[6] Jeremy J. Siegel, *Stocks for the Long Run*, Second Edition (New York: McGraw-Hill, 1998).

[7] A reasonable explanation for these trends is that the level of interest rates fell during this period. However, the same pattern emerges when yield ratios (i.e., 3-month LIBOR/3-month Treasury bill) are examined.

Exhibit 2: The Spread Between 3-Month LIBOR and 3-Month Treasury Bills
Summary Statistics for 1987-1998 (in basis points)

Year	Mean	Standard Deviation	Minimum	Maximum
1987	122.42	47.56	56.00	252.00
1988	118.91	16.68	98.00	183.00
1989	104.44	22.99	56.00	144.00
1990	65.77	23.76	38.00	159.00
1991	46.02	20.58	15.00	129.00
1992	25.52	12.75	11.00	66.00
1993	16.23	5.55	8.00	29.00
1994	34.81	15.23	11.00	78.00
1995	41.50	8.40	28.00	65.00
1996	36.40	8.15	22.00	70.00
1997	53.64	12.94	33.00	77.00
1998	64.00	19.08	40.00	132.00

Prime Rate Versus 3-Month LIBOR

Since the early 1980s, the prime rate has diminished considerably in importance owing to corporations' increased menu of financing alternatives (e.g., commercial paper, bank financing priced off LIBOR, asset securitization, etc.). Accordingly, most large corporations can borrow below the prime rate. Smaller corporations, who do not have access to alternative credit sources, pay prime rates on loans. As a result, the prime rate no longer tracks money market rates when they are declining. When money market rates increase, prime rates increase as well, albeit with a short lag.

Exhibit 3 illustrates this relationship. The graph is a time series plot of weekly observations (Friday) of the prime rate and 3-month LIBOR for the period January 1, 1987 to December 31, 1998.[8] From January 1987 to the spring of 1989, 3-month LIBOR rose steadily with the exception of a sharp drop in the wake of the October 1987 crash. The prime rate followed 3-month LIBOR up and peaked at 11.5%. During this upswing in rates, the spread between the prime rate and 3-month LIBOR remained more or less constant. As rates tumbled over the next three years, the spread between the prime rate and LIBOR widened markedly. Finally, during the Federal Reserve tightening cycle of 1994-1995, the prime rate again followed 3-month LIBOR and the spread narrowed slightly but not to the level of the late 1980s.

The disconnect between the prime rate and 3-month LIBOR is documented in Exhibit 4. Summary statistics — mean, standard deviation, minimum, and maximum — are computed for the spread (in basis points) between the prime rate and 3-month LIBOR for each of the 12 years 1987-1998. The mean spread has increased dramatically over this time period from 115.35 in 1987 to 290.27. Moreover, since 1991, the minimum spread has been at least 200 basis points.

---

[8] Source: Federal Reserve Statistical Release H.15.

Exhibit 3: Prime Rate Versus 3-Month LIBOR

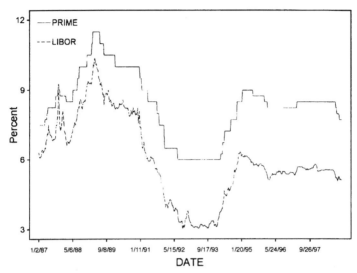

Exhibit 4: Summary Statistics for the Spread Between the Prime Rate and 3-Month LIBOR: 1987-1998 (in basis points)

Year	Mean	Standard Deviation	Minimum	Maximum
1987	115.35	24.96	37.00	155.00
1988	146.98	22.76	87.00	189.00
1989	172.37	32.39	112.00	222.00
1990	184.10	19.75	142.00	242.00
1991	253.25	26.08	202.00	305.00
1992	253.62	19.70	220.00	295.00
1993	281.74	9.09	262.00	294.00
1994	252.87	25.14	201.00	290.00
1995	290.13	20.49	216.00	315.00
1996	288.42	11.44	271.00	316.00
1997	283.71	6.41	269.00	294.00
1998	290.27	13.49	255.00	317.00

3-Month LIBOR Versus 3-Month CDs

Traditionally, Eurodollar CD rates (i.e., LIBOR) have exceeded domestic CD rates. There are several reasons for this spread. First, domestic CD liabilities are subject to reserve requirements and FDIC insurance premiums while Eurodollar CDs are not. Second, the Eurodollar CD market is much less regulated and therefore carries the perception of greater risk. Third, the gap in rates also reflects the difference in liquidity between the two markets.

Exhibit 5: 3-Month LIBOR over 3-Month CD

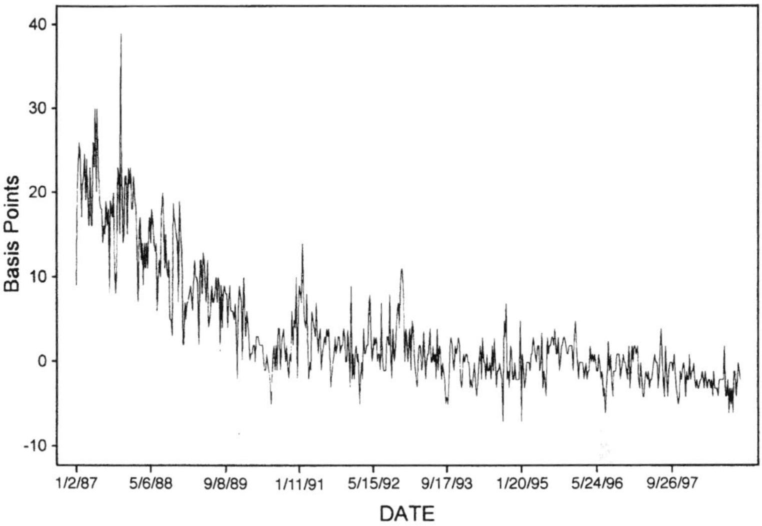

Since the late 1980s, the liquidity of the Eurodollar CD has increased dramatically and the perception of higher risk has diminished considerably. Exhibit 5 presents the spread (in basis points) between 3-month LIBOR and 3-month CDs for the period January 1987 to December 1998.[9] As before, the rates are sampled every Friday. The patterns evident from the graph are consistent with Eurodollar CDs and domestic CDs being viewed as close substitutes. Specifically, the spread's long-term trend is toward zero and there is a marked reduction in the spread's volatility.

The same pattern is evident in the summary statistics in Exhibit 6. Once again, for each calendar year in the sample period, we compute the mean, standard deviation, minimum, and maximum for the spread between 3-month LIBOR and 3-month CDs. Over the period 1987-1998, the mean spread fell from 19.52 basis points in 1987 to negative 2.23 basis points in 1998. These results suggest that Eurodollar CDs have risk/liquidity characteristics equivalent to or even slightly better than domestic CDs.

1-Year CMT, COFI, and 6-Month LIBOR

The three most common reference rates for mortgage-related floaters are 1-year CMT, COFI, and 6-month LIBOR. As of the end of July 1996, the market share by reference rate for ARMs (agency and non-agency) was 1-year CMT 58.39%, COFI 24.04%, and 6-month LIBOR 8.46%.[10] Exhibit 7 illustrates the levels of monthly

---

[9] Source: Federal Reserve Statistical Release H.15. The CD rates are an average of dealer offering rates on nationally traded CDs.

[10] Satish M. Mansukhani, "Mortgage Products Special Report," Bear, Stearns & Co. Inc. (August 27, 1996), p.6.

observations of these three reference rates for the period January 1987-December 1998. As can be seen from this exhibit, the 1-year CMT and 6-month LIBOR are highly correlated, while COFI is much more stable, lagging the other two rates. In general, a floater's reference rate will affect its duration. Other things equal, the more a security's reference rate lags market interest rates, the less it will behave like a pure floater and the more it will behave like a fixed-rate security. Accordingly, COFI-indexed securities should tend to have higher durations all else equal.

Exhibit 6: The Spread Between Three-Month LIBOR and Three-Month CDs

Summary Statistics for 1987-1998 (in basis points)

Year	Mean	Standard Deviation	Minimum	Maximum
1987	19.52	5.66	8.00	39.00
1988	12.74	4.90	2.00	22.00
1989	7.42	3.06	-2.00	13.00
1990	1.75	2.86	-5.00	10.00
1991	2.94	3.35	-3.00	14.00
1992	2.35	3.45	-5.00	11.00
1993	0.34	2.33	-5.00	5.00
1994	-0.52	2.32	-7.00	7.00
1995	0.83	2.23	-7.00	5.00
1996	-0.56	1.88	-6.00	5.00
1997	-1.06	2.00	-5.00	4.00
1998	-2.23	1.47	-6.00	2.00

Exhibit 7: 1-Year CMT, COFI, and 6-Month LIBOR

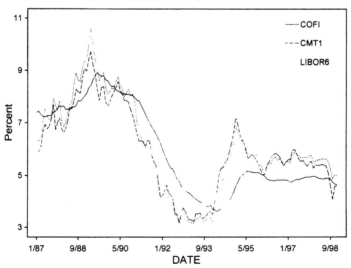

Exhibit 8: LIBOR Yield Curve

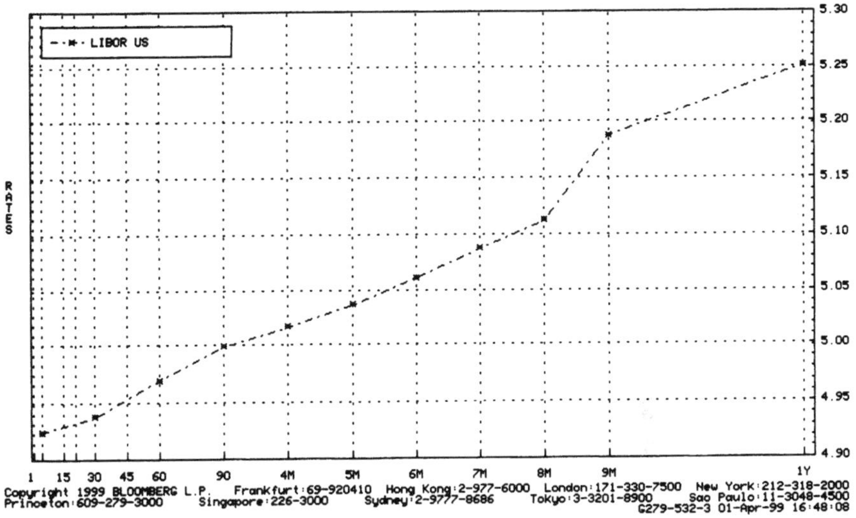

Source: Bloomberg Financial Markets

THE U.S. TREASURY YIELD CURVE AND THE LIBOR CURVE

While the reference rate for many floaters is a money market rate, the maturity of the floater itself can be 30 years or longer. Accordingly, the index spread (i.e., the additional amount that the issuer agrees to pay over the reference rate) will depend on, among other things, the U.S. Treasury yield curve and the term structure of credit spreads.[11] The yield curve is a graphical depiction between yields on Treasury securities of different maturities. Correspondingly, the term structure of credit spreads is the relationship between credit spreads and term to maturity. These relationships are discussed in Chapter 4, where we discuss the valuation of floaters.

A similar yield curve relationship exists for LIBOR. The LIBOR yield curve is the relationship between the yields on Eurodollar CDs and term to maturity. While most Eurodollar CDs are issued with original maturities of 1 year or less, issues with maturities up to five years are common. Exhibit 8 presents a LIBOR yield curve from Bloomberg.

VOLATILITY AND FLOATERS WITH EMBEDDED OPTIONS

Most floaters issued today contain embedded options. A floater may contain a cap (i.e., a maximum coupon rate regardless of the level of the reference rate) and/or

---

[11] For some floaters, the index spread is negative.

a floor (i.e., a minimum coupon rate regardless of the level of the reference rate). Caps/floors are nothing more than a package of options on interest rates. The value of the embedded options exerts a substantial influence on the value of floaters and on how they perform over time.

One of the fundamental determinants of any option's value is the volatility of the underlying asset. In other words, options feed off volatility. Accordingly, the values of caps/floors are explicitly tied to the volatility of the floater's reference rate. As can be seen from the exhibits in this chapter, the volatility of the various references changes considerably over time. The fact that volatility is not constant will have a big impact on the value of caps/floors and on the floaters' values themselves.

In the remainder of this chapter, we explain how to measure yield volatility. Volatility is measured in terms of the standard deviation or variance. Generally speaking, there are two ways to model yield volatility. The first way is by estimating historical yield volatility by some time series model. The resulting volatility is called *historical volatility*. The second way is to estimate yield volatility based on the observed prices of interest rate derivatives. Yield volatility calculated using this approach is called *implied volatility*.

Historical Volatility

The variance and standard deviation of a random variable are calculated as follows:

$$\text{Variance} = \sum_{t=1}^{T} \frac{(X_t - \bar{X})^2}{T-1} \tag{1}$$

and then

$$\text{Standard deviation} = \sqrt{\text{Variance}}$$

where

X_t = observation t on variable X
$\bar{X}$ = the sample mean for variable X
T = the number of observations in the sample

When equation (1) uses historical yield observations to obtain the variance and standard deviation, the resulting volatility is referred to as *historical volatility*. More specifically, market participants interested in estimating historical volatility look at the percentage change in daily yields. So, X_t will denote the percentage change in yield from day t and the prior day, $t-1$. If we let y_t denote the yield on day t and y_{t-1} denote the yield on day $t-1$, then X_t is the natural logarithm of percentage change in yield between two days and can be expressed as

$$X_t = 100[\text{Ln}(y_t / y_{t-1})]$$

The daily standard deviation will vary depending on the number of days selected. The appropriate number depends on the situation at hand. For example, traders concerned with overnight positions might use the last 10 trading days (i.e., two weeks). A bond portfolio manager who is concerned with longer term volatility might use the last 25 trading days (about one month).

If serial correlation of the time series is not significant, the daily standard deviation can be annualized by multiplying it by the square root of the number of days in a year. That is,

$$\text{Daily standard deviation} \times \sqrt{\text{Number of days in a year}}$$

Market practice varies with respect to the number of days in the year that should be used in the annualizing formula above. Typically, either 250 days, 260 days, or 365 days are used.

Thus, in calculating an annual standard deviation, the manager must decide on (1) the number of daily observations to use and (2) the number of days in the year to use to annualize the daily standard deviation. There are two other issues. First, what mean value should be used in calculating the standard deviation? Second, should all observations be weighted equally?

With respect to the choice of the mean value, suppose that today a trader is interested in forecasting volatility using the last 10 days of trading and updating that forecast at the end of each trading day. The trader can calculate a 10-day *moving average* of the daily percentage yield change. Rather than using a moving average, it is more appropriate to use an expectation of the average. Longerstacey and Zangari argue for use of a mean value of zero.[12] In that case, the variance as given by equation (1) simplifies to:

$$\text{Variance} = \sum_{t=1}^{T} \frac{X_t^2}{T-1} \qquad (2)$$

Turning to the second question, the daily standard deviation given by equations (1) and (2) assigns an equal weight to all observations. So, if a trader is calculating volatility based on the last 10 days of trading, for example, each day is given a weight of 10%. However, there is reason to suspect that market participants give greater weight to recent movements in yield when determining volatility. Moreover, what has been observed in several studies of the stock market is that high periods of volatility are followed by high periods of volatility.

To give greater importance to more recent information, observations further in the past should be given less weight. This can be done by revising the variance as given by equation (2) as follows:

---

[12] Jacques Longerstacey and Peter Zangari, *Five Questions about RiskMetrics™*, JP Morgan Research Publication 1995.

$$\text{Variance} = \sum_{t=1}^{T} \frac{W_t X_t^2}{T-1} \tag{3}$$

where W_t is the weight assigned to observation t such that the sum of the weights is equal to 1 and the further the observation is from today, the lower the weight. The weights should be assigned so that the forecasted volatility reacts faster to a recent major market movement and declines gradually as we move away from a major market movement.[13]

Implied Volatility

The second way to estimate yield volatility is based on the observed prices of interest rate derivatives, such as options on bond futures, or interest rate caps and floors. Yield volatility calculated using this approach is called *implied volatility*.

Implied volatility is based on some option pricing model. One of the inputs to any option pricing model in which the underlying is a Treasury security or Treasury futures contract is expected yield volatility. If the observed price of an option is assumed to be the fair price and the option pricing model is assumed to be the model that would generate that fair price, then the implied yield volatility is the yield volatility that when used as an input into the option pricing model would produce the observed option price. Because of their liquidity, options on Treasury futures, Eurodollar futures, and caps and floors on LIBOR are typically used to extract implied volatilities. However, computing implied volatilities of yield from interest rate derivatives is not as straightforward as from derivatives of, say, stock. We will not go into the technical reasons why this is so. The bottom line is that implied volatilities are not only model-dependent, but in some occasions they are also difficult to interpret, and can be misleading as well.[14]

SUMMARY

A floater's reference rate is a critical element in understanding its expected performance. In this chapter, we examined the factors that drive the relationships among four common reference rates (3-month LIBOR, 3-month Treasury bill

---

[13] The approach by JP Morgan in *RiskMetrics*™ is to use an exponential moving average. The formula for the weight W_t in an exponential moving average is:

$$W_t = (1 - \beta)\beta^t$$

where β is a value between 0 and 1. The observations are arrayed so that the closest observation is $t = 1$, the second closest is $t = 2$, etc.

[14] For a more detailed discussion of implied volatilities and their limitations, see Frank J. Fabozzi and Wai Lee, "Measuring and Forecasting Yield Volatility," Chapter 16 in Frank J. Fabozzi (ed.), *Perspectives on Interest Rate Risk Management for Money Managers and Traders* (New Hope, PA: Frank J. Fabozzi Associates, 1998).

rates, 3-month CD rates, and the prime rate). While the correlations among these rates have been quite high over the period 1987 to 1998, the spreads between various pairs of rates exhibit considerable variability. Moreover, there are identifiable long-term trends in the relationships among reference rates. For example, the emergence of LIBOR as the benchmark money market rate and, as such, the most prevalent reference rate for floaters has narrowed the spread between LIBOR and Treasury bill rates.

Since most floaters contain embedded options such as caps/floors, changes in the volatility of various reference rates over time is critical in determining the value of these floaters. The evidence presented in this chapter suggests that reference rate volatility is time-varying. As floaters become more and more complicated with the addition of multiple options, assessment of the factors that drive volatility of their reference rates will become increasingly important.

Chapter 3
Introduction to the Valuation of Floaters

In this chapter and the one to follow, we look at how to value floaters. Our focus in this chapter is on the general principles of valuation and the valuation of risky floaters that are option free. We also discuss the various interest rates that are used in the valuation process, spot rates, and forward rates. The methodology for deriving spot rates and forward rates is explained. In the next chapter we explain how to value floaters with embedded options.

GENERAL PRINCIPLES OF VALUATION

Valuation is the process of determining the fair value of a financial asset. The process is also referred to as "valuing" or "pricing" a financial asset. The fundamental principle of valuation is that the value of any financial asset is the present value of the expected cash flows. This principle applies regardless of the financial asset. Our focus in this book is on floating-rate instruments ("floaters").

Estimating Cash Flows

Cash flow is simply the cash that is expected to be received at some time from an investment. In the case of a bond, it does not make any difference whether the cash flow is interest income or repayment of principal. The cash flows of a bond are the collection of each period's cash flow.

Holding aside the risk of default, the cash flows for only a few bonds are simple to project. Noncallable Treasury securities have known cash flows. For a Treasury coupon security, the cash flows are the coupon interest payments every six months up to the maturity date and the principal payment at the maturity date. So, for example, the cash flows per $100 of par value for a 7% 10-year Treasury security are $3.5 (7%/2 × $100) every six months for the next 20 6-month periods and $100 20 6-month periods from now. Or, equivalently, the cash flows are $3.5 every six months for the next 19 6-month periods and $103.50 20 6-month periods from now.

The issuer of a bond agrees to repay the principal by the stated maturity date. The issuer can agree to repay the entire amount borrowed in one lump sum payment at the maturity date. That is, the issuer is not required to make any principal repayments prior to the maturity date. Such bonds are said to have a *bullet maturity*.

37

Bonds backed by pools of loans (mortgage-backed securities and asset-backed securities) often have a schedule of principal repayments. Such bonds are said to be *amortizing securities*. For many loans, the payments are structured so that when the last loan payment is made, the entire amount owed is fully paid off.

For any fixed-rate bond in which neither the issuer/borrower nor the investor can alter the repayment of the principal before its contractual due date, the cash flows can easily be determined assuming that the issuer does not default. Difficulty in determining a bond's cash flows arises under the following circumstances. First, either the issuer or the investor has the option to change the contractual due date of the repayment of the principal. This occurs when the bond is callable, prepayable, or putable. Second, the coupon payment is reset periodically based on some reference rate and there are restrictions on the new coupon rate (that is, there is a cap or a floor). This is a characteristic of a floater.

Discounting the Cash Flows

Once the cash flows for a bond are estimated, the next step is to determine the appropriate interest rate at which to discount those cash flows. The minimum interest rate that an investor should require is the yield available in the marketplace on a default-free cash flow. In the U.S., this is the yield on a U.S. Treasury security. The premium over the yield on a Treasury security that the investor should require should reflect the risks associated with realizing the estimated cash flows.

The traditional practice in valuation has been to discount every cash flow of a bond by the same interest rate (or discount rate). The fundamental flaw of the traditional approach is that it views each bond as the same package of cash flows. For example, consider a 10-year U.S. Treasury bond with an 8% coupon rate. The cash flows per $100 of par value would be 19 payments of $4 every six months and $104 20 6-month periods from now. The traditional practice would discount the cash flow for all 20 periods using the same interest rate.

The proper way to view the 10-year 8% coupon bond is as a package of zero-coupon instruments. Each period's cash flow should be considered a zero-coupon instrument whose maturity value is the amount of the cash flow and whose maturity date is the payment date of the cash flow. Thus, the 10-year 8% coupon bond should be viewed as 20 zero-coupon instruments. The reason that this is the proper way is because it does not allow a market participant to realize an arbitrage profit. This will be made clearer in the next chapter.

By viewing any financial asset in this way, a consistent valuation framework can be developed. For example, under the traditional approach to the valuation of fixed income securities, a 10-year zero-coupon bond would be viewed as the same financial asset as a 10-year 8% coupon bond. Viewing a financial asset as a package of zero-coupon instruments means that these two bonds would be viewed as different packages of zero-coupon instruments and valued accordingly.

Therefore, to implement the contemporary approach it is necessary to determine the theoretical rate that the U.S. Treasury would have to pay to issue a zero-coupon instrument for each maturity. Another name used for the zero-coupon rate is the *spot rate*. The spot rate can be estimated from the Treasury yield curve.

Spot Rates

The graphical depiction of the relationship between the yields on Treasury securities of different maturities is known as the *yield curve*. The Treasury yield curve is typically constructed from on-the-run Treasury issues — 3-month, 6-month, 1-year, 2-year, 5-year, 10-year, and 30-year recently auctioned issues. The first three issues are Treasury bills which are zero-coupon securities. In contrast, the four issues that mature after one year are coupon securities. Consequently, the Treasury yield curve is a combination of zero-coupon securities and coupon securities.

In the valuation of securities what is needed is the rate on zero-coupon default-free securities or, equivalently, the rate on zero-coupon Treasury securities. There are no zero-coupon Treasury securities issued by the U.S. Department of the Treasury with a maturity greater than one year. One can construct a theoretical rate that the U.S. government would have to offer if it issued zero-coupon securities with a maturity greater than one year.

There are, in fact, zero-coupon Treasury securities with a maturity greater than one year that are created by government dealer firms. These securities are called *stripped Treasury securities*. Today, all stripped Treasury securities are created by dealer firms under a Treasury Department program called STRIPS, which stands for Separate Trading of Registered Interest and Principal Securities. We shall refer to the STRIPS as *Treasury strips* or simply *strips*. For a reason discussed below, it is common to distinguish between strips based on whether they are created from the coupon payments or the principal payments. The former are called *coupon strips* and the latter are called *principal strips*. On dealer sheets, the distinction is made.[1]

It would seem logical that the observed yield on strips could be used to construct an actual spot rate curve rather than go through the procedure we will describe. There are three problems with using the observed rates on strips. First, the liquidity of the strips market is not as great as that of the Treasury coupon market. Thus, the observed rates on strips reflect a premium for liquidity. Second, the tax treatment of strips is different from that of Treasury coupon securities. Specifically, the accrued interest on strips is taxed even though no cash is received by the investor. Thus they are negative cash flow securities to taxable entities, and, as a result, their yield reflects this tax disadvantage. Finally, there are maturity sectors where non-U.S. investors find it advantageous to trade off yield for tax advantages associated with a strip. Specifically, certain foreign tax authorities allow their citizens to treat the difference between the maturity value and the purchase price as a capital gain and tax this gain at a favorable tax rate.

---

[1] Each coupon strip has its own CUSIP number. Further, coupon strips that are payable on the same date have the same CUSIP number even when stripped from different securities. Principal strips from different securities have individual CUSIP numbers even if they mature on the same date.

Some will grant this favorable treatment only when the strip is created from the principal rather than the coupon. For this reason, those who use Treasury strips to represent theoretical spot rates restrict the issues included to coupon strips.

A default-free theoretical spot rate curve can be constructed from the yield on Treasury securities. The Treasury issues that are candidates for inclusion are:

1. on-the-run Treasury issues
2. on-the-run Treasury issues and selected off-the-run Treasury issues
3. all Treasury coupon securities and bills
4. Treasury coupon strips

Once the securities that are to be included in the construction of the theoretical spot rate curve are selected, the methodology for constructing the curve must be determined. The methodology depends on the securities included. If Treasury coupon strips are used, the procedure is simple since the observed yields are the spot rates. If the on-the-run Treasury issues with or without selected off-the-run Treasury issues are used, then a methodology called bootstrapping is used. When all Treasury coupon securities and bills are used, then elaborate statistical techniques are used. We'll only discuss the bootstrapping methodology using on-the-run issues.

There is an observed yield for each of the on-the-run issues. For the coupon issues, these yields are not the yields used in the analysis when the issue is not trading at par. Instead, for each on-the-run coupon issue, the estimated yield necessary to make the issue trade at par is used. The resulting on-the-run yield curve is called the *par coupon curve*.

The goal is to construct a theoretical spot rate curve with 60 semiannual spot rates — 6-month rate to 30-year rate. Excluding the 3-month bill, there are only six maturity points available when only on-the-run issues are used. The 53 missing maturity points are extrapolated from the surrounding maturity points on the par yield curve. The simplest extrapolation method, and the one most commonly used, is linear extrapolation. Specifically, given the yield on the par coupon curve at two maturity points, the following is calculated:

$$\frac{\text{Yield at higher maturity} - \text{Yield at lower maturity}}{\text{Number of semiannual periods between the two maturity points}}$$

Then, the yield for all intermediate semiannual maturity points is found by adding to the yield at the lower maturity the amount computed above.

For example, suppose that the yield from the par yield curve for the 3-year and 5-year on-the-run issues is 6% and 6.6%, respectively. There are six semiannual periods between these two maturity points. The extrapolated yields for the 2.5, 3.0, 3.5, 4.0, and 4.5 maturity points are found as follows. Calculate

$$\frac{6.6\% - 6.0\%}{6} = 0.10\%$$

Then,

$$2.5\text{-year yield} = 6.00\% + 0.10\% = 6.10\%$$
$$3.0\text{-year yield} = 6.10\% + 0.10\% = 6.20\%$$
$$3.5\text{-year yield} = 6.20\% + 0.10\% = 6.30\%$$
$$4.0\text{-year yield} = 6.30\% + 0.10\% = 6.40\%$$
$$4.5\text{-year yield} = 6.40\% + 0.10\% = 6.50\%$$

There are two problems with using just the on-the-run issues. First, there is a large gap between some of the maturity points which may result in misleading yields for the interim maturity points when estimated using the linear extrapolation method. Specifically, the concern is with the large gap between the 5-year and 10-year maturity points and the 10-year and 30-year maturity points. The second problem is that the yields for the on-the-run issues themselves may be misleading because most are on special in the repo market. This means that the true yield is greater than the quoted (observed) yield.

Now let's look at how the par yield curve is converted into the theoretical spot rate curve. The methodology that is used is called *bootstrapping*. For simplicity, we will illustrate this methodology to calculate the theoretical spot rate curve for only 10 years. That is, 20 semiannual spot rates will be computed. Suppose that the par yield curve is the one shown in Exhibit 1.[2] Our focus is on the first three columns of this exhibit. Our goal is to explain how the values in the last two columns of the exhibit are derived.

The basic principle to obtain the theoretical spot rates is that the value of a Treasury coupon security should be equal to the value of the package of zero-coupon instruments that duplicates the coupon security's cash flows. Consider the 6-month Treasury bill in Exhibit 1. Since a Treasury bill is a zero-coupon instrument, its annualized yield of 3.00% is equal to the spot rate. Similarly, for the 1-year Treasury, the cited yield of 3.30% is the 1-year spot rate. Given these two spot rates, we can compute the spot rate for a theoretical 1.5-year zero-coupon Treasury. The price of a theoretical 1.5-year Treasury should equal the present value of the three cash flows from the 1.5-year coupon Treasury, where the yield used for discounting is the spot rate corresponding to the cash flow. Since all the coupon bonds are selling at par, the yield to maturity for each bond is the coupon rate. Using $100 as par, the cash flows for the 1.5-year coupon Treasury are:

$$0.5 \text{ year} \quad 0.035 \times \$100 \times 0.5 \qquad = \quad \$1.75$$
$$1.0 \text{ year} \quad 0.035 \times \$100 \times 0.5 \qquad = \quad \$1.75$$
$$1.5 \text{ year} \quad 0.035 \times \$100 \times 0.5 + 100 \quad = \quad \$101.75$$

The present value of the cash flows is then:

$$\frac{1.75}{(1+z_1)^1} + \frac{1.75}{(1+z_2)^2} + \frac{101.75}{(1+z_3)^3}$$

---

[2] Note that the intermediate points in this illustration were not calculated using the linear extrapolation procedure.

Exhibit 1: Par Coupon Curve for 10 Years

Period	Years	Yield to maturity (%)	Spot rate (%)	Discount function
1	0.5	3.00	3.0000	0.9852
2	1.0	3.30	3.3000	0.9678
3	1.5	3.50	3.5053	0.9492
4	2.0	3.90	3.9164	0.9254
5	2.5	4.40	4.4376	0.8961
6	3.0	4.70	4.7520	0.8686
7	3.5	4.90	4.9622	0.8424
8	4.0	5.00	5.0650	0.8187
9	4.5	5.10	5.1701	0.7948
10	5.0	5.20	5.2772	0.7707
11	5.5	5.30	5.3864	0.7465
12	6.0	5.40	5.4976	0.7222
13	6.5	5.50	5.6108	0.6979
14	7.0	5.55	5.6643	0.6764
15	7.5	5.60	5.7193	0.6551
16	8.0	5.65	5.7755	0.6341
17	8.5	5.70	5.8331	0.6134
18	9.0	5.80	5.9584	0.5895
19	9.5	5.90	6.0863	0.5658
20	10.0	6.00	6.2169	0.5421

where

z_1 = one-half the 6-month theoretical spot rate,
z_2 = one-half the 1-year theoretical spot rate, and
z_3 = one-half the 1.5-year theoretical spot rate.

Since the 6-month spot rate and 1-year spot rate are 3.00% and 3.30%, respectively, we know that:

$$z_1 = 0.0150 \quad \text{and} \quad z_2 = 0.0165$$

We can compute the present value of the 1.5-year coupon Treasury security as:

$$\frac{1.75}{(1+z_1)^1} + \frac{1.75}{(1+z_2)^2} + \frac{101.75}{(1+z_3)^3} = \frac{1.75}{(1.015)^1} + \frac{1.75}{(1.0165)^2} + \frac{101.75}{(1+z_3)^3}$$

Since the price of the 1.5-year coupon Treasury security is par, the following relationship must hold:

$$\frac{1.75}{(1.015)^1} + \frac{1.75}{(1.0165)^2} + \frac{101.75}{(1+z_3)^3} = 100$$

We can solve for the theoretical 1.5-year spot rate as follows:

$$1.7241 + 1.6936 + \frac{101.75}{(1 + z_3)^3} = 100$$

$$\frac{101.75}{(1 + z_3)^3} = 96.5822$$

$$(1 + z_3)^3 = \frac{101.75}{96.5822}$$

$$z_3 = 0.0175265 = 1.7527\%$$

Doubling this yield we obtain the bond-equivalent yield of 3.5053%, which is the theoretical 1.5-year spot rate. That rate is the rate that the market would apply to a 1.5-year zero-coupon Treasury security if, in fact, such a security existed.

Given the theoretical 1.5-year spot rate, we can obtain the theoretical 2-year spot rate. The cash flows for the 2-year coupon Treasury in Exhibit 1 are:

0.5 years	$0.039 \times \$100 \times 0.5$		= $	1.95
1.0 years	$0.039 \times \$100 \times 0.5$		= $	1.95
1.5 years	$0.039 \times \$100 \times 0.5$		= $	1.95
2.0 years	$0.039 \times \$100 \times 0.5 + 100$		= $	101.95

The present value of the cash flows is then:

$$\frac{1.95}{(1 + z_1)^1} + \frac{1.95}{(1 + z_2)^2} + \frac{1.95}{(1 + z_3)^3} + \frac{101.95}{(1 + z_4)^4}$$

where z_4 = one-half the 2-year theoretical spot rate.

Since the 6-month spot rate, 1-year spot rate, and 1.5-year spot rate are 3.00%, 3.30%, and 3.5053%, respectively, then:

$$z_1 = 0.0150, z_2 = 0.0165, \text{ and } z_3 = 0.017527$$

Therefore, the present value of the 2-year coupon Treasury security is:

$$\frac{1.95}{(1.0150)^1} + \frac{1.95}{(1.0165)^2} + \frac{1.95}{(1.017527)^3} + \frac{101.95}{(1 + z_4)^4}$$

Since the price of the 2-year coupon Treasury security is par, the following relationship must hold:

$$\frac{1.95}{(1.0150)^1} + \frac{1.95}{(1.0165)^2} + \frac{1.95}{(1.017527)^3} + \frac{101.95}{(1 + z_4)^4} = 100$$

We can solve for the theoretical 2-year spot rate as follows:

$$\frac{101.95}{(1 + z_4)^4} = 94.3407$$

$$(1 + z_4)^4 = \frac{101.95}{94.3407}$$

$$z_4 = 0.019582 = 1.9582\%$$

Doubling this yield, we obtain the theoretical 2-year spot rate bond-equivalent yield of 3.9164%.

One can follow this approach sequentially to derive the theoretical 2.5-year spot rate from the calculated values of z_1, z_2, z_3, z_4 (the 6-month, 1-year, 1.5-year, and 2-year rates), and the price and coupon of the bond with a maturity of 2.5 years. Further, one could derive the theoretical spot rate for the remaining 15 half-yearly rates.

The spot rates obtained are shown in the next-to-the-last column of Exhibit 1. They represent the term structure of default-free spot rates for maturities up to ten years for the particular par coupon curve.

Since spot rates are constructed from par rates, how are spot rates and par rates related to one another? A par rate is the average discount rate of many cash flows (those of a par bond) over many periods. For example, a 2-year par rate is a complicated average of the 6-month, 1-year, 1.5-year, and 2-year spot rates. As we will see shortly, a spot rate is the average discount rate of a single cash flow over many periods.

The Discount Function The term structure is represented by the spot rate curve. We also know that the present value of $1 at any future date, n, when discounted at the spot rate for period n is:

$$\frac{\$1}{\left[1 + \left(\dfrac{\text{Spot rate for period } n}{2}\right)\right]^n}$$

For example, the present value of $1 five years from now using the spot rate for 10 periods in Exhibit 1, 5.2772%, is

$$\frac{\$1}{\left[1 + \left(\dfrac{0.052772}{2}\right)\right]^{10}} = 0.7707$$

This value can be viewed as the time value of $1 for a default-free cash flow to be received in five years. Equivalently, it is the value of a zero-coupon default-free security with a maturity of five years and a maturity value of $1. The last column of Exhibit 1 shows the time value of $1 for each period. The set of time values for all periods is called the *discount function*.

Applying the Spot Rates to Price a Treasury Coupon Security To demonstrate how to use the spot rate curve, suppose that we want to price an 8% 10-year Treasury security. The price of this issue is the present value of the cash flows where each cash flow is discounted at the corresponding spot rate. This is illustrated in Exhibit 2. The third column shows the cash flow for each period. The fourth column shows the spot rate curve taken from Exhibit 1. The corresponding discount function is shown in the next-to-the-last column taken from Exhibit 1. Multiplying the value in the discount function column by the cash flow gives the present value of the cash flow. The sum of the present value of the cash flows is equal to 115.2619. This is the theoretical value of this issue.

Market prices for Treasury issues will differ from their theoretical values for several reasons. First, Treasury issues vary in terms of liquidity. For example, on-the-run issues are more liquid than off-the-run issues and so will command higher prices and lower yields other things equal.   Second, because of the different tax treatment of coupon interest and capital gains, higher coupon Treasury securities will trade at slightly lower prices and higher yields than lower coupon issues that are otherwise the same. Third, issues that are on special in the repo market will be priced differently from those issues in the general collateral market. Finally, issues that are "cheapest to deliver" into the Treasury bond or note futures contract will also be priced differently than other issues.

Exhibit 2: Determination of the Theoretical Price of an 8% 10-Year Treasury

Period	Years	Cash flow	Spot rate (%)	Discount function	Present Value
1	0.5	4.00	3.0000	0.9852	3.9409
2	1.0	4.00	3.3000	0.9678	3.8712
3	1.5	4.00	3.5053	0.9492	3.7968
4	2.0	4.00	3.9164	0.9254	3.7014
5	2.5	4.00	4.4376	0.8961	3.5843
6	3.0	4.00	4.7520	0.8686	3.4743
7	3.5	4.00	4.9622	0.8424	3.3694
8	4.0	4.00	5.0650	0.8187	3.2747
9	4.5	4.00	5.1701	0.7948	3.1791
10	5.0	4.00	5.2772	0.7707	3.0828
11	5.5	4.00	5.3864	0.7465	2.9861
12	6.0	4.00	5.4976	0.7222	2.8889
13	6.5	4.00	5.6108	0.6979	2.7916
14	7.0	4.00	5.6643	0.6764	2.7055
15	7.5	4.00	5.7193	0.6551	2.6205
16	8.0	4.00	5.7755	0.6341	2.5365
17	8.5	4.00	5.8331	0.6134	2.4536
18	9.0	4.00	5.9584	0.5895	2.3581
19	9.5	4.00	6.0863	0.5658	2.2631
20	10.0	104.00	6.2169	0.5421	56.3828
				Total	115.2619

The Term Structure of Credit Spreads Thus far our focus has been on the term structure of U.S. Treasury securities — default-free securities. The Treasury spot rates can then be used to value any default-free security. For a corporate bond, the theoretical price is not as easy to determine. The price of a corporate bond must reflect not only the spot rates for default-free bonds but also a risk premium to reflect default risk and any options embedded in the issue. For now, we will skip options embedded in bonds, a complexity addressed later in this chapter.

In practice, the spot rates that have been used to discount the cash flows of corporate bonds are the Treasury spot rates plus a constant credit spread. For example, if the 6-month Treasury spot rate is 3%, and the 10-year Treasury spot rate is 6%, and a suitable credit spread is deemed to be 100 basis points, then a 4% spot rate is used to discount a 6-month cash flow of a corporate bond and a 7% discount rate to discount a 10-year cash flow. The drawback of this approach is that there is no reason to expect the credit spread to be the same regardless of when the cash flow is expected to be received. Instead, it might be expected that the credit spread increases with the maturity of the corporate bond. That is, there is a term structure for credit spreads.

In practice, the difficulty in estimating a term structure for credit spreads is that unlike Treasury securities in which there is a wide-range of maturities from which to construct a Treasury spot rate curve, there are no issuers that offer a sufficiently wide range of corporate zero-coupon securities to construct a zero-coupon spread curve. Robert Litterman and Thomas Iben of Goldman Sachs describe a procedure to construct a generic zero-coupon spread curve by credit rating and industry using data provided from a trading desk.[3]

Typically the credit spread increases with maturity. The shape of the term structure is not the same for all credit ratings. The lower the credit rating, the steeper the term structure. One implication of an upward-sloping term structure for credit spreads is that it is inappropriate to discount the cash flows from a corporate bond at a constant spread to the Treasury spot rate curve. The short-term cash flows will be undervalued, and the long-term cash flows will be overvalued.

When the generic zero spreads for a given credit quality and in a given industry are added to the default-free spot rates, the resulting credit term structure is used to value bonds of issuers of the same credit quality in the industry sector. This term structure is referred to as the *benchmark spot rate curve* or *benchmark zero-coupon rate curve*.

Forward Rates

Market participants typically have different views about what they expect future interest rates to be. Under a certain theory of the term structure of interest rates known as the pure expectations theory and based on arbitrage arguments, the mar-

---

[3] Robert Litterman and Thomas Iben, "Corporate Bond Valuation and the Term Structure of Credit Spreads," *Journal of Portfolio Management* (Spring 1991), pp. 52-64.

ket's consensus of future interest rates can be extrapolated from the Treasury yield curve. These rates are called *forward rates*.[4]

Examples of forward rates that can be calculated from the Treasury yield curve are the:

- 6-month forward rate six months from now
- 6-month forward rate three years from now
- 1-year forward rate one year from now
- 3-year forward rate two years from now
- 5-year forward rate three years from now

Since the forward rates are extrapolated from the Treasury yield curve, these rates are sometimes referred to as *implicit forward rates*.

To illustrate the process of extrapolating 6-month forward rates, we will use the yield curve and corresponding spot rate curve from Exhibit 1. Consider an investor who has a 1-year investment horizon and is faced with the following two alternatives:

Alternative 1: Buy a 1-year Treasury bill, or

Alternative 2: Buy a 6-month Treasury bill, and when it matures in six months buy another 6-month Treasury bill.

The investor will be indifferent toward the two alternatives if they produce the same return over the 1-year investment horizon. The investor knows the spot rate on the 6-month Treasury bill and the 1-year Treasury bill. However, he does not know what yield will be available on a 6-month Treasury bill that will be purchased six months from now. That is, he does not know the 6-month forward rate six months from now. Given the spot rates for the 6-month Treasury bill and the 1-year Treasury bill, the forward rate on a 6-month Treasury bill is the rate that equalizes the dollar return between the two alternatives.

To see how that rate can be determined, suppose that an investor purchased a 6-month Treasury bill for X. At the end of six months, the value of this investment would be:

$$X(1 + z_1)$$

where z_1 is one-half the bond-equivalent yield (BEY) of the theoretical 6-month spot rate.

Let f represent one-half the forward rate (expressed as a BEY) on a 6-month Treasury bill available six months from now. If the investor were to renew his investment by purchasing that bill at that time, then the future dollars available at the end of one year from the X investment would be:

---

[4] The statement that forward rates reflect the market's consensus of future interest rates is strictly true only if investors do not demand an additional risk premium for holding bonds with longer maturities and that investors' preference for positive convexity does not influence the yield curve's shape.

Exhibit 3: Graphical Depiction of the 6-Month Forward Rate Six Months from Now

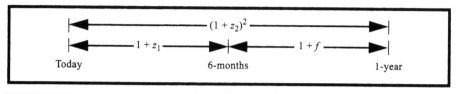

$$X(1+z_1)(1+f)$$

Now consider the alternative of investing in a 1-year Treasury bill. If we let z_2 represent one-half the BEY of the theoretical 1-year spot rate, then the future dollars available at the end of one year from the $\$X$ investment would be:

$$X(1+z_2)^2$$

This is depicted in Exhibit 3.

Now, we are prepared to analyze the investor's choices and what this says about forward rates. The investor will be indifferent toward the two alternatives confronting him if he makes the same dollar investment ($\$X$) and receives the same future dollars from both alternatives at the end of one year. That is, the investor will be indifferent if:

$$X(1+z_1)(1+f) = X(1+z_2)^2$$

Solving for f, we get:

$$f = \frac{(1+z_2)^2}{(1+z_1)} - 1$$

Doubling f gives the BEY for the 6-month forward rate six months from now.

We can illustrate the use of this formula with the theoretical spot rates shown in Exhibit 1. From that exhibit, we know that:

6-month bill spot rate = 0.030, therefore z_1 = 0.0150
1-year bill spot rate   = 0.033, therefore z_2 = 0.0165

Substituting into the formula, we have:

$$f = \frac{(1.0165)^2}{(1.0150)} - 1 = 0.0180 = 1.8\%$$

Therefore, the forward rate on a 6-month Treasury security is 3.6% (1.8% × 2) BEY.

Let's confirm our results. If X is invested in the 6-month Treasury bill at 1.5% and the proceeds then reinvested at the 6-month forward rate of 1.8%, the total proceeds from this alternative would be:

$$X(1.015)(1.018) = 1.03327\,X$$

Investment of $X in the 1-year Treasury bill at one-half the 1-year rate, 1.0165%, would produce the following proceeds at the end of one year:

$$X(1.0165)^2 = 1.03327\,X$$

Both alternatives have the same payoff if the 6-month Treasury bill yield six months from now is 1.8% (3.6% on a BEY). This means that if an investor is guaranteed a 1.8% yield (3.6% BEY) on a 6-month Treasury bill six months from now, he will be indifferent toward the two alternatives.

Forward rates can also be interpreted as equating the holding period return of buying and holding a 6-month bill and the holding period return of buying a 1-year bill and selling it after six months. The latter strategy is known as "riding the yield curve." In our example, since the yield curve is upward sloping and *if it does not change* over the next six months, the 1-year bill will earn a higher return because of the increase in price due to the decrease in yield relative to the forecast at which it is priced. Accordingly, investors will earn an additional return. The forward rate tells us how much the 6-month spot rate must rise over the next six months to offset this additional return.

For example, suppose an investor purchases a 1-year bill with maturity value of $100 currently yielding 3.3% on a bond-equivalent basis. The 1-year bill's price is $96.7799. Further, suppose the investor sells the bill after six months. If the 6-month spot rate rises to 3.6%, the 1-year bill (which now has six months until maturity) is priced at $98.2318. If this occurs, the investor's holding period return is 1.5% (3% BEY). Note this is same return the investor would have obtained by buying and holding the 6-month bill. Thus, buying and holding the 6-month bill and riding the yield curve for six months with the 1-year bill will have the same holding period returns over the next six months.

The same line of reasoning can be used to obtain the 6-month forward rate beginning at any time period in the future. For example, the following can be determined:

- the 6-month forward rate three years from now
- the 6-month forward rate five years from now

The notation that we use to indicate 6-month forward rates is $_1f_m$ where the subscript 1 indicates a 1-period (6-month) rate and the subscript m indicates the period beginning m periods from now. When m is equal to zero, this means the current rate. Thus, the first 6-month forward rate is simply the current 6-month spot rate. That is,

$$_1f_0 = z_1$$

Exhibit 4: Six-Month Forward Rates: The Short-Term Forward Rate Curve

Notation	Forward Rate
$_1f_0$	3.00
$_1f_1$	3.60
$_1f_2$	3.92
$_1f_3$	5.15
$_1f_4$	6.54
$_1f_5$	6.33
$_1f_6$	6.23
$_1f_7$	5.79
$_1f_8$	6.01
$_1f_9$	6.24
$_1f_{10}$	6.48
$_1f_{11}$	6.72
$_1f_{12}$	6.97
$_1f_{13}$	6.36
$_1f_{14}$	6.49
$_1f_{15}$	6.62
$_1f_{16}$	6.76
$_1f_{17}$	8.10
$_1f_{18}$	8.40
$_1f_{19}$	8.72

The general formula for determining a 6-month forward rate is:

$$_1f_m = \frac{(1 + z_{m+1})^{m+1}}{(1 + z_m)^m} - 1$$

For example, suppose that the 6-month forward rate four years (8 6-month periods) from now is sought. In terms of our notation, m is 8 and we seek $_1f_8$. The formula is then:

$$_1f_8 = \frac{(1 + z_9)^9}{(1 + z_8)^8} - 1$$

From Exhibit 1, since the 4-year spot rate is 5.065% and the 4.5-year spot rate is 5.1701%, z_8 is 2.5325% and z_9 is 2.58505%. Then,

$$_1f_8 = \frac{(1.0258505)^9}{(1.025325)^8} - 1 = 3.005\%$$

Doubling this rate gives a 6-month forward rate four years from now of 6.01%.

Exhibit 4 shows all of the 6-month forward rates for the Treasury yield curve and corresponding spot rate curve shown in Exhibit 1. The set of these forward rates is the *short-term forward-rate curve*.

Relationship between Spot Rates and Short-Term Forward Rates Suppose an investor invests $\$X$ in a 3-year zero-coupon Treasury security. The total proceeds three years (six periods) from now would be:

$$X(1 + z_6)^6$$

The investor could instead buy a 6-month Treasury bill and reinvest the proceeds every six months for three years. The future dollars or dollar return will depend on the 6-month forward rates. Suppose that the investor can actually reinvest the proceeds maturing every six months at the calculated 6-month forward rates shown in Exhibit 4. At the end of three years, an investment of $\$X$ would generate the following proceeds:

$$X(1 + z_1)(1 + {_1}f_1)(1 + {_1}f_2)(1 + {_1}f_3)(1 + {_1}f_4)(1 + {_1}f_5)$$

Since the two investments must give the same proceeds at the end of four years, the two previous equations can be equated:

$$X(1 + z_6)^6 = X(1 + z_1)(1 + {_1}f_1)(1 + {_1}f_2)(1 + {_1}f_3)(1 + {_1}f_4)(1 + {_1}f_5)$$

Solving for the 3-year (6-period) spot rate, we have:

$$z_6 = [(1 + z_1)(1 + {_1}f_1)(1 + {_1}f_2)(1 + {_1}f_3)(1 + {_1}f_4)(1 + {_1}f_5)]^{\frac{1}{6}} - 1$$

This equation tells us that the 3-year spot rate depends on the current 6-month spot rate and the five 6-month forward rates. In fact, the right-hand side of this equation is a geometric average of the current 6-month spot rate and the five 6-month forward rates.

Let's use the values in Exhibits 1 and 4 to confirm this result. Since the 6-month spot rate in Exhibit 1 is 3%, z_1 is 1.5% and therefore

$$z_6 = [(1.015)(1.018)(1.0196)(1.02575)(1.0327)(1.03165)]^{\frac{1}{6}} - 1$$
$$= 0.023761 = 2.3761\%$$

Doubling this rate gives 4.7522%. This agrees with the spot rate shown in Exhibit 1.

In general, the relationship between a T-period spot rate, the current 6-month spot rate, and the 6-month forward rates is as follows:

$$z_T = [(1 + z_1)(1 + {_1}f_1)(1 + {_1}f_2) \dots (1 + {_1}f_{T-1})]^{1/T} - 1$$

Therefore, discounting at the forward rates will give the same present value as discounting at spot rates. This means that calculating the zero-volatility spread over the Treasury spot rate curve is the same as calculating the zero-volatility spread over the Treasury forward rate curve.

To summarize, a par rate is the average discount rate of many cash flows (those of a par bond) over many periods. A spot rate is the average discount rate of a single cash flow over many periods. A forward rate is the rate used to discount a single cash flow back one period. Accordingly, a 1-period forward rate is the fundamental unit of yield curve analysis.

Forward Rates for Any Period We can take the analysis of forward rates further. It is not necessary to limit ourselves to 6-month forward rates. The Treasury yield curve can be used to calculate the forward rate for any time in the future for any investment horizon. Before we defined $_1f_m$ as the 1-period (or 6-month) forward rate m periods from now. We will now let $_nf_m$ be the forward rate for an investment of n periods beginning m periods from now.

Forward Rate as a Hedgeable Rate A natural question about forward rates is how well they do at predicting future interest rates. Studies have demonstrated that forward rates do not do a good job at predicting future interest rates.[5] For example, Michele Kreisler and Richard Worley present evidence that suggests there is little or no relationship between the yield curve's slope (i.e., implied forward rates) and subsequent interest rate movements. In other words, increases in rates are as likely to follow positively sloped yield curves as flat or inverted yield curves.[6] Then, why the big deal about understanding forward rates? The reason is that forward rates indicate how an investor's expectations must differ from the market consensus in order to make the correct decision.

A forward rate may not be realized. That is irrelevant. The fact is that a forward rate indicates to the investor if his expectation about a rate in the future is less than the corresponding forward rate, then he would be better off investing now to lock in the forward rate. For this reason, as well as others explained later, some market participants prefer not to talk about forward rates as being market consensus rates. Instead they refer to forward rates as being *hedgeable rates*.

VALUING A RISKY FLOATER

We begin our valuation discussion with the simplest possible case — a default risk-free floater with no embedded options. Suppose the floater pays cash flows quarterly and the coupon formula is 3-month LIBOR flat. The coupon reset and payment dates are assumed to coincide. Under these idealized circumstances, the floater's price will always equal par on the coupon reset dates. This result holds because the floater's new coupon rate is always reset to reflect the current market rate (e.g., 3-month LIBOR). Accordingly, on each coupon reset date, any change in interest rates (via the reference rate) is also reflected in the size of the floater's coupon payment.

---

[5] Eugene F. Fama, "Forward Rates as Predictors of Future Spot Rates," *Journal of Financial Economics* (1976), pp. 361-377.
[6] Michele A. Kreisler and Richard B. Worley. "Value Measures for Managing Interest-Rate Risk." in Frank J. Fabozzi (ed.), *Managing Fixed Income Portfolios* (New Hope, PA: Frank J. Fabozzi Associates, 1997).

Exhibit 5: Bloomberg Security Decription of a Merrill Lynch Floater Maturing June 24, 2003

```
5                                                      P066 Corp   D E S
S E C U R I T Y   D E S C R I P T I O N            Page 1/ 3
MERRILL LYNCH      MER Float 06/03    N O T   P R I C E D
ISSUER INFORMATION            IDENTIFIERS              1) Additional Sec Info
Name MERRILL LYNCH & CO       Common    008850305      2) Floating Rates
Type Finance-Invest Bnkr/Brkr ISIN    US590188JC35      3) Identifiers
Market of Issue GLOBAL        CUSIP      590188JC3      4) Ratings
SECURITY INFORMATION          RATINGS                  5) Fees/Restrictions
Country USA      Currency USD Moody's     Aa3           6) Prospectus
Collateral Type NOTES         S&P         AA-           7) Sec. Specific News
Calc Typ ( 21)FLOAT RATE NOTE FI          AA            8) Involved Parties
Maturity  6/24/2003 Series    ISSUE SIZE               9) Custom Notes
NORMAL                        Amt Issued             10) Issuer Information
Coupon5.15        FLOATING QUARTLY USD 750,000.00  (M) 11) Pricing Sources
QUARTL US LIB+15      ACT/360 Amt Outstanding         12) Prospectus Request
Announcement Dt  6/17/98      USD 750,000.00      (M)
Int. Accrual Dt  6/24/98      Min Piece/Increment
1st Settle Date  6/24/98         1,000.00/  1,000.00
1st Coupon Date  9/24/98      Par Amount    1,000.00
Tss Pr 99.912  Reoffer   99.912 LEAD MANAGER/EXCHANGE
                              ML                      65) Old DES
HAVE PROSPECTUS               LUXEMBOURG              66) Send as Attachment
CPN RATE=3MO US$LIBOR +15BP. UNSEC'D. DISC MARGIN: 17BP OVER 3MO LIBOR.
```

Source: Bloomberg Financial Markets

The discussion is easily expanded to include risky floaters (e.g., corporate floaters) without a call feature or other embedded options. We will illustrate the valuation of a risky floater with a non-callable floating-rate note issued by Merrill Lynch (ticker symbol "MER 06/03") that matures June 24, 2003. The Security Description Screen (DES) from Bloomberg is presented in Exhibit 5. This floater delivers cash flows quarterly employing a coupon formula equal to 3-month LIBOR plus 15 basis points and does not possess a cap or a floor. As before, the coupon reset and payment dates are assumed to be the same. This floater pays a spread of 15 basis points above the reference rate (i.e., the quoted margin) to compensate the investor for the risks (e.g., default, liquidity, etc.) associated with this security. The quoted margin is established on the floater's issue date and is fixed to maturity. If the market's evaluation of the risk of holding the floater does not change, the risky floater will be repriced to par on each coupon reset date just as with the default-free floater. This result holds as long as the issuer's risk can be characterized by a constant markup over the risk-free rate.[7]

The more likely scenario, however, is that the market's perception of the security's risk will change over time. A perceived change in the floater's risk manifests itself in a divergence between the quoted margin (which is fixed at issue) and the spread the market requires for bearing the security's risks — henceforth, the *required margin*. When this divergence occurs, the risky floater will not be repriced to par on

---

[7] See Jess Yawitz, Howard Kaufold, Thomas Maciroski, and Michael Smirlock, "The Pricing and Duration of Floating-Rate Bonds," *Journal of Portfolio Management* (Summer 1987), pp. 49-56.

the coupon reset date. If the required margin increases (decreases) relative to the quoted margin, the floater will be repriced at a discount (premium) to par value. Intuitively, the pricing expression for a risky floater can be thought of as possessing two components: (1) a floater whose quoted margin and required margin are the same and (2) a "differential risk annuity" that delivers payments equal to the difference between the quoted margin and the required margin multiplied by the par value. Note it is the differential risk annuity that causes the floater's price to deviate from par on a coupon reset date. Specifically, if the required margin is above (below) the quoted margin, then the differential risk annuity will deliver negative (positive) cash flows and the floater's price will be reset at a discount (premium) to its par value.

We will illustrate this process using the Merrill Lynch floater from Exhibit 5. For ease of exposition, we will invoke some simplifying assumptions. First, the issue will be priced on a coupon reset date. Second, although this floater has an ACT/360 day-count convention, for simplicity we will assume that each quarter has 91 days. Third, we will assume initially that the LIBOR yield curve is flat such that all implied 3-month LIBOR forward rates are the same.[8] Note the same principles apply with equal force when these assumptions are relaxed.

Exhibit 6: Valuing a Risk Floater When the Market's Required Margin Equals the Quoted Margin*

(1) Coupon Period	(2) Day Count	(3) Forward Rate (%)	(4) Quoted Margin (%)	(5) Cash Flow	(6) Required Margin (%)	(7) Discount Factor	(8) PV of Cash Flow
0	91	5.00				1.000000	
1	91	5.00	0.15	$1.301806	0.15	0.987149	$1.285076
2	91	5.00	0.15	1.301806	0.15	0.974464	1.268562
3	91	5.00	0.15	1.301806	0.15	0.961941	1.252260
4	91	5.00	0.15	1.301806	0.15	0.949579	1.236168
5	91	5.00	0.15	1.301806	0.15	0.937377	1.220282
6	91	5.00	0.15	1.301806	0.15	0.925331	1.204600
7	91	5.00	0.15	1.301806	0.15	0.913439	1.189120
8	91	5.00	0.15	1.301806	0.15	0.901701	1.173839
9	91	5.00	0.15	1.301806	0.15	0.890113	1.158755
10	91	5.00	0.15	1.301806	0.15	0.878675	1.143864
11	91	5.00	0.15	1.301806	0.15	0.867383	1.129164
12	91	5.00	0.15	1.301806	0.15	0.856237	1.114654
13	91	5.00	0.15	1.301806	0.15	0.845233	1.100329
14	91	5.00	0.15	1.301806	0.15	0.834371	1.086189
15	91	5.00	0.15	1.301806	0.15	0.823649	1.072231
16	91	5.00	0.15	101.301800	0.15	0.813065	82.264910
						Price =	100.000000

* Assumes 3-month LIBOR remains constant at 5%

[8] We will relax this assumption shortly.

Let's value the Merrill Lynch floater on June 24, 1999. From Exhibit 5, we know this floater's coupon rate is equal to 3-month plus 15 basis points and delivers cash flows quarterly. Since this floater matures on June 24, 2003, there are 16 coupon payments remaining. Assume that 3-month LIBOR is 5% and will remain at that level until the floater's maturity. Finally, suppose the required margin is also 15 basis points so the quoted margin and the required margin are the same. Exhibit 6 illustrates the valuation process.

The first column in Exhibit 6 simply lists the quarterly periods. Next, column (2) lists the number of days in each quarterly coupon period assumed to be 91 days. Column (3) indicates the assumed current value of 3-month LIBOR. In period 0, 3-month LIBOR is the current 3-month spot rate. In periods 1 through 16, these rates are implied 3-month LIBOR forward rates derived from the current LIBOR yield curve.[9] For ease of exposition, we will call these rates *forward rates*. Recall for a floater, the coupon rate is set at the beginning of the period and paid at the end. For example, the coupon rate in the first period depends on the value of 3-month LIBOR at period 0 plus the quoted margin. In this first illustration, 3-month LIBOR is assumed to remain constant at 5%. Column (4) is the quoted margin of 15 basis points and remains fixed to maturity.

The cash flow is found by multiplying the coupon rate and the maturity value (assumed to be 100). However, the coupon rate (the forward rate in the previous period plus the quoted margin) must be adjusted for the number of days in the quarterly payment period. The formula to do so is:

$$\frac{\text{Coupon rate} \times \text{Number of days in period}}{360} \times 100$$

In addition to the projected cash flow, in period 16 the investor receives the maturity value of 100. The projected cash flows of the Merrill Lynch floater are shown in Column (5).

It is from the assumed values of 3-month LIBOR (i.e., the current spot rate and the implied forward rates) and the required margin in Column (6) that the discount rate that will be used to determine the present value of the cash flows will be calculated. The discount factor is found as follows:[10]

$$\frac{\text{Discount factor in the previous period}}{1 + (\text{Fwd. rate in previous period} + \text{Required margin}) \times \text{No. of days in period}/360}$$

The discount factors are shown in Column (7).

Finally, Column (8) is the present value of each of the cash flows and is computed by taking the product of the cash flow in Column (5) and the discount factor in Column (7). The floater's value is the sum of these present values and appears at the bottom of Column (8). Thus, a floater whose quoted margin and market's required margin are the same trades at par.

---

[9] The implied LIBOR forward rates can also be determined using Eurodollar CD futures contracts as described in Chapter 6.

[10] The formulas presented below are adapted from Chapter 6 of Ravi E. Dattatreya, Raj E.S. Venkatesh, and Vijaya E. Venkatesh, *Interest Rate & Currency Swaps* (Chicago: Probus Publishing, 1994).

Exhibit 7: Valuing a Risk Floater When the Market's Required Margin Equals the Quoted Margin*

(1) Coupon Period	(2) Day Count	(3) Forward Rate (%)	(4) Quoted Margin (%)	(5) Cash Flow	(6) Required Margin (%)	(7) Discount Factor	(8) PV of Cash Flow
0	91	5.00				1.000000	
1	91	5.01	0.15	1.301806	0.15	0.987149	$1.285076
2	91	5.02	0.15	1.304333	0.15	0.974439	1.270994
3	91	5.03	0.15	1.306861	0.15	0.961869	1.257029
4	91	5.04	0.15	1.309389	0.15	0.949437	1.243182
5	91	5.05	0.15	1.311917	0.15	0.937143	1.229453
6	91	5.06	0.15	1.314444	0.15	0.924984	1.215840
7	91	5.07	0.15	1.316972	0.15	0.912961	1.202344
8	91	5.08	0.15	1.319500	0.15	0.901071	1.188963
9	91	5.09	0.15	1.322028	0.15	0.889314	1.175698
10	91	5.10	0.15	1.324556	0.15	0.877689	1.162547
11	91	5.11	0.15	1.327083	0.15	0.866194	1.149511
12	91	5.12	0.15	1.329611	0.15	0.854828	1.136588
13	91	5.13	0.15	1.332139	0.15	0.843590	1.123779
14	91	5.14	0.15	1.337194	0.15	0.832458	1.113159
15	91	5.15	0.15	1.339722	0.15	0.821453	1.100519
16	91	5.16	0.15	101.342300	0.15	0.810573	82.145320
						Price =	100.000000

* Assumes 3-month LIBOR increases 1 basis point per quarter until maturity.

It is important to stress that this result holds *regardless of the path 3-month LIBOR takes in the future*. To see this, we replicate the process described in Exhibit 6 once again with one important exception. Rather than remaining constant, we assume that 3-month LIBOR forward rates increase by 1 basis point per quarter until the floater's maturity. These calculations are displayed in Exhibit 7. As before, the present value of the floater's projected cash flows is 100. When the market's required margin equals the quoted margin, any increase/decrease in the floater's projected cash flows will result in an offsetting increase/decrease in the floater's discount factors leaving the total present value of the cash flow equal to par.

Now let's consider the case when the required margin does not equal the quoted margin. A risky floater can be separated into two components.[11] Namely, a floater selling at par (i.e., the required margin equals the floater's quoted margin) and a "differential risk annuity" that causes the floater to deviate from par. A differential risk annuity is a series of constant payments (until a floater's maturity date) equal to the difference between the quoted margin and the required margin multiplied by the par value. A position in a risky floater can be described as a long position in a par floater and a long (short) position in a differential risk annuity. A

---

[11] See Steven I. Dym, "A Generalized Approach to Price and Duration of Non-Par Floating-Rate Notes," *The Journal of Portfolio Management* (Summer 1998), pp. 102-107.

long (short) position in the differential risk annuity indicates that the required margin has decreased (increased) since the floater's issue date. Accordingly, the price of a risky floater is equal to par plus the present value of the differential risk annuity when the required margin and the quoted margin are not the same.

To illustrate, we will value the same Merrill Lynch floater assuming that the required margin is now 20 basis points. For this to occur, some dimension of the floater's risk must have increased since the floater's issuance. Now in order to be reset to par, the Merrill Lynch floater would hypothetically have to possess a coupon rate equal to 3-month LIBOR plus 20 basis points. Since the quoted margin is fixed, the floater's price must fall to reflect the market's perceived increase in the security's risk.

Exhibit 8 illustrates the calculation. Once again for simplicity, we assume that 3-month LIBOR remains unchanged at 5% and there are 91 days in each coupon period. Since a risky floater can be thought of as par plus the differential risk annuity, all that is necessary is to take the present value of the annuity. Each annuity payment is computed as follows:

Differential risk annuity payment

$$= \frac{((\text{Quoted margin} - \text{Required margin}) \times \text{Number of days in period})}{360} \times 100$$

Exhibit 8: Valuing the Differential Risk Annuity When the Market's Required Margin is Greater Than the Quoted Margin[*]

(1) Coupon Period	(2) Day Count	(3) Forward Rate (%)	(4) Quoted Margin	(5) Required Margin (%)	(6) Cash Flow	(7) Discount Factor	(8) PV of Cash Flow
0	91	5.00				1.000000	
1	91	5.00	0.15	0.20	−0.01264	0.987026	−0.01247
2	91	5.00	0.15	0.20	−0.01264	0.974221	−0.01231
3	91	5.00	0.15	0.20	−0.01264	0.961581	−0.01215
4	91	5.00	0.15	0.20	−0.01264	0.949106	−0.01200
5	91	5.00	0.15	0.20	−0.01264	0.936792	−0.01184
6	91	5.00	0.15	0.20	−0.01264	0.924638	−0.01169
7	91	5.00	0.15	0.20	−0.01264	0.912642	−0.01153
8	91	5.00	0.15	0.20	−0.01264	0.900801	−0.01139
9	91	5.00	0.15	0.20	−0.01264	0.889115	−0.01124
10	91	5.00	0.15	0.20	−0.01264	0.877579	−0.01109
11	91	5.00	0.15	0.20	−0.01264	0.866194	−0.01095
12	91	5.00	0.15	0.20	−0.01264	0.854956	−0.01081
13	91	5.00	0.15	0.20	−0.01264	0.843864	−0.01067
14	91	5.00	0.15	0.20	−0.01264	0.832915	−0.01053
15	91	5.00	0.15	0.20	−0.01264	0.822109	−0.01039
16	91	5.00	0.15	0.20	−0.01264	0.811443	−0.01026
						Total Present Value =	−0.1813

[*] Assumes 3-month LIBOR remains constant at 5%

The quoted margin and required margin are in Columns (4) and (5), respectively. These cash flows are contained in Column (6). The discount factors are computed as described previously with the exception of the larger required margin. The discount factors appear in Column (7). The present value of the each cash flow is in Column (8) and is just the product of the cash flow (Column (6)) and its corresponding discount factor (Column (7)). The present value of the differential risk annuity is −0.1813 and is shown at the bottom of Column (8).

Once the present value of the differential risk annuity is determined, the price of the risky Merrill Lynch floater is simply the sum of 100 (price of the floater per $100 of par value when the quoted margin and required margin are the same) and the present value of the differential risk annuity. In our example,

Price of risky floater = 100 + (−0.1813) = 99.8187

When the required margin exceeds the quoted margin, the floater will be priced at a discount to par value. However, the size of the discount will depend on the assumed path 3-month LIBOR will take in the future.[12]

The next illustration takes up the case when the required margin is less than the quoted margin. For example, we will value the Merrill Lynch floater assuming the required margin is now 10 basis points and everything else is assumed to remain the same. Exhibit 9 presents the calculation of the differential risk annuity. Note the difference between the quoted margin (Column (4)) and the required margin (Column (5)) is positive and therefore produces a positive annuity payment (Column (6)). The discount factors (Column (7)) are computed as previously described except for the lower required margin. The present values of the differential risk annuity payment appear in Column (8) and their total appears at the bottom of the column.

In this instance, the price of the Merrill Lynch floater is given by:

Price of risky floater = 100 + 0.1817 = 100.1817

When the required margin is less than the quoted margin, the floater will be priced at a premium to par value. Note, the size of the premium is also interest-rate path dependent.

---

[12] Raymond J. Iwanowski, "An Investor's Guide to Floating-Rate Notes: Conventions, Mathematics, and Relative Valuation," Chapter 9 in Thomas S.Y. Ho (ed.), *Fixed Income Solutions* (Chicago: Irwin Professional Publishing, 1996).

Exhibit 9: Valuing the Differential Risk Annuity When the Market's Required Margin is Less Than the Quoted Margin[*]

(1) Coupon Period	(2) Day Count	(3) Forward Rate (%)	(4) Quoted Margin (%)	(5) Required Margin (%)	(6) Cash Flow	(7) Discount Factor	(8) PV of Cash Flow
0	91	5.00				1.000000	
1	91	5.00	0.15	0.10	0.01264	0.987272	0.01248
2	91	5.00	0.15	0.10	0.01264	0.974707	0.01232
3	91	5.00	0.15	0.10	0.01264	0.962301	0.01216
4	91	5.00	0.15	0.10	0.01264	0.950053	0.01201
5	91	5.00	0.15	0.10	0.01264	0.937961	0.01186
6	91	5.00	0.15	0.10	0.01264	0.926024	0.01170
7	91	5.00	0.15	0.10	0.01264	0.914237	0.01156
8	91	5.00	0.15	0.10	0.01264	0.902601	0.01141
9	91	5.00	0.15	0.10	0.01264	0.891113	0.01127
10	91	5.00	0.15	0.10	0.01264	0.879772	0.01112
11	91	5.00	0.15	0.10	0.01264	0.868574	0.01098
12	91	5.00	0.15	0.10	0.01264	0.857520	0.01084
13	91	5.00	0.15	0.10	0.01264	0.846605	0.01070
14	91	5.00	0.15	0.10	0.01264	0.835830	0.01056
15	91	5.00	0.15	0.10	0.01264	0.825192	0.01043
16	91	5.00	0.15	0.10	0.01264	0.814689	0.01030

Total Present Value = 0.1817

[*] Assumes 3-month LIBOR remains constant at 5%

Chapter 4

Valuing Floaters with Embedded Options

G iven the underlying principles and concepts in the valuation process explained in the previous chapter, we turn our attention to the valuation of risky floaters with embedded options. Once recognition is given to an embedded option, a valuation model that considers the volatility of interest rates must be adopted. The model used to value fixed-rate bonds with embedded options is the lattice model. We explain this model and demonstrate how it can be extended to value five floating-rate structures: (1) a capped floater, (2) a range note, (3) a callable capped floater, (4) an indexed amortizing note, and (5) a ratchet bond. We defer a discussion of the valuation of floating-rate mortgage-backed and asset-backed securities until Chapter 10.

VALUATION OF BONDS WITH EMBEDDED OPTIONS

A lattice model can be used to value fixed-rate coupon bonds with embedded options. A lattice model permits interest rates to change each period based on a volatility assumption. An interest rate tree is employed to value bonds. The tree is constructed such that the values it produces are consistent with the volatility assumption and is calibrated to the market prices of the relevant on-the-run Treasury issues (i.e., the tree does not permit arbitrage and hence is referred to as an *arbitrage-free tree*). A special case of the lattice model is the binomial model. While our illustrations in this chapter use the binomial model, the principles are the same for other lattice models.

VALUING OPTION-FREE BONDS

We begin with a review of the valuation of option-free bonds. We must determine the on-the-run or benchmark yield curve for the particular issuer whose bonds we

The first part of this chapter that describes the valuation model is coauthored with Andrew J. Kalotay and George O. Williams and draws from Andrew J. Kalotay, George O. Williams, and Frank J. Fabozzi, "A Model for Valuing Bonds and Embedded Options," *Financial Analysts Journal* (May-June 1993), pp. 35-46. The part of this chapter that covers the extension of the valuation model to five floating-rate structures is coauthored with Michael Dorigan and Andrew J. Kalotay and draws from Michael Dorigan, Frank J. Fabozzi, and Andrew J. Kalotay, "Valuation of Floating-Rate Bonds," *Perspectives in Fixed Income Portfolio Management: Volume 2* (New Hope, PA: Frank J. Fabozzi Associates, 2000).

want to value. The starting point is the Treasury's on-the-run yield curve. To obtain a particular issuer's on-the-run yield curve, an appropriate credit is added to the yields of each on-the-run Treasury issue. The credit spread need not be constant for all maturities. For example, the credit spread may increase with maturity. In our illustration, we use the following hypothetical on-the-run issue for an issuer:

Maturity	Yield to maturity	Market Price
1 year	3.5%	100
2 years	4.2%	100
3 years	4.7%	100
4 years	5.2%	100

Each bond is trading at par value (100) so the coupon rate is equal to the yield to maturity. We will simplify the illustration by assuming annual-pay bonds.

The spot rates can be shown to be:[1]

Year	Spot Rate
1	3.5000%
2	4.2147%
3	4.7345%
4	5.2707%

The corresponding 1-year forward rates are:

Current 1-year forward rate	3.500%
1-year forward rate one year from now	4.935%
1-year forward rate two years from now	5.784%
1-year forward rate three years from now	6.893%

Now consider an option-free bond with four years remaining to maturity and a coupon rate of 6.5%. The value of this bond can be calculated in one of two ways, both producing the same value. First, the cash flows can be discounted at the spot rates as shown below:

$$\frac{6.5}{(1.035)^1} + \frac{6.5}{(1.042147)^2} + \frac{6.5}{(1.047345)^3} + \frac{100+6.5}{(1.052707)^4} = 104.643$$

The second way is to discount by the 1-year forward rates as shown below:

$$\frac{6.5}{(1.035)} + \frac{6.5}{(1.035)(1.04935)} + \frac{6.5}{(1.035)(1.04935)(1.05784)}$$

$$+ \frac{100+6.5}{(1.035)(1.04935)(1.05784)(1.06893)} = 104.643$$

This result holds, of course, because the n-year spot rate is the geometric average of the 1-year forward rates.

---

[1] The methodology used to obtain the spot rate is bootstrapping. See Chapter 2 in Frank J. Fabozzi, *Valuation of Fixed Income Securities and Derivatives* (New Hope, PA: Frank J. Fabozzi Associates, 1998).

Exhibit 1: Four-Year Binomial Interest Rate Tree

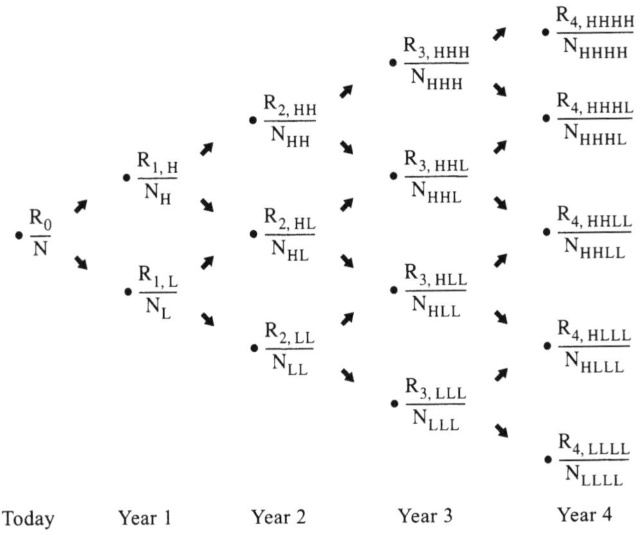

| Today | Year 1 | Year 2 | Year 3 | Year 4 |

BINOMIAL INTEREST RATE TREE

Once we allow for an embedded option such that the option's value depends on the level of interest rates, consideration must be given to future interest rate volatility. This can be done by introducing a *binomial interest rate tree*. This tree is nothing more than a graphical depiction of the 1-period or short rates over time based on some assumption about interest rate volatility. How this tree is constructed is explained below.

Exhibit 1 shows an example of a binomial interest rate tree. In this tree, each node (bold circle) represents a time period that is equal to one year (in our illustration) from the node to its left. Each node is labeled with an N, representing node, and a subscript. For now, we denote the higher "branch" of the tree with an "H" and the lower with an "L." It is important to distinguish between the notation used to identify nodes and that used to describe a "path" to a certain node. For example, N_{HHL} can be reached by traversing the tree in an HHL pattern, i.e., move higher, then higher, then lower. But an HLH pattern would still place you at N_{HHL}. To capture path dependence, as it is known, requires the addition of at least one other variable, referred to as a *state variable*. We will see this in the sections on indexed amortizing notes and ratchet bonds later in this chapter.

Look first at the point denoted by just N in Exhibit 1. This is the root of the tree and is nothing more than the current 1-year spot rate, or equivalently the current 1-year rate, which we denote by R_0. In the binomial model what is assumed in creating this tree is that the 1-year rate can take on two possible values the next year and the two rates have the same probability of occurring. One rate will be higher than the other. It is assumed that the 1-year rate can evolve over time based on a random process called a *lognormal random walk with a certain volatility.*

We use the following notation to describe the tree in the first year. Let

σ = assumed volatility of the 1-year rate

$R_{1,L}$ = the lower 1-year rate one year from now

$R_{1,H}$ = the higher 1-year rate one year from now

The relationship between $R_{1,L}$ and $R_{1,H}$ is as follows:

$$R_{1,H} = R_{1,L}(e^{2\sigma})$$

where e is the base of the natural logarithm 2.71828.

For example, suppose that $R_{1,L}$ is 4.4448% and σ is 10% per year, then:

$$R_{1,H} = 4.4448\%(e^{2 \times 0.10}) = 5.4289\%$$

In the second year, there are three possible values for the 1-year rate, which we will denote as follows:

$R_{2,LL}$ = 1-year rate in second year assuming the lower rate in the first year and the lower rate in the second year

$R_{2,HH}$ = 1-year rate in second year assuming the higher rate in the first year and the higher rate in the second year

$R_{2,HL}$ = 1-year rate in second year assuming the higher rate in the first year and the lower rate in the second year or equivalently the lower rate in the first year and the higher rate in the second year

The relationship between $R_{2,LL}$ and the other two 1-year rates is as follows:

$$R_{2,HH} = R_{2,LL}(e^{4\sigma}) \quad \text{and} \quad R_{2,HL} = R_{2,LL}(e^{2\sigma})$$

So, for example, if $r_{2,LL}$ is 4.6958%, then assuming once again that σ is 10%, then

$$R_{2,HH} = 4.6958\%(e^{4 \times 0.10}) = 7.0053\%$$

and

$$R_{2,HL} = 4.6958\%(e^{2 \times 0.10}) = 5.7354\%$$

In the third year there are four possible values for the 1-year rate, which are denoted as follows: $R_{3,HHH}$, $R_{3,HHL}$, $R_{3,HLL}$, and $R_{3,LLL}$, and whose first three values are related to the last as follows:

$$R_{3,HHH} = R_{3,LLL}(e^{6\sigma})$$
$$R_{3,HHL} = R_{3,LLL}(e^{4\sigma})$$
$$R_{3,HLL} = R_{3,LLL}(e^{2\sigma})$$

Exhibit 2: Four-Year Binomial Interest Rate Tree with One-Year Rates*

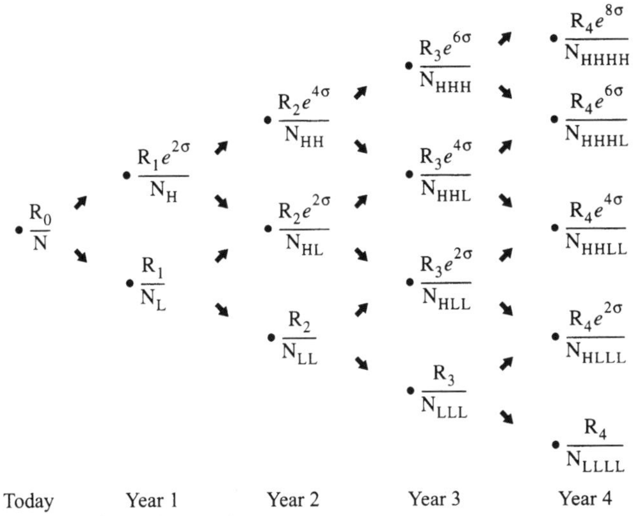

Today   Year 1   Year 2   Year 3   Year 4

* R_t equals forward 1-year lower rate.

Exhibit 1 shows the notation for a 4-year binomial interest rate tree. We can simplify the notation by letting R_t be the 1-year rate t years from now for the lower rate since all the other short rates t years from now depend on that rate. Exhibit 2 shows the interest rate tree using this simplified notation.

Before we go on to show how to use this binomial interest rate tree to value bonds, let's focus on two issues here. First, what does the volatility parameter σ represent? Second, how do we find the value of the bond at each node?

Volatility and the Standard Deviation

It can be shown that the standard deviation of the 1-year rate is equal to $R_0\sigma$.[2] The standard deviation is a statistical measure of volatility. It is important to see that the process that we assume in generating the binomial interest rate tree (or equivalently the short rates), implies that volatility is measured relative to the current level of rates. For example, if σ is 10% and the 1-year rate (R_0) is 4%, then the standard deviation of the 1-year rate is 4% × 10% = 0.4% or 40 basis points. However, if the current 1-year rate is 8%, the standard deviation of the 1-year rate would be 8% × 10% or 80 basis points.

___

[2] This can be seen by noting that

$$e^{2\sigma} \approx 1 + 2\sigma$$

Then the standard deviation of the 1-year rate is

$$\frac{Re^{2\sigma} - R}{2} \approx \frac{R + 2\sigma R - R}{2} = \sigma R$$

Exhibit 3: Calculating the Value at a Node: 1

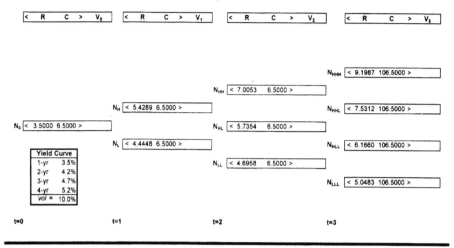

Determining the Value at a Node

To explain how to determine the value at a node, we will use the following notation at each node:

$$[<R \quad C> \quad V_t]$$

where

R = interest rate from the binomial interest rate tree at each node
C = cash flow to be paid in the next period
V_t = value of the bond at period t

We denote the value of the bond at period t at node N_* by $V_t[N_*]$.

For all the nodes at the period just before the bond matures, the cash flow to be paid in the next period is the maturity value plus the last coupon payment. For the nodes prior to that period, the cash flow to be paid in the next period is just the coupon payment.

For example, for our 4-year 6.5% coupon bond, there will be four nodes at $t = 3$ (period before maturity): N_{HHH}, N_{HHL}, N_{HLL}, and N_{LLL}. At each node, C is equal to 106.5. This amount is the maturity value of 100 plus the last coupon payment of 6.5. For the prior period, $t = 2$, the value for C is the coupon payment of 6.5 for all three nodes (N_{HH}, N_{HL}, and N_{LL}). The same is true for the value of C at all other nodes at $t = 1$ and $t = 0$.

Exhibit 3 shows the tree that would be used to value the 4-year 6.5% coupon bond using the notation given above. We'll see how we get the value for R at each node later. Notice that at each node the value at the node is not shown. It is that value at each node that we will explain how to compute.

Exhibit 4: Calculating the Value at a Node: 2

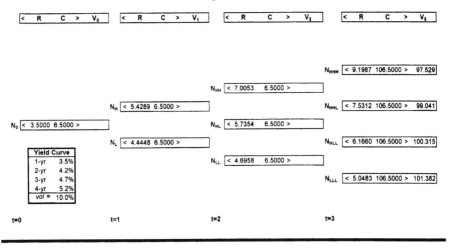

To do so, consider node N_{HHL}. At that node the cash flow to be paid in the next period (i.e., at maturity) is 106.50. The value of the bond at that period, V_3 [N_{HHL}], is found by discounting the cash flow using an appropriate discount rate. The appropriate discount rate is the R at that node. In our illustration, R at N_{HHL} is 7.5312%. Thus,

$$V_3[N_{HHL}] = \frac{106.50}{1.075312} = 99.041$$

The same procedure is used to get the value for V_3 at the three other nodes in Exhibit 3. Exhibit 4 is the same as Exhibit 3 with the value for V_3 included.

Now let's look at period 2. To get the value at a node for V_2 the following must be done. First, the future cash flow must be computed. The future cash flow at a node is equal to the cash flow paid in the next period, C, plus the value of the bond at the node to the right. There are two nodes to the right. Each is assumed to have an equal probability of occurrence. For example, consider N_{HL}. The two future cash flows at N_{HL} are

$6.5 + V_3$ [N_{HHL}] $= 6.5 + 99.041 = 105.541$
$6.5 + V_3$ [N_{HLL}] $= 6.5 + 100.315 = 106.815$

Each of the expected cash flows is then discounted at the value for R at the node and the two present values are averaged. Using N_{HL} again, R is 5.7354%. Therefore, V_2 [N_{HL}] is equal to:

$$V_2[N_{HL}] = 0.5\left(\frac{105.541}{1.057354}\right) + 0.5\left(\frac{106.815}{1.057354}\right) = 100.418$$

Similarly, the value for V_t at all of the nodes at $t = 2$, $t = 1$, and $t = 0$ is computed. The value at $t = 0$, V_0 is the value of the bond.

Exhibit 5: The 1-Year Rates for Year 1
Using the 2-Year 4.2% On-the-Run Issue: First Trial

<R C> V_0		<R C> V_1

$$N_H \quad \boxed{<5.8017 \ 104.2> \ 98.486}$$

$$N_0 \quad \boxed{<3.5000 \ 4.2> \ 99.691}$$

$$N_L \quad \boxed{<4.7500 \ 104.2> \ 99.475}$$

$t = 0$ $\qquad\qquad$ $t = 1$

Constructing the Binomial Interest Rate Tree

To see how to construct the binomial interest rate tree, let's use the assumed on-the-run yields presented earlier. We will assume that volatility, σ, is 10% and construct a 2-year tree using the 2-year bond with a coupon rate of 4.2%.

Exhibit 5 shows the relevant binomial interest rate tree. We'll see how all the values reported in the exhibit are obtained. The root rate for the tree, R_0, is simply the current 1-year rate, 3.5%.

In the first year there are two possible 1-year rates, the higher rate and the lower rate. What we want to find is the two 1-year rates that will be consistent with the volatility assumption, the process that is assumed to generate the short rates, and the observed market value of the bond. There is no simple formula for this. It must be found by an iterative process (i.e., trial-and-error). The steps are described and illustrated below.

Step 1: Select a value for R_1. Recall that R_1 is the lower 1-year rate. In this first trial, we *arbitrarily* selected a value of 4.75%.

Step 2: Determine the corresponding value for the higher 1-year rate. As explained earlier, this rate is related to the lower 1-year rate as follows: $R_1 \, e^{2\sigma}$. Since R_1 is 4.75%, the higher 1-year rate is 5.8017% (= 4.75% $e^{2\times0.10}$). This value is reported in Exhibit 5 at node N_H.

Step 3: Compute V_1 for the two nodes. This value at each node is determined as explained above. The two values are

$$V_1[N_H] = \frac{104.2}{1.058017} = 98.486$$

$$V_1[N_L] = \frac{104.2}{1.0475} = 99.475$$

Step 4: Calculate V_0 as follows:
Future cash flows:

$$4.2 + V_1[N_H] = 4.2 + 98.486 = 102.686$$
$$4.2 + V_1[N_L] = 4.2 + 99.475 = 103.675$$

$$V_0 = 0.5\left(\frac{102.686}{1.035}\right) + 0.5\left(\frac{103.675}{1.035}\right) = 99.691$$

Exhibit 6: The 1-Year Rates for Year 1 Using the 2-Year 4.2% On-the-Run Issue

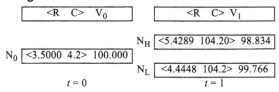

Step 5: Compare the value in Step 4 to the bond's market value. If the two values are the same, then the R_1 used in this trial is the one we seek. This is the 1-year rate that would then be used in the binomial interest rate tree for the lower rate and used to calculate the corresponding higher rate. If, instead, the value found in Step 4 is not equal to the market value of the bond, this means that the value R_1 in this trial is not the 1-year rate that is consistent with (1) the volatility assumption, (2) the process assumed to generate the 1-year rate, and (3) the observed market value of the bond. In this case, the five steps are repeated with a different value for R_1.

When R_1 is 4.75%, a value of 99.691 results in Step 4 which is less than the observed market price of 100. Therefore, 4.75% is too large and the five steps must be repeated trying a lower rate for R_1.

Let's jump right to the correct rate for R_1 in this example and rework steps 1 through 5. This occurs when R_1 is 4.4448%. The corresponding binomial interest rate tree is shown in Exhibit 6.

Step 1: In this trial we select a value of 4.4448% for R_1, the lower 1-year rate.

Step 2: The corresponding value for the higher 1-year rate is 5.4289% (= $4.4448\% \, e^{2\times0.10}$).

Step 3: V_1 for the two nodes is:

$$V_1[N_H] = \frac{104.2}{1.044448} = 98.834$$

$$V_1[N_L] = \frac{104.2}{1.054289} = 99.766$$

Step 4: The average present value is 100, which is the value at the node. To verify this, V_0 is calculated once again as follows:

Future cash flows:

$4.2 + V_1[N_H] = 4.2 + 98.834 = 103.034$

$4.2 + V_1[N_L] = 4.2 + 99.766 = 103.966$

$$V_0 = 0.5\left(\frac{103.034}{1.035}\right) + 0.5\left(\frac{103.966}{1.035}\right) = 100$$

Step 5: Since the average present value is equal to the observed market price of 100, R_1 or $R_{1,L}$ is 4.4448%, and $R_{1,H}$ is 5.4289%.

We can "grow" this tree for one more year by determining R_2. Now we will use the 3-year on-the-run issue, the 4.7% coupon bond, to get R_2. The same five steps are used in an iterative process to find the 1-year rates in the tree two years from now. The objective is now to find the value of R_2 that will produce a bond value of 100 (since the 3-year on-the-run issue has a market price of 100) and is consistent with (1) a volatility assumption of 10%, (2) a current 1-year rate of 3.5%, and (3) the two rates one year from now of 4.4448% (the lower rate) and 5.4289% (the higher rate).

As can be seen from Exhibit 7, the value of R_2, or equivalently $R_{2,LL}$, which will produce the desired result is 4.6958%. We showed earlier that the corresponding rates $R_{2,HL}$ and $R_{2,HH}$ would be 5.7354% and 7.0053%, respectively.

Valuing an Option-Free Bond Using the Binomial Model

The procedure for determining the value of a bond using a lattice is referred to as the *backward induction method* or *recursive valuation method*. Exhibit 8 shows the 1-year rates or binomial interest rate tree that can then be used to value any bond for this issuer (fixed or floating) with a maturity up to four years. To illustrate how to use the binomial interest rate tree, consider a 6.5% option-free bond with four years remaining to maturity. Also assume that the issuer's on-the-run yield curve is the one given earlier and hence the appropriate binomial interest rate tree is the one in Exhibit 8. Exhibit 9 shows the various values in the discounting process, and produces a bond value of 104.643.

It is important to note that this value is identical to the bond value found earlier when we discounted at either the spot rates or the 1-year forward rates. We should expect to find this result since our bond is option free. This clearly demonstrates that the valuation model is consistent with the standard valuation model for an option-free bond.

Exhibit 7: The 1-Year Rates for Year 2 Using the 3-Year 4.7% On-the-Run Issue

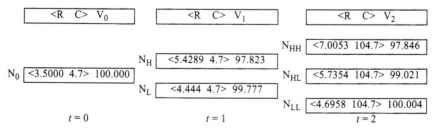

N_0 <3.5000 4.7> 100.000

N_H <5.4289 4.7> 97.823

N_L <4.444 4.7> 99.777

N_{HH} <7.0053 104.7> 97.846

N_{HL} <5.7354 104.7> 99.021

N_{LL} <4.6958 104.7> 100.004

$t = 0$ $t = 1$ $t = 2$

Exhibit 8: 4-Year Binomial Tree

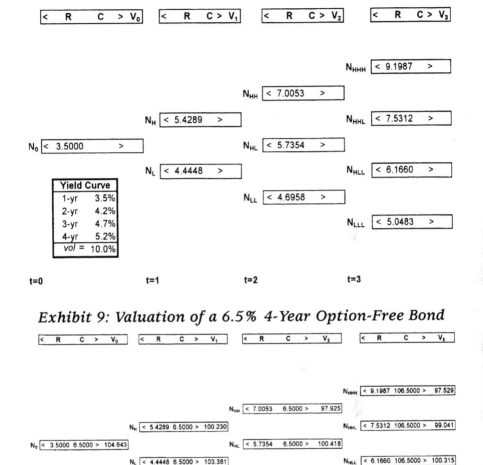

Exhibit 9: Valuation of a 6.5% 4-Year Option-Free Bond

VALUING CAPPED FLOATING-RATE BONDS

Now that we have some experience with the recursive valuation method, we can turn our attention to the valuation of floaters. Consider a floater with a coupon indexed to the 1-year rate (the reference rate) plus a spread. For our purposes, assume a 25 basis point spread (i.e., quoted margin) to the reference rate. In Exhibit

10, we use the tree from Exhibit 8 and, as was the case with the option-free fixed-rate coupon bond, at each node we have entered the cash flow expected at the end of each period. Using the same valuation method as before, we can find the value at each node. Consider N_{HLL}.

$$V_3[N_{HLL}] = 0.5\left(\frac{100 + 6.416}{1.06166}\right) + 0.5\left(\frac{100 + 6.416}{1.06166}\right) = 100.235$$

Stepping back one period

$$V_2[N_{LL}] = 0.5\left(\frac{100.235 + 4.9458}{1.046958}\right) + 0.5\left(\frac{100.238 + 4.9458}{1.046958}\right) = 100.465$$

Following this same procedure, we arrive at the price of 100.893. How would this change if the interest rate on the bond were capped?

Assume that the cap is 7.25%. Exhibit 11 provides a picture of the effects of the cap on the value of the bond. As rates move higher there is a possibility that the current reference rate exceeds the cap. Such is the case at N_{HHH} and N_{HHL}. The coupon is subject to the following constraint:

$$C_t = \max[R_t, 7.25\%]$$

As a result of the cap, the value of the bond in the upper nodes at $t = 4$ falls below par. Explicitly,

$$V_3[N_{HHH}] = 0.5\left(\frac{100 + 7.25}{1.09187}\right) + 0.5\left(\frac{100 + 7.25}{1.091987}\right) = 98.215$$

Exhibit 10: Valuation of a Floating-Rate Bond with No Cap

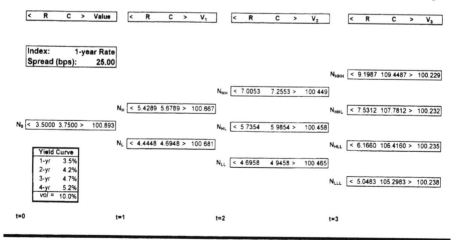

Exhibit 11: Valuation of a Capped Floating-Rate Bond

<	R	C	>	Value		<	R	C	>	V₁		<	R	C	>	V₂		<	R	C	>	V₃

Index:	1-year Rate
Cap (%):	7.25
Spread (bps):	25.00

N_{HHH} | < 9.1987 107.2500 > | 98.215 |

N_{HH} | < 7.0053   7.2500 > | 99.273 |

N_H | < 5.4289 5.6789 > | 99.998 |

N_{HHL} | < 7.5312 107.2500 > | 99.738 |

N_0 | < 3.5000 3.7500 > | 100.516 |

N_{HL} | < 5.7354   5.9854 > | 100.224 |

N_L | < 4.4448 4.6948 > | 100.569 |

N_{HLL} | < 6.1660 106.4160 > | 100.235 |

N_{LL} | < 4.6958   4.9458 > | 100.465 |

N_{LLL} | < 5.0483 105.2983 > | 100.238 |

Yield Curve	
1-yr	3.5%
2-yr	4.2%
3-yr	4.7%
4-yr	5.2%
vol =	10.0%

t=0   t=1   t=2   t=3

Valuing recursively through the tree, we arrive at the current value of the capped floater, 100.516. This last calculation gives us a means for pricing the cap. Without a cap, the bond is priced at 100.893. With the cap, it is priced at 100.516. The difference between these two prices is the value of the cap, 0.377. It is important to note that the price of the cap is *volatility dependent*. Any change in the volatility would result in a different valuation for the cap. The greater the volatility, the higher is the price of the option, and *vice versa*.

What if an issuer wanted to offer this bond at par? In such a case, an adjustment has to be made to the coupon. To lower the price from 100.516 to par, a lower spread over the reference rate need only be offered to investors. Suppose the issuer decides that the coupon will be the 1-year rate plus 5 basis points. It turns out that this is not enough. Take a look at Exhibit 12. It shows the relationship between the spread over the 1-year reference rate and the bond price. At a spread of 8.70 bps over the 1-year reference rate the bond will be priced at par. The spread of 8.7 bps is also volatility dependent.

Now let's move on to another structure where the coupon floats with a reference rate, but is again restricted. In this next case, a range is set in which the bond pays the reference rate, but, outside of the range, no coupon is paid.

VALUING A RANGE NOTE

A range note is a floater that pays the reference rate only if the rate falls within a specified band. If the reference rate falls outside the band, whether the lower or upper boundary, no coupon is paid. Typically, the band increases over time.

To illustrate, suppose that the reference rate is, again, the 1-year rate. Suppose further that the band (or coupon schedule) is defined as in Exhibit 13. Exhibit 14 holds our tree and the cash flows expected at each node. Either the 1-

year reference rate is paid at each node, or nothing. In the case of this 3-year note, there are a number of states in which no coupon is paid. Using our recursive valuation method, we can work back through the tree to the current value, 98.963.

Exhibit 12: Spread to Index to Price Cap at Par

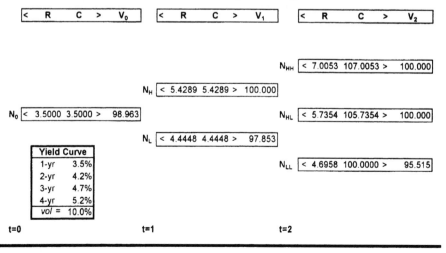

Exhibit 13: Coupon Schedule (Bands) for a Range Note

	Year 1	Year 2	Year 3
Lower Limit	3.00%	4.00%	5.00%
Upper Limit	5.00%	6.25%	8.00%

Exhibit 14: Valuation of a Range Floater

| < R C > V₀ | < R C > V₁ | < R C > V₂ |

N_{HH} | < 7.0053 107.0053 > 100.000 |

N_H | < 5.4289 5.4289 > 100.000 |

N_0 | < 3.5000 3.5000 > 98.963 |

N_{HL} | < 5.7354 105.7354 > 100.000 |

N_L | < 4.4448 4.4448 > 97.853 |

Yield Curve	
1-yr	3.5%
2-yr	4.2%
3-yr	4.7%
4-yr	5.2%
vol =	10.0%

N_{LL} | < 4.6958 100.0000 > 95.515 |

t=0   t=1   t=2

Exhibit 15: Valuation of a Callable Floating-Rate Bond with a 7.25% Cap

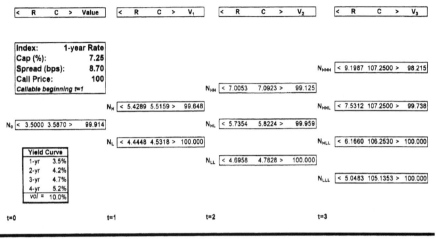

CALLABLE CAPPED FLOATING-RATE BONDS

Now consider a call option on the capped floater. We must be careful to specify the appropriate rules for calling the bond on the valuation tree. For our purposes, any time the bond has a value above par, the bond will be called. (Here we assume a par call to simplify the illustration.)

Before we get into these details, it is important to motivate the need for a call on a floating-rate bond. The value of a cap to the issuer increases as market rates near the cap and there is the potential for rates to exceed the cap prior to maturity. As rates decline, so does the value of the cap, eventually approaching zero. The problem for the issuer in this case is the additional basis-point spread it is paying for a cap that now has no value. Thus, when rates decline, a call has value to the issuer because it can call and reissue at current rates without the spread attributable to the cap.

Suppose that the capped floater is callable at par any time after the first year. Exhibit 15 provides details on the effect of the call option on valuation of the capped floater. Again it is assumed that for this callable bond, when the market price exceeds par in a recursive valuation model, the bond is called. In the case of our 4-year bond, you can see that the price of the bond at the previously mentioned nodes N_{LL}, N_{LLH}, and N_{LLL} is now 100 in Exhibit 15, the call price. The effect of the call option on the value is also evident with today's value for the bond moving to 99.914.

As with the case of a cap, the by-product of this analysis is the value of the call option on a capped floater. We now have the fair value of the capped floater versus the callable capped floater. So, the call option has a value of $100 - 99.914 = 0.086$.

Exhibit 16: Spread to Index to Price Callable Cap at Par

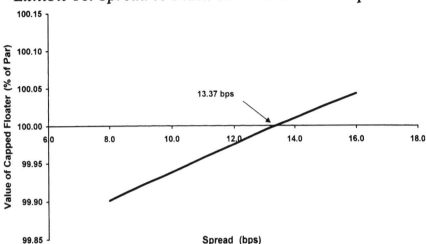

How would one structure the issue so that it is priced at par? Again, the issuer would have to offer the bondholder additional spread over the reference rate and the 8.7 basis points the holder is already receiving for accepting the cap. In this case, an additional 4.67 basis points is required, moving the total spread over the 1-year reference rate to 13.37 basis points. As before, we arrive at this 4.67 basis point spread through an iterative process described above for the structuring of a cap. Exhibit 16 shows the relationship between the spread and the value of the capped floater.

To summarize, the callable capped floater offers benefits to the issuer, but there is a cost. To avoid increasing payments as rates rise, the issuer can put a cap on the bond. However, investors will demand compensation in the form of higher coupon payments, i.e., a higher spread to the reference rate.

This spread is a burden that the bond issuer would like to avoid paying if rates decline and the cap has no value due to the low rates. A call option allows the issuer to retire the capped floater and reissue at lower rates. Again, the bondholder recognizes that the benefit to the issuer is a detriment to the bondholder and demands additional compensation, a higher spread.

Once the spread is determined, valuation of the callable capped floater is a simple application of the recursive valuation process with which we have utilized throughout this chapter. The coupon payments are defined at each node and the call option exercised at nodes where the market price exceeds the call price. All that is left is the discounting of the cash flow period-by-period back to the present to arrive at a value for the instrument, as we have just seen in Exhibits 11 and 15.

Now let's take a look at the indexed amortizing note for a couple of new valuation twists.

INDEXED AMORTIZING NOTES[3]

In this section we examine an indexed amortizing note (IAN), a bond whose principal payments are a prescribed function of the path of interest rates. Typically, principal payments are structured to accelerate in low rate environments. A typical IAN structure is described below.

Assume that the IAN has a 4-year maturity and pays investors a 6% interest rate on the outstanding principal, P, in years 1, 2, 3, and 4. Regardless of what happens to interest rates, there is no principal payment the first year (the "lock-out" period). In years 2 and 3, the amount of principal paid depends on the level of the 1-year rate. If the 1-year rate is below 5%, 75% of the remaining balance is repaid; if the rate is between 5% and 6%, 50% of the balance is repaid; if the rate exceeds 6%, there is no principal payment. If a principal payment made in accordance with this formula brings the outstanding balance below 20% of the amount originally issued (which we take to be 100.0), the entire bond is retired immediately (This is referred to as the "clean-up" provision). At maturity in year 4 any remaining principal is amortized. The formula below summarizes the amortization schedule for the note:

$$\text{time } t \text{ principal payment} = \begin{cases} 0 & \text{if } t = 1 \\ 0.75P & \text{if } t = 2 \text{ or } 3, R < 5\% \text{ and } 0.25P > 20 \\ 0.50P & \text{if } t = 2 \text{ or } 3, 5\% < R < 6\% \text{ and } 0.50P > 20 \\ 0 & \text{if } t = 2 \text{ or } 3, \text{ and } R > 6\% \\ P & \text{Otherwise.} \end{cases}$$

The IAN is a "path dependent" security. For a path dependent security knowledge of interest rates, at any time, call it t^*, in the valuation process does not provide sufficient information to calculate the cash flow generated by the security at that time. Contrast this with the floaters we just completed reviewing in the previous section. In that case knowledge of the current interest rate was all that was needed to calculate the cash flow to noteholders each period

Path dependence arises because the outstanding amount of the IAN depends on prior interest rates. In the case of path dependence, the cash flow also depends in some manner on the level of the factor at all points in time t prior to the calculation date, i.e., $t < t^*$. In other words, for IANs, how interest rates got to their current level over time is relevant.

There are a number of securities that possess this characteristic. A CMO is another example of a path-dependent security. One must know the amount of the underlying mortgage pool still outstanding at time t^* to calculate the time t^* cash flow of a CMO. This, however, depends on the prior prepayment experience which, in turn, is driven by the path of interest rates over the prior period.

As explained in Chapter 10, Monte Carlo simulation is the usual method of valuing these path dependent securities. However, this technique offers a num-

---

[3] This section of the chapter is adapted from C. Douglas Howard, "Valuing Path-Dependent Securities: Some Numerical Examples," Chapter 4 in Frank J. Fabozzi (ed.), *Advances in Fixed Income Valuation Modeling and Risk Management* (New Hope, PA: Frank Fabozzi Associates, 1997).

ber disadvantages. It is computationally intensive. It does not comply with arbitrage-free principles. Finally, the path sampling that is part of every Monte Carlo analysis leads to inconsistent results. All of this can be avoided with an application of recursive valuation.

Recursive Valuation

Consider each node as an interest rate state which we now label as $<R>$, where R is the rate in that state. Thus, $<7.0053>$ represents the interest rate state at N_{HH}. To value the IAN recursively, we partition the interest rate states as they exist at each node in the tree established in Exhibit 3 by further specifying how much of the IAN's principal, P, is outstanding *before* the principal payment of that year. The state $<7.0053>$, for example, is partitioned into $<7.0053, 100>$, $<7.0053, 50>$, $<7.0053, 25>$ and $<7.0053, 0>$. This additional variable, whose values partition the state as specified by the value of the stochastic interest rate variable, is referred to as a non-stochastic state variable and its range of attainable values is referred to as the state space.[4]

Exhibit 17 displays the expanded tree in which these interest rate states are explicit. (There is additional information included in the exhibit that we can ignore it for now.) Note that some states, such as $<5.0483, 100>$, cannot be reached. The bond will be entirely amortized by the time it reaches this state. If this is not apparent to you yet, it will be soon as we run through an example below. This phenomenon whereby certain states are not attainable will not make our forthcoming calculations incorrect, it just means that we will do some unnecessary calculations.

Exhibit 17: Valuation Tree with Partitioned Interest Rate States and Cash Flows

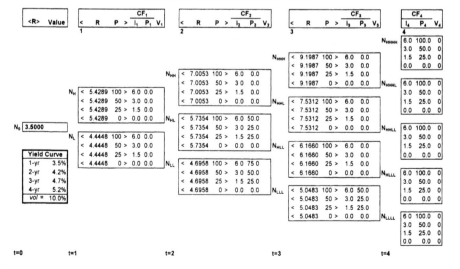

---

[4] The term "stochastic" simply refers to a random variable that varies with time.

Exhibit 18: 6% Indexed Amortizing Bond
Valuation on Entire State Space

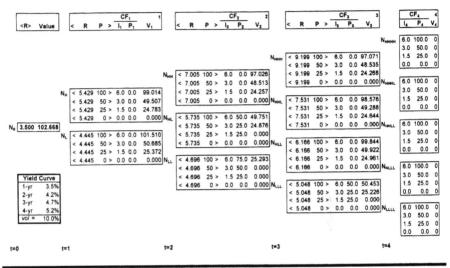

Once the time t 1-year rate and amount outstanding (prior to current-period principal payment) are *both* specified as, say, $<R, P>$, the time t cash flow can easily be calculated. The interest component is just 0.06P. The principal component of the cash flow is deduced from the value of P, the lockout period, the amortization table, and the clean-up provision, rules provided in the formula above. The state-dependent cash flow is the sum of interest and principal.

As before, we begin our recursive calculations at the right end of the lattice. Exhibit 18 shows, for periods 1 through 4, the cash flow $CF_i<R, P>$ just described broken out as principal, P_t, and interest, I_t. For now, the present value of subsequent cash flows, $V_t<R, P>$ (shown just to the right of the cash flow figures), is left blank.

Note, again, that $V_4<R, P> = 0$ for all R and P since there is no cash flow after year 4. Since the IAN matures in period 4, the cash flow is simply the sum of the amount outstanding and interest on that amount — a calculation that is independent of the 1-year rate at period 4.

The situation is more complicated in period 3. Here the amortization schedule and the amount outstanding interact to determine the cash flow. Consider, for example, the calculations corresponding to state $<5.0483, 50>$. The interest payment of 3 is calculated as 0.06×50.0. Also, since $5.0 < 5.0483 < 6.0$, 50% of the outstanding amount is prepaid in period 3. This principal payment of 25.0 leaves 25.0 still outstanding — an amount which exceeds the clean-up provision. The state $<5.0483, 50>$ cash flow is therefore $25.0 + 3.0 = 28.0$. Next we calculate $V3<5.0483, 50>$. Since 50.0 of principal was outstanding (before the period 3 payment) and 25.0 is paid off in period 3, the amount outstanding changes to 25.0. Thus, only the cash flows of the partitioned states with a principal value of 25 need to be discounted.

$$V_3<5.0483, 50> = \frac{0.5(1.5 + 25 + 0) + 0.5(1.5 + 25 + 0)}{1.050483} = 25.2265$$

This number can be found in Exhibit 18, along with all of the other figures compiled via the recursive process.

Compare this with the analogous calculations for state <5.0483, 25> in period 3. The interest cash flow is $0.06 \times 25.0 = 1.5$. The principal payment specified by the amortization schedule is again 50% of the amount outstanding which results in a payment of $12.5 = 25.0 \times 50\%$. This would leave only 12.5 remaining outstanding, however, so the clean-up provision requires that the entire amount of 25.0 be retired leaving nothing outstanding. Thus,

$$V_3<5.0483, 25> = \frac{0.5(0 + 0 + 0) + 0.5(0 + 0 + 0)}{1.050483} = 0$$

The calculations in period 2 follow the same procedure. For example, in state <5.7354, 100>, the principal payment is 50.0, generating a cash flow of 6.0+50.0=56.0 and leaving 50.0 remaining outstanding. Hence, one moves from state <5.7354, 100> in period 2 to either <7.5312, 50> or <6.1660, 50> in period 3, each with equal likelihood. Thus,

$$V_3<5.7354,100> = \frac{0.5(6 + 0 + 49.2880) + 0.5(3 + 0 + 49.9218)}{1.057354} = 49.7515$$

Similarly, in period 1, one moves from state <4.4448, 100> to either < 4.6958, 100> or <5.7354, 100> in period 2, each with equal likelihood. Thus, $CF_1(<4.4448, 100>) = 0.06 \times 100.0 = 6$ (plus 0 principal) and

$$V_1<4.4448,100> = \frac{0.5(6 + 50 + 49.7515) + 0.5(6 + 75 + 25.2928)}{1.04448}$$

$$= 101.5102$$

Finally, at time 0, there is only today's state <3.5000, 100> to calculate. From this state we move to either <4.4448, 100> or <5.4289, 100>, each with probability 1/2. The value of the IAN is

$$V_0<3.5000,100> = \frac{0.5(6 + 0 + 99.0136) + 0.5(6 + 0 + 101.5102)}{1.03500}$$

$$= 102.6685$$

Selecting the Necessary State Space

As we previously observed, only the amounts in the list <0, 25, 50, 100> can be outstanding at any point in time. This is because the IAN starts with 100.0 outstanding and this list is closed under the rules of principal amortization (including the clean-up provision). (For example, if we amortize 50% of 50.0 we get 25.0 outstanding, another number in the list.) In general, it may not be so easy to construct an exhaustive list of possible states or, commonly, the list of possible states may be very large. An effective numerical procedure is to partition the range of the state space (in this case, the range is from 0 to 100 outstanding) into a manageable number of "buckets," say 0, 20-30, 30-40, . . ., 90-100. Sometimes a surprisingly small number of buckets can lead to a very good approximation of the precise answer.

Notice also that not all the states can be reached. For example, in periods 1 and 2 only those states with 100.0 outstanding are reached. This is because the lockout provision prevents any amortization until year 2. Thus, even in year 2, the amount outstanding prior to that year's amortization must be 100.0.

From the standpoint of computational efficiency, it may be better to first pass *forward* through the lattice to determine which states are actually reachable. This is demonstrated in Exhibit 19 where we have highlighted the region of each period's state space that is actually reachable. Following this, during the recursive process described above, it is only necessary to calculate the CF_i and PV_i values for those states that are flagged as reachable in the forward pass. In our IAN example, this would result in substantial savings in computational time.

Consider Exhibit 20(a). The number of valuations necessary in period 3 has been reduced to 6. In Exhibit 20(b), the roll back passes into period 2 where, now, only three calculations are necessary. Exhibit 20(c) provides the full recursive analysis whereby we arrive at the same value for the IAN as in Exhibit 18, but in this case with fewer calculations.

Exhibit 19: 6% Indexed Amortizing Bond
Identification of Attainable States

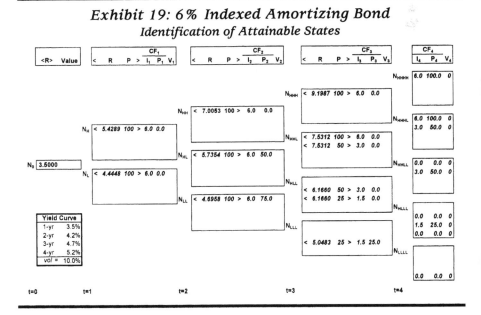

Exhibit 20: 6% Indexed Amortizing Bond
(a) Recursive Valuation: Step 1 on Attainable States

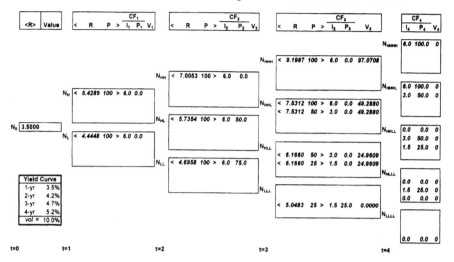

(b) Recursive Valuation: Step 2 on Attainable States

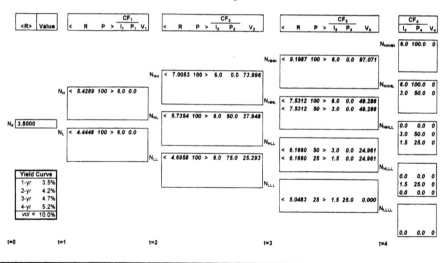

Exhibit 20 (Continued)
(c) Recursive Valuation: Step 3 on Attainable States

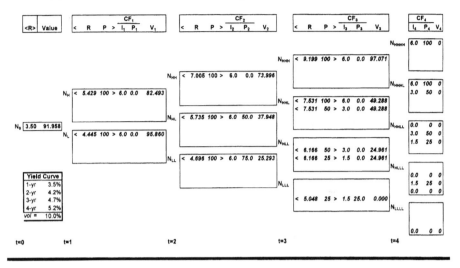

A *caveat* is necessary. In some situations, this forward pass may take more time than it saves. It may be better to compromise and avoid only some of the unused state space by (non-time-consuming) ad hoc reasoning. In the case of the IAN, for example, the unnecessary states in periods 1 and 2 could be avoided simply by recognizing the effects of the lockout provision. The best computational strategy will certainly depend on the application.

RATCHET BONDS

In this final section, we introduce a structure that is relatively new to the capital markets. To value it, we will need to draw on all of the knowledge we have gained from our look at callable capped floaters and IANs. The ratchet bond carries a floating coupon that is capped and path dependent. It is designed to replace the callable bond in the capital structure of debt issuers. We have covered the mechanics in the previous sections, so we can move quickly to the analysis of the ratchet structure. Since the ratchet bond is new, a few words are necessary to motivate its creation and usefulness to debt issuers.[5]

Consider an issuer that relies on callable bonds on an on-going basis to fund its activities. What cash flow pattern emerges from this financing strategy? The answer depends on the path of interest rates. If rates trend upward, the bond

---

[5] A more detailed discussion of ratchet bonds can be found in Andrew Kalotay and Leslie Abreo, "Ratchet Bonds: Maximum Refunding Efficiency at Minimum Transaction Cost," *Journal of Applied Corporate Finance*, Spring 1999, pp 40-47.

will remain outstanding and pay the stated coupon to maturity. If rates decline, the bond will eventually be called and refunded, presumably with another callable bond. As a result of the refunding, interest payments decline from previous levels. If rates continue to fall, the process repeats: the refunding issue is itself called and refunded. Thus, funding via callable bonds gives rise to interest payments that decline if rates decline and remain unchanged if rates rise.

The ratchet bond is designed to replicate the cash flow pattern generated by a series of conventional callable bonds. It is an adjustable (i.e., floating) rate structure on which the coupon rate is periodically reset at a fixed spread over an index, e.g., 10-year Constant Maturity Treasury (CMT). The coupon "ratchets" only downward; it cannot increase.

To illustrate the valuation process, we will make a change to our interest rate environment. For the ratchet bond analysis, the par yield curve is assumed to be flat at 3.5%. The short-rate volatility remains at 10%. Exhibit 21 holds the new binary tree on which valuation will proceed.

Now, consider a ratchet bond that pays a coupon equal to the 1-year rate, set in advance, plus 24 bps (i.e., a spread to the index or reference rate). There is a two-year lockout period during which the coupon cannot reset. This last feature is equivalent to the call protection afforded by conventional callable bonds. Working with the rule that the coupon can only move (ratchet) down, we can pass forward through the tree and establish cash flows at each node. This forward pass is presented in Exhibit 22 where notation follows that from previous figures.

Exhibit 21: Binomial Tree for Ratchet Bond Valuation

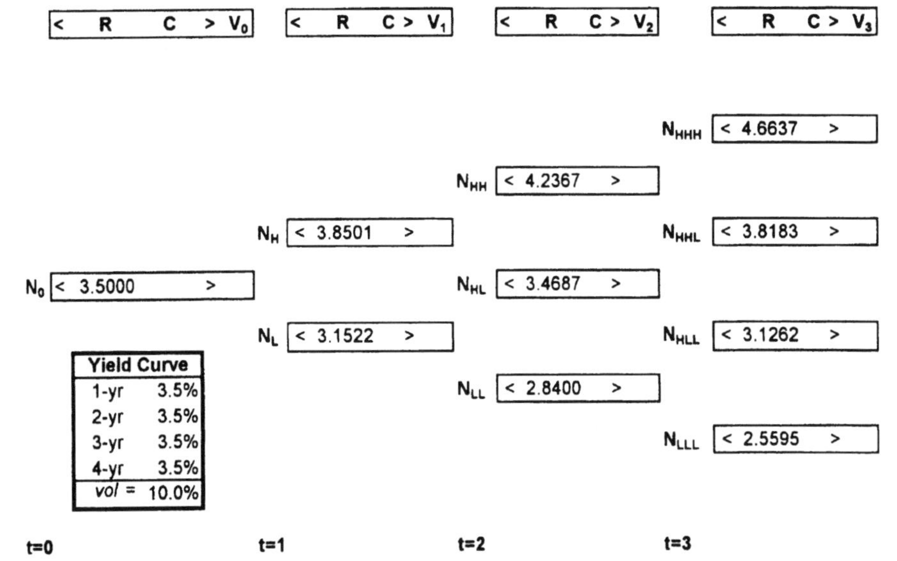

| $<$ R C $> V_0$ | $<$ R C $> V_1$ | $<$ R C $> V_2$ | $<$ R C $> V_3$ |

N_{HHH} $<$ 4.6637 $>$

N_{HH} $<$ 4.2367 $>$

N_H $<$ 3.8501 $>$ N_{HHL} $<$ 3.8183 $>$

N_0 $<$ 3.5000 $>$ N_{HL} $<$ 3.4687 $>$

N_L $<$ 3.1522 $>$ N_{HLL} $<$ 3.1262 $>$

Yield Curve	
1-yr	3.5%
2-yr	3.5%
3-yr	3.5%
4-yr	3.5%
vol =	10.0%

N_{LL} $<$ 2.8400 $>$

N_{LLL} $<$ 2.5595 $>$

t=0   t=1   t=2   t=3

Exhibit 22: Coupon Payments for 4-Year Ratchet Bond
Coupon is 24 bp spread to 1-year rate

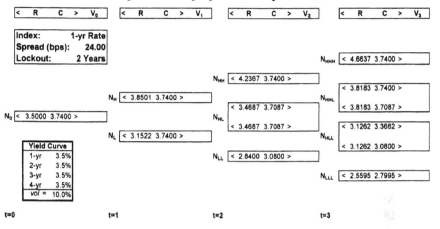

Exhibit 23: Value of 4-Year Ratchet Bond

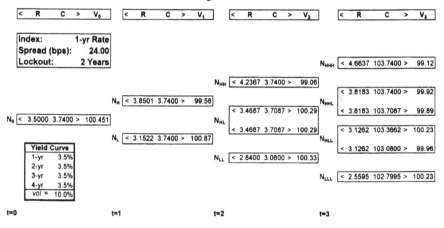

Path dependence is apparent as you move through the tree. Consider node N_{HHL}, which actually represents the current state for three different paths: HHL, HLH and LHH. Depending on the path taken, the coupon is either 3.7400 (in the case of HHL) or 3.7087 (for HLH and LHH). How is this the case? At node N_{HL} (or N_{LH} if you prefer) the lockout provision has expired and the current 1-year rate is 3.4687%. If the 24 bps spread is added to the rate, a coupon of 3.7087% is set for the bond for the next period. By this same procedure, the 3.08% coupon is set at N_{LL} (2.8400 + 0.2400 = 3.0800).

Once the cash flows are in place, the recursive valuation can begin. Exhibit 23 provides the full valuation, rolling back period-by-period to arrive at the 100.45 value of the ratchet bond.

Exhibit 24: Spread to Index to Price Ratchet Bond at Par

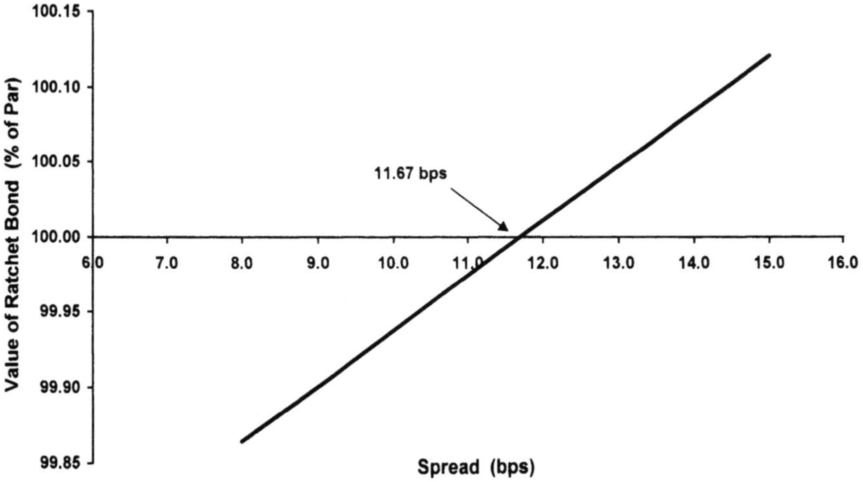

The structuring of the ratchet bond is analogous to that of a callable capped floater. If we want the ratchet bond priced at par, then we must adjust the spread to find a level that prices the bond at 100. Obviously, 24 bps is too large enough. We follow an iterative procedure to arrive at the appropriate figure.

Exhibit 24 provides the result of the iterations. The spread at which the bond is priced at par is 11.67 bps over the reference rate, leading to an at-issue coupon just below 3.62%. Note the change in the coupon at various nodes from the coupons in Exhibit 23.

Chapter 5

Spread Measures and Spread Duration

articipants in the floater market commonly refer to various "spread" measures that an issue is trading over its reference rate. These measures include spread for life, adjusted simple margin, adjusted total margin, discount margin, and option-adjusted spread. Each of these measures is explained in this chapter along with their limitations. In addition, we will discuss the concept of spread duration. We begin with a discussion of the concept of current yield and how to compare floaters with different reset dates.

CURRENT YIELD

The current yield of a floater is calculated by dividing the security's annual dollar cash flow (assuming that the reference rate does not change over the security's life) by the market price. The formula for the current yield is

$$\text{Current yield} = \frac{\text{Annual dollar cash flow}}{\text{Price}} \qquad (1)$$

To illustrate the calculation, suppose that the coupon reset formula for a 6-year floater selling for $99.3098 is 6-month LIBOR plus 80 basis points (i.e., the quoted margin). The coupon rate is reset every six months. Assume the current value for the reference rate is 10%. The calculation is shown below:

$$\text{Annual dollar cash flow} = \$100 \times 0.1080 = \$10.80$$

$$\text{Current yield} = \frac{\$10.80}{\$99.3098} = 0.10875 = 10.875\%$$

Current yield possesses a number of drawbacks as a potential return measure. First, the measure assumes that the reference rate will not change over the security's life. Second, current yield considers only coupon interest and no other source of return that will affect an investor's yield.[1] Simply put, the current yield

---

[1] To see this, assume the current yield is a yield to perpetuity, the annual dollar cash flow is a perpetual annuity payment, and the security's price is the present value of the perpetual annuity. By rearranging terms such that the price equals the annual coupon payment divided by the current yield, we obtain the present value of a perpetual annuity formula.

assumes that the floater delivers a perpetual annuity. Third, current yield ignores the potential impact of any embedded options.

Comparing Floaters with Different Reset Dates

To compare the current yields of two floaters with different coupon reset dates, an adjustment known as the *weighted average rate* is utilized. The comparison requires two assumptions: (1) the coupon payments of the two floaters are determined using the same reference rate and (2) the frequency with which the coupon payments are reset is the same (e.g., semiannually, monthly, etc.). It is presumed that two floaters that share these attributes will produce the same current yield regardless of their respective terms to maturity.

The weighted average rate is simply the weighted average coupon rate over some anticipated holding period where the weights are the fraction of the holding period prior to the coupon reset date and the fraction of the holding period subsequent to the coupon reset date. (The holding period is assumed to contain only one coupon reset date. Accordingly, it is presumed an investor is considering the purchase of a floater as an alternative to a money market instrument.) On the reset date, it is assumed the new coupon rate is the current value of the reference rate adjusted for a spread. The formula for the weighted average rate is given by:

Weighted average rate

$$= \frac{(\text{Current coupon} \times w) + [\text{Assumed new coupon} \times (1 - w)]}{\text{Number of days in the holding period}} \qquad (2)$$

where w is the number of days to the coupon reset date divided by the number of days in the anticipated holding period. The floater's current yield is then determined by dividing the weighted average rate by the market price.

To illustrate the calculation, suppose an investor is considering the purchase of one of two floaters for an anticipated holding period of 180 days. The purchase candidates are two issues with identical coupon reset formulas of 6-month LIBOR plus 90 basis points. Security A has a current coupon of 6.80%, matures in three years, and is trading at 99.50. Conversely, Security B has a current coupon of 7%, matures in five years, and is trading at 99.125. These two securities also differ in coupon reset dates: Security A resets in 30 days while Security B resets in 90 days. Suppose the current value of the reference rate (6-month LIBOR) is 6.20%. Accordingly, the assumed new coupon rate for both Securities A and B is 7.10% since they share the same quoted margin.

The weighted average rate for Security A and the accompanying current yield using the weighted average rate is computed below:

$$\text{Weighted average rate} = \frac{(6.80\% \times 30) + (7.10\% \times 150)}{180} = 7.05\%$$

Annual dollar cash flow $= \$100 \times 0.0705 = \$7.05$

$$\text{Current yield using weighted average rate} = \frac{\$7.05}{\$99.50} = 0.07085 = 7.085\%$$

The weighted average rate for Security B and the accompanying current yield using the weighted average rate is computed below:

$$\text{Weighted average rate} = \frac{(7\% \times 90) + (7.10\% \times 90)}{180} = 7.05\%$$

Annual dollar cash flow = $100 \times 0.0705 = \$7.05$

$$\text{Current yield using weighted average rate} = \frac{\$7.05}{\$99.125} = 7.11\%$$

Although Security A carries a lower coupon rate, it resets sooner to the higher rate. As a result, the current yield of the two securities is closer than one would expect.

MARGIN MEASURES

There are several yield spread measures or *margins* that are routinely used to evaluate floaters. The four margins commonly used are spread for life, adjusted simple margin, adjusted total margin, and discount margin. We will illustrate the calculations of these margins with a floating-rate note issued by Enron Corp. (ticker symbol "ENE 03/00") that matures March 30, 2000. This issue contains no embedded options. The floater has a coupon formula equal to 3-month LIBOR plus 45 basis points and delivers cash flows quarterly. The Yield Analysis screen (YA) from Bloomberg is presented in Exhibit 1. We will illustrate the calculation of each of the four margin measures in turn.

Spread for Life

When a floater is selling at a premium/discount to par, a potential buyer of a floater will consider the premium or discount as an additional source of dollar return. *Spread for life* (also called *simple margin*) is a measure of potential return that accounts for the accretion (amortization) of the discount (premium) as well as the constant index spread over the security's remaining life. Spread for life is calculated using the following formula:

$$\text{Spread for life} = \left[\frac{100(100 - P)}{\text{Maturity}} + \text{Quoted margin} \right] \frac{100}{P} \tag{3}$$

where P is the market price (per $100 of par value) and Maturity is in years using the appropriate day-count convention. The quoted margin is measured in basis points.

To illustrate this calculation, the Enron floater has a current coupon of 5.45, matures in 345 days or 0.9583 of a year using an ACT/360. Although there is no current market quote available for this floater as indicated by the words "NOT PRICED" at the top center of the screen, we will use the Bloomberg default price of 99.99 for the current market price P. The simple margin is calculated as follows

$$\text{Spread for life} = \left[\frac{100(100 - 99.99)}{0.9583} + 45 \right] \frac{100}{99.99} = 46.0481 \text{ basis points}$$

Exhibit 1: Bloomberg's Yield Analysis Screen for Enron Floater

```
2                                                        DG41 Corp   Y A
ENTER ALL VALUES AND HIT <GO>.
ENRON CORP           ENE Float 03/00    N O T   P R I C E D
                     F L O A T I N G   R A T E   N O T E S
```

I N P U T S		DATE	FIX RATE	DATE	FIX RATE	DATE	FIX RATE
SETTLE DATE	4/20/99	3/30/99	5.45000				
MATURITY	3/30/00	6/30/99					
PREV PAY DATE	3/30/99						
NEXT PAY DATE	6/30/99						
REDEMPTION	100.0000						
CPN FREQUENCY	4						
REFIX FREQ	4						
BENCHMARK US00	-3 MNTH						
ASSUMED INDEX	5.0000						
QUOTED MARGIN	45.000						
REPO TO 6/30/99	4.9755	FACE AMOUNT(M)	1000	M/M EQUIV TO NEXT FIX			
INDEX TO 6/30/99	4.9755	PRINCIPAL	999900.00	PRICE @ FIX = 99.991			
P R I C E S		ACCRUED INTEREST	3179.17	ON 6/30/99- 71 DAYS			
PRICE	99.99000	TOTAL	1003079.17	CD(ACT/360) = 5.438			
NEUTRAL PRICE	99.99089			FIX PRICES? (Y/N) N			
ADJUSTED PRICE	99.90031	M A R G I N S					
ADJUSTED SIMPLE MARGIN	55.458 BPS	(5.555)	SPREAD FOR LIFE				
ADJUSTED TOTAL MARGIN	55.957 BPS	(5.560)	46.06 BPS				
DISCOUNT MARGIN	46.231 BPS	(5.462)	VOLATILITY = 0.00				

Source: Bloomberg Financial Markets

At the bottom of the YA screen in Exhibit 1 is a box labeled "MARGINS." The Enron floater's spread for life is 46.06. The slight difference between our calculation and Bloomberg's is likely due to rounding error. Note also that spread for life considers only the accretion/amortization of the discount/premium over the floater's remaining term to maturity and considers neither the level of the coupon rate nor the time value of money.

Adjusted Simple Margin

The *adjusted simple margin* (also called *effective margin*) is an adjustment to spread for life. This adjustment accounts for a one-time cost of carry effect when a floater is purchased with borrowed funds. Suppose a security dealer has purchased $10 million of a particular floater. Naturally, the dealer has a number of alternative ways to finance the position — borrowing from a bank, repurchase agreement, etc. Regardless of the method selected, the dealer must make a one-time adjustment to the floater price to account for the cost of carry from the settlement date to next coupon reset date. Given a particular financing rate, a carry-adjusted forward price can be determined as of the next coupon reset date. Once the carry-adjusted price is determined, the floater's adjusted price is simply the carry-adjusted price discounted to the settlement date by the reference rate. As before, the reference rate is assumed to remain constant until maturity. Note the cost of carry adjustment is simply an adjustment to the purchase price of the floater. If the cost of carry is positive (negative), the purchase price will be adjusted downward (upward). A floater's adjusted price is calculated as below:

$$\text{Adjusted price} = P - \frac{[(\text{Coupon rate})100 - (P + AI)rf]w}{[1 + (w)(rr_{\text{avg}})]} \qquad (4)$$

where

Coupon rate = current coupon rate of the floater (in decimal)
P = market price (per \$100 of par value)
AI = accrued interest (per \$100 of par value)
rf = financing rate (e.g., the repo rate) (in decimal)

$$w = \frac{\text{Number of days between settlement and the next coupon payent}}{\text{Number of days in a year using the appropriate day-count}}$$

rr_{avg} = assumed (average) value for the reference rate until maturity (in decimal)

To illustrate this calculation, we revisit the Enron floater. The following information is taken from the YA screen in Exhibit 1. The market price is 99.99 is taken from the "PRICES" box on the left-hand side of the screen. For the coupon rate, we use 0.0545 (in decimal) which is located under "FIX RATE." The accrued interest is 0.3179 (per \$100 of par value). Under "INPUTS", we find the repo rate (0.049755) to the next coupon reset date. There 71 days between the settlement date (4/20/99) and the next coupon reset date (6/30/99) and the day count is ACT/360. Given this information, $w = 71/360$ or 0.1972. Lastly, the assumed value of the reference rate until maturity (rr_{avg}) is simply the current value of the reference rate which is 0.05 (in decimal) and is labeled "ASSUMED INDEX" under the "INPUTS" section.

$$\text{Adjusted price} = 99.99 - \frac{[(0.0545)100 - (99.99 + 0.3179)0.049755]0.1972}{[1 + (0.1972)(0.05)]}$$

$$= 99.90033$$

The adjusted price as computed by Bloomberg is 99.90031 and is found under "PRICES."

Once the adjusted price is determined, the adjusted simple margin is computed using the formula below.

$$\text{Adjusted simple margin} = \left[\frac{100(100 - P_A)}{\text{Maturity}} + \text{Quoted margin} \right] \frac{100}{P_A} \qquad (5)$$

where P_A is the adjusted price, Maturity is measured in years using the appropriate day-count convention, and Quoted margin is measured in basis points.

To compute the adjusted simple margin for the Enron floater, we gather the following information from Exhibit 1. We use the adjusted price of 99.90031 for P_A. There are 345 days between the settlement date (4/20/99) and the maturity date (3/30/00). Since the day count convention is ACT/360, the maturity is 345/360 or

0.9583. The quoted margin of 45 basis points is obtained from the "INPUTS" box. Plugging this information into equation (5), we obtain the adjusted simple margin.

$$\text{Adjusted simple margin} = \left[\frac{100(100 - 99.90031)}{0.9583} + 45 \right] \frac{100}{99.90031} \quad (6)$$

$$= 55.458 \text{ basis points}$$

The adjusted simple margin from Bloomberg is 55.458 which is also located in the "MARGINS" box at the bottom of Exhibit 1.

Adjusted Total Margin

The *adjusted total margin* (also called *total adjusted margin*) adds one additional refinement to the adjusted simple margin. Specifically, the adjusted total margin is the adjusted simple margin plus the interest earned by investing the difference between the floater's par value and the adjusted price.[2] The current value of the reference rate (i.e., the assumed index) is assumed to be the investment rate. The adjusted total margin is calculated using the following expression:

Adjusted total margin

$$= \left[\frac{100(100 - P_A)}{\text{Maturity}} + \text{Quoted margin} + 100(100 - P_A)rr_{avg} \right] \frac{100}{P_A} \quad (7)$$

The notation used is the same as given above.

For the Enron floater we used in previous illustrations, the adjusted total margin is:

Adjusted total margin

$$= \left[\frac{100(100 - 99.90031)}{0.9583} + 45 + 100(100 - 99.90031)0.05 \right] \frac{100}{99.90031}$$

$$= 55.957 \text{ basis points}$$

In Exhibit 1, Bloomberg's adjusted total margin is 55.957 which is obtained from the "MARGINS" box.

Discount Margin

One common method of measuring potential return that employs discounted cash flows is *discount margin*. This measure indicates the average spread or margin over the reference rate the investor can expect to earn over the security's life given a particular assumption of the path the reference rate will take to maturity. The assumption that the future levels of the reference rate are equal to today's

---

[2] When the floater's adjusted price is greater than 100, the additional increment is negative and represents the interest forgone.

level is the usual assumption. The procedure for calculating the discount margin is as follows:

Step 1. Determine the cash flows assuming that the reference rate does not change over the security's life.

Step 2. Select a margin.

Step 3. Discount the cash flows found in Step 1 by the current value of the reference rate plus the margin selected in Step 2.

Step 4. Compare the present value of the cash flows as calculated in Step 3 to the price. If the present value is equal to the security's price, the discount margin is the margin assumed in Step 2. If the present value is not equal to the security's price, go back to Step 2 and select a different margin.

For a security selling at par, the discount margin is simply the quoted margin.

For example, suppose that a 6-year floater selling for $99.3098 pays the reference rate plus a quoted margin of 80 basis points. The coupon resets every 6 months. Assume that the current value of the reference rate is 10%.

Exhibit 2 presents the calculation of the discount margin for this security. Each period in the security's life is enumerated in Column (1), while the Column (2) shows the current value of the reference rate.[3] Column (3) sets forth the security's cash flows. For the first 11 periods, the cash flow is equal to the reference rate (10%) plus the quoted margin of 80 basis points multiplied by 100 and then divided by 2. In last 6-month period, the cash flow is $105.40 — the final coupon payment of $5.40 plus the maturity value of $100. Different assumed margins appear at the top of the last five columns. The rows below the assumed margin indicate the present value of each period's cash flow for that particular value of assumed margin. Finally, the last row gives the total present value of the cash flows for each assumed margin.

For the five assumed margins, the present value of the cash flows is equal to the floater's price ($99.3098) when the assumed margin is 96 basis points. Accordingly, the discount margin on a semiannual basis is 48 basis points and correspondingly 96 basis points on an annual basis. (Notice that the discount margin is 80 basis points (i.e., the quoted margin) when the floater is selling at par.)

Now that we have a sense about how to calculate discount margin, let's return to our Enron floater in Exhibit 1. The floater is trading at 99.99 with a coupon rate of 5.45% as of the last coupon reset date, 3/30/99. Accrued interest on this floater from the last coupon date (3/30/99) to the settlement date (4/20/00) is 0.3179 (per $100 of par value) which appears in the box in the middle of the screen. Given this information, we know the floater's full price (i.e., flat price plus accrued interest) is 100.307917 (per $100 of par value). In the box labeled "MARGINS" at the bottom of the screen, we see that the discount margin is 46.231 basis points. Accordingly, if we discount the floater's four remaining quarterly cash flows using

---

[3] For simplicity, we assume the coupon periods are of equal length.

an annual discount of 5.46321% (i.e., the reference rate plus the discount margin), we should recover the floater's full price of 100.307917 (per $100 of par value).

The Enron floater has four remaining quarterly cash flows of $1.3625 [(0.0545 × 100)/4] delivered on 6/30/99, 9/30/99, 12/30/99, and 3/30/99. In addition, on the day the floater matures (3/30/00) the investor will receive the floater's terminal cash flow of $100 (per $100 of par value). Since the floater is being valued between coupon payment dates, we determine the present value of cash flows received over fractional coupon periods using an ACT/360 day count convention. The present value calculation is as follows:

$$100.3156$$
$$= \frac{\$1.3625}{1.0546321^{71/360}} + \frac{\$1.3625}{1.0546321^{163/360}} + \frac{\$1.3625}{1.0546321^{254/360}} + \frac{\$101.3625}{1.0546321^{345/360}}$$

This calculation is within rounding error of Bloomberg's full price of 100.3079 (per $100 of par value).

There are several drawbacks of the discount margin as a measure of potential return from holding a floater. First and most obvious, the measure assumes the reference rate will not change over the security's life. Second, the price of a floater for a given discount margin is sensitive to the path that the reference rate takes in the future except in the special case when the discount margin equals the quoted margin.

Exhibit 2: Calculation of the Discount Margin for a Floater

Floater: Maturity = 6 years
Coupon rate = Reference rate + 80 basis points
Resets every 6 months
Maturity value = $100

(1)	(2)	(3)	(4)	(5)	(6)	(7)	(8)
			Assumed Margin				
Period	Rate (%)	Flow ($)*	80	84	88	96	100
1	10	5.40	$5.1233	$5.1224	$5.1214	$5.1195	$5.1185
2	10	5.40	4.8609	4.8590	4.8572	4.8535	4.8516
3	10	5.40	4.6118	4.6092	4.6066	4.6013	4.5987
4	10	5.40	4.3755	4.3722	4.3689	4.3623	4.3590
5	10	5.40	4.1514	4.1474	4.1435	4.1356	4.1317
6	10	5.40	3.9387	3.9342	3.9297	3.9208	3.9163
7	10	5.40	3.7369	3.7319	3.7270	3.7171	3.7122
8	10	5.40	3.5454	3.5401	3.5347	3.5240	3.5186
9	10	5.40	3.3638	3.3580	3.3523	3.3409	3.3352
10	10	5.40	3.1914	3.1854	3.1794	3.1673	3.1613
11	10	5.40	3.0279	3.0216	3.0153	3.0028	2.9965
12	10	105.40	56.0729	55.9454	55.8182	55.5647	55.4385
		Present value =	$100.00	$99.8269	$99.6541	$99.3098	$99.1381

* For periods 1-11: Cash flow = 100(Reference rate + 80 basis points) (0.5)
  For period 12: Cash flow = 100(Reference rate + 80 basis points) (0.5) + 100

To see the significance of the second drawback, it is useful to partition the value of an option-free floater into two parts: (1) the present value of the security's cash flows (i.e., coupon payments and maturity value) if the discount margin equals the quoted margin and (2) the present value of an annuity which pays the difference between the quoted margin and the discount margin multiplied by 100 and divided by the number of periods per year.

$$P = 100 + \sum_{i=1}^{n} \frac{100(qm - dm)/m}{(1 + y_i + dm)^i} \tag{8}$$

where

P = price of the floater (per \$100 of par value)

qm = quoted margin

dm = discount margin

y_i = assumed value of the reference rate in period i

n = number of periods until maturity

m = number of periods per year

In this framework, one can easily see as before that if the quoted margin is equal to the discount margin, the second term is zero and the floater will be valued at par. If the index spread is greater than (less than) the discount margin, the second term is positive (negative) and the floater will be valued at a premium (discount).

This framework is also quite useful for addressing the question: for a given discount margin, how does the present value of the floater's cash flows change given different assumptions about how the reference rate is expected to change in the future? [4] Consider a floater that pays interest semiannually with the following characteristics:

Maturity   = 3 years
Coupon rate   = 6-month LIBOR + 50 basis points
Maturity value = \$100

For ease of exposition, assume that we value the security on its coupon anniversary date. Let's consider two paths that 6-month LIBOR can take in the next three years. In the first path, we assume that 6-month LIBOR will remain unchanged at say, 5.25%. In the second path, we assume that 6-month LIBOR will increase by 10 basis points each period for the next three years (i.e., 5.25%, 5.35%, 5.45%, 5.55%, 5.65%, 5.75%). Finally, we will value the floater assuming three different values (in basis points) for the discount margin: 0, 50 and 100. The values for the floaters associated with each discount margin and under each interest rate path are given in Exhibit 3.

---

[4] For further discussion, see Raymond J. Iwanowski, "An Investor's Guide to Floating-Rate Notes: Conventions, Mathematics, and Relative Valuation," in Thomas S. Y. Ho (ed.), *Fixed Income Solutions* (Burr Ridge, IL: Irwin Professional Publishing, 1996).

Exhibit 3: Bond Values Assuming Different Discounted Margins and Alternative Interest Rate Paths

	Assumed Interest Rate Path	
Discounted Margin	6-month LIBOR remains constant at 5.25%	6-month LIBOR increases 10 bp each period
100	98.6512	98.6549
50	100	100
0	101.3713	101.3676

There are several implications that we can draw from the results in Exhibit 3. First, as discussed previously, when the discount margin equals the quoted margin, the value of the floater equals 100 regardless of the assumed interest rate path. This result holds because any change in the discount rate is exactly offset by a corresponding increase/decrease in the coupon. In other words, the second term in equation (6).

$$\sum_{i=1}^{n} \frac{100(qm-dm)/m}{(1+y_i+dm)^i} \tag{9}$$

is always equal to zero so the security will sell at par. However, when the discount margin differs from the quoted margin, the present value of the security's cash flows will depend on the assumed interest rate path.

For example, suppose the reference rate is expected to increase as in Exhibit 2. What happens to the size of the discount/premium of a floater? When the discount margin is less than the quoted margin, the second term in equation (6) will be smaller because the cash flows are growing at a slower rate than the discount rate. If this occurs, the security will have a smaller premium than under the assumption of an unchanged reference rate. Conversely, when the discount margin is larger than the quoted margin, the effect is reversed. A smaller discount and a higher price will result owing to the fact that the cash flows are growing at a faster rate than the discount rate. These effects are even more pronounced as the term to maturity increases. This illustration clearly demonstrates that the discount margin possesses an important shortcoming as a measure of relative value.

Option-Adjusted Spread

The spread measures discussed thus far fail to recognize any embedded options that may be present in a floater. A spread measure that takes into account embedded options is called an *option-adjusted spread*. Here is how it is computed.

In Chapter 4, we explained how to value a floater with an embedded option. In the binomial tree, the cash flows at any node are discounted at the appropriate rate on the binomial tree. The product of the valuation model is the theoretical value of the floater. The option-adjusted spread (OAS) enters the picture when we compare the security's theoretical value to the market price. Because of perceived differences in risk (default, liquidity, etc.) between the security being valued and the on-the-run benchmark securities used to construct the binomial tree, the theoretical value will usually differ from the market price. Suppose we are valuing a floater which is less liquid than the on-the-run benchmark securities. As a result, the floater's theoretical value (which ignores the difference in liquidity) is higher than its market price. We conclude the discount rates from the binomial tree used to determine the floater's theoretical value are "too low." The option-adjusted spread is the spread that is added to each discount rate in the tree so that the valuation model produces a value equal to the market price. The reason why the spread is "option adjusted" is because the cash flows shown in the binomial tree are those that result after they are adjusted for any embedded options. For example, if the floater has a cap, the cash flows in the binomial tree take into account the cap.

The interpretation of the option-adjusted spread depends on what the benchmark is. Specifically, in our illustrations of the binomial model in Chapter 4, the on-the-run yield curve used was that of the issuer. Thus, the option-adjusted spread is the additional spread over the spot rates for the issuer after adjusting for the embedded options. Many times, however, the Treasury on-the-run yield curve is used to generate the binomial tree. In that case, the option-adjusted spread is the spread over the Treasury spot rate curve after adjusting for the embedded options. In fact, some vendors allow the user to generate a tree based on the LIBOR yield curve. When the LIBOR yield curve is the benchmark, the OAS is the spread over that curve after adjusting for the floater's embedded options. Some market participants prefer to use the LIBOR yield curve because they are interested in the spread over their LIBOR-based funding costs.

Despite its widespread use, the OAS has a number of limitations.[5] Among the more significant are as follows. First, OAS is model-dependent. Specifically, changing the interest rate process and/or the volatility assumption will produce a different OAS even with the same yield curve. Second, adding a constant number of basis points to each node on an interest rate tree produces an interest rate distribution that is inconsistent with the model's assumptions. For example, adding a constant spread to each node on a binomial (i.e., lognormal) tree produces an interest rate distribution that is no longer lognormal. Third, a security's true OAS will decline to zero as its maturity date approaches. Yet, estimated OAS is assumed to remain constant over time.

SPREAD DURATION

In Chapter 4 we explained that duration is a measure of the sensitivity of a security to changes in interest rates. A useful interpretation is that it is the approxi-

---

[5] See, for example, David Babbel and Stavros Zenios, "Pitfalls in the Analysis of Option-Adjusted Spreads," *Financial Analysts Journal* (July/August 1992), pp. 65-69 and Robert Kopprasch, "Option-Adjusted Spread Analysis: Going Down the Wrong Path?," *Financial Analysts Journal* (May/June 1994), pp. 42-47.

mate percentage change in a security's price for a 100 basis point change in interest rates.

For a floater, the price will change if either the reference rate changes and/or the required margin changes. Index duration is a measure of the responsiveness of a change in a floater's price to a change in the reference rate (i.e., index). In Chapter 4, we explained how index duration is computed.

Spread duration is a measure of the responsiveness of a floater's price to a change in the required margin or required spread. The question is, what spread? We discussed several spread/margin measures in this chapter. The spread/margin measure used by market participants is the option-adjusted spread and so spread duration is computed using the valuation model described in Chapter 4.

Recall that to calculate duration, the value of a security is revalued after shifting rates up and down a small number of basis points. In the case of spread duration, the OAS is changed. That is, spread duration is calculated as follows:

$$\text{Spread duration} = \frac{\text{Price at lower OAS} - \text{Price at higher OAS}}{2(\text{Initial price})(\text{Change in OAS used to compute prices})}$$

Specifically, the OAS is decreased a small number of basis points and the new OAS is used to obtain the rates on the binomial tree that will be used for discounting. Given the new rates on the binomial tree, the floater is valued. This gives the price of the floater at the lower OAS for the spread duration formula. Next, the OAS is increased by the same number of basis point and the new rates are obtained for the binomial tree. These higher rates are then used to value the floater, producing the price at the higher OAS that is used in the spread duration formula.

Chapter 6

Relative Value Analysis Using the Interest Rate Swap Market

A swap contract is a mechanism for transforming the nature of cash flows. In its simplest and most prevalent form, a swap contract is an agreement by two parties to exchange interest payments based on a notional amount. Normally, one party makes payments based on a fixed coupon rate while the counterparty makes payments that float with a reference rate. For corporations, especially financial institutions, swaps are an invaluable tool for asset/liability management. For investors, swaps markets are an increasingly important source of information for relative value analysis for both floating-rate and fixed-rate securities. This chapter will focus on this latter dimension.

Swap markets help investors assess the relative value of a complicated security (e.g., collared floater) in two basic ways. First, the cash flows of a floater can be converted into a synthetic fixed-rate security using swaps. Once transformed into a fixed-rate security, its yield can then be compared to the yields on other comparable fixed-rate instruments. Second, the cash flows of a complicated security can be converted into a synthetic fixed-rate security using a combination of swaps and options.

In order to gain an understanding about how swaps markets are used to gauge the relative value of floaters, we must first review some basic principles about how swap contracts are structured. We will also review some basic swap terminology and conventions. Valuation of swaps is also discussed before we turn our attention to a swap-based analysis of floaters.

INTEREST RATE SWAPS

In an *interest rate swap*, two parties (called *counterparties*) agree to exchange periodic interest payments. The dollar amount of the interest payments exchanged is based on some predetermined dollar principal, which is called the *notional amount*. The dollar amount each counterparty pays to the other is the agreed-upon periodic interest rate times the notional amount. The only dollars that are exchanged between the parties are the interest payments, not the notional amount. Accordingly, the notional principal serves only as a scale factor to translate an interest rate into a cash flow. In the most common type of swap, one party agrees to pay the other party fixed interest payments at designated dates for the life of the contract. This party is referred to as the *fixed-rate payer.* The other party, who agrees to make interest rate payments that float with some reference rate, is referred to as the *floating-rate payer.*

The reference rates that have been used for the floating rate in an interest rate swap are various money market rates: Treasury bill rate, the London inter-bank offered rate, commercial paper rate, bankers acceptances rate, certificates of deposit rate, the federal funds rate, and the prime rate. The most common is the London interbank offered rate (LIBOR). LIBOR is the rate at which prime banks offer to pay on Eurodollar deposits available to other prime banks for a given maturity. There is not just one rate but a rate for different maturities. For example, there is a 1-month LIBOR, 3-month LIBOR, and 6-month LIBOR.

To illustrate an interest rate swap, suppose that for the next five years party X agrees to pay party Y 10% per year, while party Y agrees to pay party X 6-month LIBOR (the reference rate). Party X is a fixed-rate payer/floating-rate receiver, while party Y is a floating-rate payer/fixed-rate receiver. Assume that the notional amount is $50 million, and that payments are exchanged every six months for the next five years. This means that every six months, party X (the fixed-rate payer/floating-rate receiver) will pay party Y $2.5 million (10% times $50 million divided by 2). The amount that party Y (the floating-rate payer/fixed-rate receiver) will pay party X will be 6-month LIBOR times $50 million divided by 2. If 6-month LIBOR is 7%, party Y will pay party X $1.75 million (7% times $50 million divided by 2). Note that we divide by two because one-half year's interest is being paid.

Interest rate swaps are over-the-counter instruments. This means that they are not traded on an exchange. An institutional investor wishing to enter into a swap transaction can do so through either a securities firm or a commercial bank that trans-acts in swaps.[1] These entities can do one of the following. First, they can arrange or broker a swap between two parties that want to enter into an interest rate swap. In this case, the securities firm or commercial bank is acting in a brokerage capacity.

The second way in which a securities firm or commercial bank can get an institutional investor into a swap position is by taking the other side of the swap. This means that the securities firm or the commercial bank is a dealer rather than a broker in the transaction. Acting as a dealer, the securities firm or the commercial bank must hedge its swap position in the same way that it hedges its position in other securities. Also it means that the swap dealer is the counterparty to the transaction.

The risks that the two parties take on when they enter into a swap is that the other party will fail to fulfill its obligations as set forth in the swap agreement. That is, each party faces default risk. The default risk in a swap agreement is called *counterparty risk*. In any agreement between two parties that must perform according to the terms of a contract, counterparty risk is the risk that the other

---

[1] Don't get confused here about the role of commercial banks. A bank can use a swap in its asset/liability management. Or, a bank can transact (buy and sell) swaps to clients to generate fee income. It is in the latter sense that we are discussing the role of a commercial bank in the swap market here.

party will default. With futures and exchange-traded options the counterparty risk is the risk that the clearinghouse established to guarantee performance of the contracts will default. Market participants view this risk as small. In contrast, counterparty risk in a swap can be significant.

Because of counterparty risk, not all securities firms and commercial banks can be swap dealers. Several securities firms have established subsidiaries that are separately capitalized so that they have a high credit rating which permit them to enter into swap transactions as a dealer.

Thus, it is imperative to keep in mind that any party who enters into a swap is subject to counterparty risk.

INTERPRETING A SWAP POSITION

There are two ways that a swap position can be interpreted: (1) a package of forward/futures contracts and (2) a package of cash flows from buying and selling cash market instruments.

Package of Forward Contracts

Consider the hypothetical interest rate swap used earlier to illustrate a swap. Let's look at party X's position. Party X has agreed to pay 10% and receive 6-month LIBOR. More specifically, assuming a $50 million notional amount, X has agreed to buy a commodity called "6-month LIBOR" for $2.5 million. This is effectively a 6-month forward contract where X agrees to pay $2.5 million in exchange for delivery of 6-month LIBOR. The fixed-rate payer is effectively long a 6-month forward contract on 6-month LIBOR. The floating-rate payer is effectively short a 6-month forward contract on 6-month LIBOR. There is therefore an implicit forward contract corresponding to each exchange date.

Consequently, interest rate swaps can be viewed as a package of more basic interest rate derivative instruments — forwards. The pricing of an interest rate swap will then depend on the price of a package of forward contracts with the same settlement dates in which the underlying for the forward contract is the same reference rate.

While an interest rate swap may be nothing more than a package of forward contracts, it is not a redundant contract for several reasons. First, maturities for forward or futures contracts do not extend out as far as those of an interest rate swap; an interest rate swap with a term of 15 years or longer can be obtained. Second, an interest rate swap is a more transactionally efficient instrument. By this we mean that in one transaction an entity can effectively establish a payoff equivalent to a package of forward contracts. The forward contracts would each have to be negotiated separately. Third, the interest rate swap market has grown in liquidity since its establishment in 1981; interest rate swaps now provide more liquidity than forward contracts, particularly long-dated (i.e., long-term) forward contracts.

Exhibit 1: Cash Flows for the Purchase of a 5-Year Floating-Rate Bond Financed by Borrowing on a Fixed-Rate Basis

Transaction:
- Purchase for $50 million a 5-year floating-rate bond:
  floating rate = LIBOR, semiannual pay
- Borrow $50 million for five years:
  fixed rate = 10%, semiannual payments

Six Month Period	Cash Flow (In Millions of Dollars) From:		
	Floating-rate Bond*	Borrowing Cost	Net
0	−$50	+$50.0	$0
1	+ (LIBOR$_1$/2) × 50	−2.5	+ (LIBOR$_1$/2) × 50 − 2.5
2	+ (LIBOR$_2$/2) × 50	−2.5	+ (LIBOR$_2$/2) × 50 − 2.5
3	+ (LIBOR$_3$/2) × 50	−2.5	+ (LIBOR$_3$/2) × 50 − 2.5
4	+ (LIBOR$_4$/2) × 50	−2.5	+ (LIBOR$_4$/2) × 50 − 2.5
5	+ (LIBOR$_5$/2) × 50	−2.5	+ (LIBOR$_5$/2) × 50 − 2.5
6	+ (LIBOR$_6$/2) × 50	−2.5	+ (LIBOR$_6$/2) × 50 − 2.5
7	+ (LIBOR$_7$/2) × 50	−2.5	+ (LIBOR$_7$/2) × 50 − 2.5
8	+ (LIBOR$_8$/2) × 50	−2.5	+ (LIBOR$_8$/2) × 50 − 2.5
9	+ (LIBOR$_9$/2) × 50	−2.5	+ (LIBOR$_9$/2) × 50 − 2.5
10	+ (LIBOR$_{10}$/2) × 50 + 50	−52.5	+ (LIBOR$_{10}$/2) × 50 − 2.5

* The subscript for LIBOR indicates the 6-month LIBOR as per the terms of the floating-rate bond at time t.

Package of Cash Market Instruments

To understand why a swap can also be interpreted as a package of cash market instruments, consider an investor who enters into the transaction below:

- buy $50 million par of a 5-year floating-rate bond that pays 6-month LIBOR every six months
- finance the purchase by borrowing $50 million for five years at a 10% annual interest rate paid every six months.

The cash flows for this transaction are set forth in Exhibit 1. The second column of the exhibit shows the cash flows from purchasing the 5-year floating-rate bond. There is a $50 million cash outlay and then ten cash inflows. The amount of the cash inflows is uncertain because they depend on future LIBOR. The next column shows the cash flows from borrowing $50 million on a fixed-rate basis. The last column shows the net cash flows from the entire transaction. As the last column indicates, there is no initial cash flow (no cash inflow or cash outlay). In all ten 6-month periods, the net position results in a cash inflow of LIBOR and a cash outlay of $2.5 million. This net position, however, is identical to the position of a fixed-rate payer/floating-rate receiver.

It can be seen from the net cash flow in Exhibit 1 that a fixed-rate payer has a cash market position that is equivalent to a long position in a floating-rate bond and a short position in a fixed-rate bond — the short position being the equivalent of borrowing by issuing a fixed-rate bond.

What about the position of a floating-rate payer? It can be easily demonstrated that the position of a floating-rate payer is equivalent to purchasing a fixed-rate bond and financing that purchase at a floating-rate, where the floating rate is the reference rate for the swap. That is, the position of a floating-rate payer is equivalent to a long position in a fixed-rate bond and a short position in a floating-rate bond.

TERMINOLOGY, CONVENTIONS, AND MARKET QUOTES

Here we review some of the terminology used in the swaps market and explain how swaps are quoted. The date that the counterparties commit to the swap is called the *trade date*. The date that the swap begins accruing interest is called the *effective date*, while the date that the swap stops accruing interest is called the *maturity date*. How often the floating-rate is changed is called the *reset frequency*.

While our illustrations assume that the timing of the cash flows for both the fixed-rate payer and floating-rate payer will be the same, this is rarely the case in a swap. An agreement may call for the fixed-rate payer to make payments annually but the floating-rate payer to make payments more frequently (semiannually or quarterly). Also, the way in which interest accrues on each leg of the transaction differs, because there are several day count conventions in the fixed-income markets.

Normally, the fixed interest payments are paid on the basis of a 30/360 day count; floating-rate payments are paid on the basis of an actual/360 day count. Accordingly, the fixed interest payments will differ slightly owing to the differences in the lengths of coupon periods. The floating payments will differ owing to day counts as well as movements in the reference rate.

The terminology used to describe the position of a party in the swap markets combines cash market jargon and futures market jargon, given that a swap position can be interpreted as a position in a package of cash market instruments or a package of futures/forward positions. As we have said, the counterparty to an interest rate swap is either a fixed-rate payer or floating-rate payer. Exhibit 2 describes these positions in several ways.

The first two expressions in Exhibit 2 to describe the position of a fixed-rate payer and floating-rate payer are self-explanatory. To understand why the fixed-rate payer is viewed as short the bond market, and the floating-rate payer is viewed as long the bond market, consider what happens when interest rates change. Those who borrow on a fixed-rate basis will benefit if interest rates rise because they have locked in a lower interest rate. But those who have a short bond position will also benefit if interest rates rise. Thus, a fixed-rate payer can be said to be short the bond market. A floating-rate payer benefits if interest rates fall. A long position in a bond also benefits if interest rates fall, so terminology describing a floating-rate payer as long the bond market is not surprising. From our discussion of the interpretation of a swap as a package of cash market instruments, describing a swap in terms of the sensitivities of long and short cash positions follows naturally.

The convention that has evolved for quoting swaps levels is that a swap dealer sets the floating rate equal to the reference rate and then quotes the fixed rate that will apply. To illustrate this convention, consider the following 10-year swap terms available from a dealer:

- *Floating-rate payer:*
  Pay floating rate of 3-month LIBOR quarterly.
  Receive fixed rate of 8.75% semiannually.
- *Fixed-rate payer:*
  Pay fixed rate of 8.85% semiannually
  Receive floating rate of 3-month LIBOR quarterly.

The offer price that the dealer would quote the fixed-rate payer would be to pay 8.85% and receive LIBOR "flat." (The word flat means with no spread.) The bid price that the dealer would quote the floating-rate payer would be to pay LIBOR flat and receive 8.75%. The bid-offer spread is 10 basis points.

In order to solidify our intuition, it is useful to think of the swap market as a market where two counterparties trade the floating reference rate in a series of exchanges for a fixed price. In effect, the swap market is a market to buy and sell LIBOR. So, buying a swap (pay fixed/receive floating) can be thought of as buying LIBOR on each reset date for the fixed rate agreed to on the trade date. Conversely, selling a swap (receive fixed/pay floating) is effectively selling LIBOR on each reset date for a fixed rate agreed to on the trade date. In this framework, a dealer's bid-offer spread can be easily interpreted. Using the numbers presented above, the bid price of 8.75% is the price the dealer will pay to the counterparty to receive 3-month LIBOR. In other words, buy LIBOR at the bid. Similarly, the offer price of 8.85% is the price the dealer receives from the counterparty in exchange for 3-month LIBOR. In other words, sell LIBOR at the offer.

Exhibit 2: Describing the Counterparties to a Swap

Fixed-rate Payer	Floating-rate Payer
• pays fixed rate in the swap	• pays floating rate in the swap
• receives floating in the swap	• receives fixed in the swap
• is short the bond market	• is long the bond market
• has bought a swap	• has sold a swap
• is long a swap	• is short a swap
• has established the price sensitivities of a longer-term liability and a floating-rate asset	• has established the price sensitivities of a longer-term asset and a floating-rate liability

Source: Robert F. Kopprasch, John Macfarlane, Daniel R. Ross, and Janet Showers, "The Interest Rate Swap Market: Yield Mathematics, Terminology, and Conventions," Chapter 58 in Frank J. Fabozzi and Irving M. Pollack (eds.), *The Handbook of Fixed Income Securities* (Homewood, IL: Dow Jones-Irwin, 1987).

The fixed rate is some spread above the Treasury yield curve with the same term to maturity as the swap. In our illustration, suppose that the 10-year Treasury yield is 8.35%. Then the offer price that the dealer would quote to the fixed-rate payer is the 10-year Treasury rate plus 50 basis points versus receiving LIBOR flat. For the floating-rate payer, the bid price quoted would be LIBOR flat versus the 10-year Treasury rate plus 40 basis points. The dealer would quote such a swap as 40-50, meaning that the dealer is willing to enter into a swap to receive LIBOR and pay a fixed rate equal to the 10-year Treasury rate plus 40 basis points; and it would be willing to enter into a swap to pay LIBOR and receive a fixed rate equal to the 10-year Treasury rate plus 50 basis points. The difference between the Treasury rate paid and received is the bid-offer spread.[2]

VALUING INTEREST RATE SWAPS

In an interest rate swap, the counterparties agree to exchange periodic interest payments. The dollar amount of the interest payments exchanged is based on the notional principal. In the most common type of swap, there is a fixed-rate payer receiver and a fixed-rate receiver. The convention for quoting swap rates is that a swap dealer sets the floating rate equal to the reference rate and then quotes the fixed rate that will apply.

Computing the Payments for a Swap

While in the previous section we described in general terms the payments by the fixed-rate payer and fixed-rate receiver, we did not give any details. That is, we explained that if the swap rate is 6% and the notional amount is $100 million, then the fixed-rate payment will be $6 million for the year and the payment is then adjusted based on the frequency of settlement. So, if settlement is semiannual, the payment is $3 million. If it is quarterly, it is $1.5 million. Similarly, the floating-rate payment would be found by multiplying the reference rate by the notional amount and then scaled based on the frequency of settlement.

It was useful to show the basic features of an interest rate swap using quick calculations for the payments such as described above and then explaining how the parties to a swap either benefit or hurt when interest rates changes. However, we are going to show how to value a swap in this section To value a swap it is necessary to determine the present value of the fixed-rate payments and the present value of the floating-rate payments. The difference between these two present values is the value of a swap. As will be explained below, whether the value is positive (i.e., an asset) or negative (i.e., a liability) will depend on the party.

---

[2] A question that commonly arises is why is the fixed rate of a swap quoted as a fixed spread above a Treasury rate when Treasury rates are not used directly in swap valuation? Because of the timing difference between the quote and settlement, quoting the fixed-rate side as a spread above a Treasury rate allows the swap dealer to hedge against changing interest rates.

At the inception of the swap, the terms of the swap will be such that the present value of the floating-rate payments is equal to the present value of the fixed-rate payments. That is, the value of the swap is equal to zero at the inception of the swap. This is the fundamental principle in determining the swap rate (i.e., the fixed rate that the fixed-rate payer will make).

Here is a roadmap of the presentation. First we will look at how to compute the floating-rate payments. We will see how the future values of the reference rate are determined to obtain the floating rate for the period. From the future values of the reference rate we will then see how to compute the floating-rate payments taking into account the number of days in the payment period. Next we will see how to calculate the fixed-rate payments given the swap rate. Before we look at how to calculate the value of a swap, we will see how to calculate the swap rate. This will require an explanation of how the present value of any cash flow in an interest rate swap is computed. Given the floating-rate payments and the present value of the floating-rate payments, the swap rate can be determined by using the principle that the swap rate is the fixed rate that will make the present value of the fixed-rate payments equal to the present value of the floating-rate payments. Finally, we will see how the value of swap is determined after the inception of a swap.

Calculating the Floating-Rate Payments

For the first floating-rate payment, the amount is known. For all subsequent payments, the floating-rate payment depends on the value of the reference rate when the floating rate is determined. To illustrate the issues associated with calculating the floating-rate payment, we will assume that

- a swap starts today, January 1 of year 1(swap settlement date)
- the floating-rate payments are made quarterly based on "actual/360"
- the reference rate is 3-month LIBOR
- the notional amount of the swap is $100 million
- the term of the swap is three years

The quarterly floating-rate payments are based on an "actual/360" day count convention. This convention means that 360 days are assumed in a year and that in computing the interest for the quarter the actual number of days in the quarter are used. The floating-rate payment is set at the beginning of the quarter but paid at the end of the quarter — that is, the floating-rate payments are made in arrears. Suppose that today 3-month LIBOR is 4.05%. Let's look at what the fixed-rate payer will receive on March 31 of year 1 — the date when the first quarterly swap payment is made. There is no uncertainty about what the floating-rate payment will be. In general, the floating-rate payment is determined as follows:

$$\text{notional amount} \times (3\text{-month LIBOR}) \times \frac{\text{no. of days in period}}{360}$$

In our illustration, assuming a non-Leap year, the number of days from January 1 of year 1 to March 31 of year 1 (the first quarter) is 90. If 3-month LIBOR is 4.05%, then the fixed-rate payer will receive a floating-rate payment on March 31 of year 1 equal to:

$$\$100,000,000 \times 0.0405 \times \frac{90}{360} = \$1,012,500$$

Now the difficulty is in determining the floating-rate payment after the first quarterly payment. That is, for the 3-year swap there will be 12 quarterly floating-rate payments. So, while the first quarterly payment is known, the next 11 are not. However, there is a way to hedge the next 11 floating-rate payments by using a futures contract. Specifically, the futures contract used to hedge the future floating-rate payments in a swap whose reference rate is 3-month LIBOR is the Eurodollar CD futures contract. We will digress to discuss this contract.

The Eurodollar CD Futures Contract As explained earlier in the chapter, a swap position can be interpreted as a package of forward/futures contracts or a package of cash flows from buying and selling cash market instruments. It is the former interpretation that will be used as the basis for valuing a swap. In the case of a LIBOR-based swap, the appropriate futures contract is the Eurodollar CD futures contract. For this reason, we will describe this important contract.

Eurodollar certificates of deposit (CDs) are denominated in dollars but represent the liabilities of banks outside the United States. The contracts are traded on both the International Monetary Market of the Chicago Mercantile Exchange and the London International Financial Futures Exchange. The rate paid on Eurodollar CDs is the London interbank offered rate (LIBOR).

The 3-month Eurodollar CD is the underlying instrument for the Eurodollar CD futures contract. The contract is for $1 million of face value and is traded on an index price basis. The index price basis in which the contract is quoted is equal to 100 minus the annualized LIBOR futures rate. For example, a Eurodollar CD futures price of 94.00 means a 3-month LIBOR futures rate of 6% (100 minus 6%).

The Eurodollar CD futures contract is a cash settlement contract. That is, the parties settle in cash for the value of a Eurodollar CD based on LIBOR at the settlement date.

The Eurodollar CD futures contract allows the buyer of the contract to lock in the rate on 3-month LIBOR today for a future 3-month period. For example, suppose that on February 1, 2000 an investor purchases a Eurodollar CD futures contract that settles in March 2000. Suppose that the LIBOR futures rate for this contract is 5%. This means that the investor has agreed to effectively invest in a 3-month Eurodollar CD that pays a rate of 5%. Specifically, the investor has locked in a rate for a 3-month investment of 5% beginning March 2000. If the investor on February 1, 2000 purchased a contract that settles in September 2001 and the LIBOR futures rate is 5.4%, the investor has locked in the rate on a 3-month investment beginning September 2001.

From the perspective of the seller of a Eurodollar CD futures contract, the seller is agreeing to lend funds for three months at some future date at the LIBOR futures rate. For example, suppose on February 1, 2000 a bank sells a Eurodollar CD futures contract that settles in March 2000 and the LIBOR futures rate is 5%. The bank locks in a borrowing rate of 5% for three months beginning in March 2000. If the settlement date is September 2001 and the LIBOR futures rate is 5.4%, the bank is locking in a borrowing rate of 5.4% for the 3-month period beginning September 2001.

The key point here is that the Eurodollar CD futures contract allows a participant in the financial market to lock in a 3-month rate on an investment or a 3-month borrowing rate. The 3-month rate begins in the month that the contract settles.

Determining Future Floating-Rate Payments Now let's return to our objective of determining the future floating-rate payments. These payments can be locked in over the life of the swap using the Eurodollar CD futures contract. We will show how these floating-rate payments are computed using this contract.

We will begin with the next quarterly payment — from April 1 of year 1 to June 30 of year 1. This quarter has 91 days. The floating-rate payment will be determined by 3-month LIBOR on April 1 of year 1 and paid on June 30 of year 1. Where might the fixed-rate payer look to today (January 1 of year 1) to project what 3-month LIBOR will be on April 1 of year 1? One possibility is the Eurodollar CD futures market. There is a 3-month Eurodollar CD futures contract for settlement on June 30 of year 1. That futures contract will have the market's expectation of what 3-month LIBOR on April 1 of year 1 is. For example, if the futures price for the 3-month Eurodollar CD futures contract that settles on June 30 of year 1 is 95.85, then as explained above, the 3-month Eurodollar futures rate is 4.15%. We will refer to that rate for 3-month LIBOR as the "forward rate." Therefore, if the fixed-rate payer bought 100 of these 3-month Eurodollar CD futures contract on January 1 of year 1 (the inception of the swap) that settles on June 30 of year 1, then the payment that will be locked in for the quarter (April 1 to June 30 of year 1) is

$$\$100,000,000 \times 0.0415 \times \frac{91}{360} = \$1,049,028$$

(Note that each futures contract is for $1 million and hence 100 contracts have a notional amount of $100 million.) Similarly, the Eurodollar CD futures contract can be used to lock in a floating-rate payment for each of the next 10 quarters. Once again, it is important to emphasize that the reference rate at the beginning of period t determines the floating-rate that will be paid for the period. However, the floating-rate payment is not made until the end of period t.

Exhibit 3 shows this for the 3-year swap. Shown in Column (1) is when the quarter begins and in Column (2) when the quarter ends. The payment will be received at the end of the first quarter (March 31 of year 1) and is $1,012,500. That is the known floating-rate payment as explained earlier. It is the only payment that is known. The information used to compute the first payment is in Column (4) which shows the current 3-month LIBOR (4.05%). The payment is shown in the last column, Column (8).

Notice that Column (7) numbers the quarters from 1 through 12. Look at the heading for Column (7). It identifies each quarter in terms of the end of the quarter. This is important because we will eventually be discounting the payments (cash flows). We must take care to understand when each payment is to be exchanged in order to properly discount. So, for the first payment of $1,012,500 it is going to be received at the end of quarter 1. When we refer to the time period for any payment, the reference is to the end of quarter. So, the fifth payment of $1,225,000 would be identified as the payment for period 5, where period 5 means that it will be exchanged at the end of the fifth quarter.

Calculating the Fixed-Rate Payments

The swap will specify the frequency of settlement for the fixed-rate payments. The frequency need not be the same as the floating-rate payments. For example, in the 3-year swap we have been using to illustrate the calculation of the floating-rate payments, the frequency is quarterly. The frequency of the fixed-rate payments could be semiannual rather than quarterly.

In our illustration we will assume that the frequency of settlement is quarterly for the fixed-rate payments, the same as with the floating-rate payments. The day count convention is the same as for the floating-rate payment, "actual/360". The equation for determining the dollar amount of the fixed-rate payment for the period is:

$$\text{notional amount} \times (\text{swap rate}) \times \frac{\text{no. of days in period}}{360}$$

Exhibit 3: Floating-Rate Payments Based on Initial LIBOR and Eurodollar CD Futures

(1) Quarter starts	(2) Quarter ends	(3) Number of days in quarter	(4) Current 3-month LIBOR	(5) Eurodollar CD futures price	(6) Forward rate	(7) Period = End of quarter	(8) Floating-rate payment at end of quarter
Jan 1 year 1	Mar 31 year 1	90	4.05%		—	1	1,012,500
Apr 1 year 1	June 30 year 1	91		95.85	4.15%	2	1,049,028
July 1 year 1	Sept 30 year 1	92		95.45	4.55%	3	1,162,778
Oct 1 year 1	Dec 31 year 1	92		95.28	4.72%	4	1,206,222
Jan 1 year 2	Mar 31 year 2	90		95.10	4.90%	5	1,225,000
Apr 1 year 2	June 30 year 2	91		94.97	5.03%	6	1,271,472
July 1 year 2	Sept 30 year 2	92		94.85	5.15%	7	1,316,111
Oct 1 year 2	Dec 31 year 2	92		94.75	5.25%	8	1,341,667
Jan 1 year 3	Mar 31 year 3	90		94.60	5.40%	9	1,350,000
Apr 1 year 3	June 30 year 3	91		94.50	5.50%	10	1,390,278
July 1 year 3	Sept 30 year 3	92		94.35	5.65%	11	1,443,889
Oct 1 year 3	Dec 31 year 3	92		94.24	5.76%	12	1,472,000

Exhibit 4: Fixed-Rate Payments for
Several Assumed Swap Rates

(1)	(2)	(3)	(4)	(5)	(6)	(7)	(8)	(9)
		Number	Period =	Fixed-rate payment if				
Quarter	Quarter	of days in	End of	swap rate is assumed to be				
starts	ends	quarter	quarter	4.9800%	4.9873%	4.9874%	4.9875%	4.9880%
Jan 1 year 1	Mar 31 year 1	90	1	1,245,000	1,246,825	1,246,850	1,246,875	1,247,000
Apr 1 year 1	June 30 year 1	91	2	1,258,833	1,260,679	1,260,704	1,260,729	1,260,856
July 1 year 1	Sept 30 year 1	92	3	1,272,667	1,274,532	1,274,558	1,274,583	1,274,711
Oct 1 year 1	Dec 31 year 1	92	4	1,272,667	1,274,532	1,274,558	1,274,583	1,274,711
Jan 1 year 2	Mar 31 year 2	90	5	1,245,000	1,246,825	1,246,850	1,246,875	1,247,000
Apr 1 year 2	June 30 year 2	91	6	1,258,833	1,260,679	1,260,704	1,260,729	1,260,856
July 1 year 2	Sept 30 year 2	92	7	1,272,667	1,274,532	1,274,558	1,274,583	1,274,711
Oct 1 year 2	Dec 31 year 2	92	8	1,272,667	1,274,532	1,274,558	1,274,583	1,274,711
Jan 1 year 3	Mar 31 year 3	90	9	1,245,000	1,246,825	1,246,850	1,246,875	1,247,000
Apr 1 year 3	June 30 year 3	91	10	1,258,833	1,260,679	1,260,704	1,260,729	1,260,856
July 1 year 3	Sept 30 year 3	92	11	1,272,667	1,274,532	1,274,558	1,274,583	1,274,711
Oct 1 year 3	Dec 31 year 3	92	12	1,272,667	1,274,532	1,274,558	1,274,583	1,274,711

It is the same equation as for determining the floating-rate payment except that the swap rate is used instead of the reference rate (3-month LIBOR in our illustration). For example, suppose that the swap rate is 4.98% and the quarter has 90 days. Then the fixed-rate payment for the quarter is:

$$\$100,000,000 \times 0.0498 \times \frac{90}{360} = \$1,245,000$$

If there are 92 days in a quarter, the fixed-rate payment for the quarter is:

$$\$100,000,000 \times 0.0498 \times \frac{92}{360} = \$1,272,667$$

Note that the rate is fixed for each quarter but the dollar amount of the payment depends on the number of days in the period.

Exhibit 4 shows the fixed-rate payments based on different assumed values for the swap rate. The first three columns of the exhibit show the same information as in Exhibit 3 — the beginning and end of the quarter and the number of days in the quarter. Column (4) simply uses the notation for the period. That is, period 1 means the end of the first quarter, period 2 means the end of the second quarter, and so on. The other columns of the exhibit show the payments for each assumed swap rate.

Calculation of the Swap Rate

Now that we know how to calculate the payments for the fixed-rate and floating-rate sides of a swap where the reference rate is 3-month LIBOR given (1) the current value for 3-month LIBOR, (2) the expected 3-month LIBOR from the Euro-dollar CD futures contract, and (3) the assumed swap rate, we can demonstrate how to compute the swap rate.

At the initiation of an interest rate swap, the counterparties are agreeing to exchange future payments and no upfront payments by either party are made. This means that the swap terms must be such that the present value of the payments to be made by the counterparties must be at least equal to the present value of the payments that will be received. In fact, to eliminate arbitrage opportunities, the present value of the payments made by a party will be equal to the present value of the payments received by that same party. *The equivalence (or no arbitrage) of the present value of the payments is the key principle in calculating the swap rate.*

Since we will have to calculate the present value of the payments, let's show how this is done.

Calculating the Present Value of the Floating-Rate Payments

As explained earlier, we must be careful about how we compute the present value of payments. In particular, we must carefully specify (1) the timing of the payment and (2) the interest rates that should be used to discount the payments. We already addressed the first issue. In constructing the exhibit for the payments, we indicated that the payments are at the end of the quarter. So, we denoted the time periods with respect to the end of the quarter.

Now let's turn to the interest rates that should be used for discounting. In Chapter 3, we emphasized two things. First, every cash flow should be discounted at its own discount rate using a spot rate. So, if we discounted a cash flow of $1 using the spot rate for period t, the present value would be:

$$\text{present value of \$1 to be received in period } t = \frac{\$1}{(1 + \text{spot rate for period } t)^t}$$

The second thing we emphasized is that forward rates are derived from spot rates so that if we discounted a cash flow using forward rates rather than a spot rate, we would come up with the same value. That is, the present value of $1 to be received in period t can be rewritten as:

present value of $1 to be received in period $t =$

$$\frac{\$1}{(1 + \text{forward rate for period } 1)(1 + \text{forward rate for period } 2) \cdots (1 + \text{forward rate for period } t)}$$

We will refer to the present value of $1 to be received in period t as the *forward discount factor*. In our calculations involving swaps, we will compute the forward discount factor for a period using the forward rates. These are the same forward rates that are used to compute the floating-rate payments — those obtained from the Eurodollar CD futures contract. We must make just one more adjustment. We must adjust the forward rates used in the formula for the number of days in the period (i.e., the quarter in our illustrations) in the same way that we made this adjustment to obtain the payments. Specifically, the forward rate for a period, which we will refer to as the period forward rate, is computed using the following equation:

$$\text{period forward rate} = \text{annual forward rate} \times \left(\frac{\text{days in period}}{360} \right)$$

For example, look at Exhibit 3. The annual forward rate for period 4 is 4.72%. The period forward rate for period 4 is:

$$\text{period forward rate} = 4.72\% \times \left(\frac{92}{360} \right) = 1.2062\%$$

Column (5) in Exhibit 5 shows the annual forward rate for all 12 periods (reproduced from Exhibit 3) and Column (6) shows the period forward rate for all 12 periods. Note that the period forward rate for period 1 is 4.05%, the known rate for 3-month LIBOR.

Also shown in Exhibit 5 is the forward discount factor for all 12 periods. These values are shown in the last column. Let's show how the forward discount factor is computed for periods 1, 2, and 3. For period 1, the forward discount factor is:

$$\text{forward discount factor} = \frac{\$1}{(1.010125)} = 0.98997649$$

For period 2,

$$\text{forward discount factor} = \frac{\$1}{(1.010125)(1.010490)} = 0.97969917$$

For period 3.

$$\text{forward discount factor} = \frac{\$1}{(1.010125)(1.010490)(1.011628)}$$
$$= 0.96843839$$

Given the floating-rate payment for a period and the forward discount factor for the period, the present value of the payment can be computed. For example, from Exhibit 3 we see that the floating-rate payment for period 4 is $1,206,222. From Exhibit 5, the forward discount factor for period 4 is 0.95689609. Therefore, the present value of the payment is:

present value of period 4 payment = $1,206,222 × 0.95689609 = $1,154,229

Exhibit 6 shows the present value for each payment. The total present value of the 12 floating-rate payments is $14,052,917. Thus, the present value of the payments that the fixed-rate payer will receive is $14,052,917 and the present value of the payments that the fixed-rate receiver will make is $14,052,917.

Determination of the Swap Rate

The fixed-rate payer will require that the present value of the fixed-rate payments that must be made based on the swap rate not exceed the $14,052,917 payments to be received from the floating-rate payments. The fixed-rate receiver will require that the present value of the fixed-rate payments to received be at least as great as the $14,052,917 that must be paid. This means that both parties will require a present value for the fixed-rate payments to be $14,052,917. If that is the case, the present value of the fixed-rate payments is equal to the present value of the floating-rate payments and therefore the value of the swap is zero for both parties at the inception of the swap. The interest rates that should be used to compute the present value of the fixed-rate payments are the same interest rates as those used to discount the floating-rate payments.

Exhibit 5: Calculating the Forward Discount Factor

(1)	(2)	(3)	(4)	(5)	(6)	(7)
Quarter starts	Quarter ends	Number of days in quarter	Period = End of quarter	Forward rate	Period forward rate	Forward discount factor
Jan 1 year 1	Mar 31 year 1	90	1	4.05%	1.0125%	0.98997649
Apr 1 year 1	June 30 year 1	91	2	4.15%	1.0490%	0.97969917
July 1 year 1	Sept 30 year 1	92	3	4.55%	1.1628%	0.96843839
Oct 1 year 1	Dec 31 year 1	92	4	4.72%	1.2062%	0.95689609
Jan 1 year 2	Mar 31 year 2	90	5	4.90%	1.2250%	0.94531597
Apr 1 year 2	June 30 year 2	91	6	5.03%	1.2715%	0.93344745
July 1 year 2	Sept 30 year 2	92	7	5.15%	1.3161%	0.92132183
Oct 1 year 2	Dec 31 year 2	92	8	5.25%	1.3417%	0.90912441
Jan 1 year 3	Mar 31 year 3	90	9	5.40%	1.3500%	0.89701471
Apr 1 year 3	June 30 year 3	91	10	5.50%	1.3903%	0.88471472
July 1 year 3	Sept 30 year 3	92	11	5.65%	1.4439%	0.87212224
Oct 1 year 3	Dec 31 year 3	92	12	5.76%	1.4720%	0.85947083

Exhibit 6: Present Value of the Floating-Rate Payments

(1)	(2)	(3)	(4)	(5)	(6)
Quarter starts	Quarter ends	Period = End of quarter	Forward discount factor	Floating-rate payment at end of quarter	PV of floating-rate payment
Jan 1 year 1	Mar 31 year 1	1	0.98997649	1,012,500	1,002,351
Apr 1 year 1	June 30 year 1	2	0.97969917	1,049,028	1,027,732
July 1 year 1	Sept 30 year 1	3	0.96843839	1,162,778	1,126,079
Oct 1 year 1	Dec 31 year 1	4	0.95689609	1,206,222	1,154,229
Jan 1 year 2	Mar 31 year 2	5	0.94531597	1,225,000	1,158,012
Apr 1 year 2	June 30 year 2	6	0.93344745	1,271,472	1,186,852
July 1 year 2	Sept 30 year 2	7	0.92132183	1,316,111	1,212,562
Oct 1 year 2	Dec 31 year 2	8	0.90912441	1,341,667	1,219,742
Jan 1 year 3	Mar 31 year 3	9	0.89701471	1,350,000	1,210,970
Apr 1 year 3	June 30 year 3	10	0.88471472	1,390,278	1,229,999
July 1 year 3	Sept 30 year 3	11	0.87212224	1,443,889	1,259,248
Oct 1 year 3	Dec 31 year 3	12	0.85947083	1,472,000	1,265,141
				Total	14,052,917

To show how to compute the swap rate, we begin with the basic relationship for no arbitrage to exist:

PV of floating-rate payments = PV of fixed-rate payments

We know the value for the left-hand side of the equation.
If we let

SR = swap rate

and

$Days_t$ = number of days in the payment period t

then the fixed-rate payment for period t is equal to:

$$\text{notional amount} \times SR \times \frac{Days_t}{360}$$

The present value of the fixed-rate payment for period t is found by multiplying the previous expression by the forward discount factor. If we let FDF_t denote the forward discount factor for period t, then the present value of the fixed-rate payment for period t is equal to:

$$\text{notional amount} \times SR \times \frac{Days_t}{360} \times FDF_t$$

We can now sum up the present value of the fixed-rate payment for each period to get the present value of the floating-rate payments. Using the Greek symbol sigma, Σ, to denote summation and letting N be the number of periods in the swap, then the present value of the fixed-rate payments can be expressed as:

$$\sum_{t=1}^{N} \text{notional amount} \times SR \times \frac{Days_t}{360} \times FDF_t$$

This can also be expressed as

$$SR \sum_{t=1}^{N} \text{notional amount} \times \frac{Days_t}{360} \times FDF_t$$

The condition for no arbitrage is that the present value of the fixed-rate payments as given by the expression above is equal to the present value of the floating-rate payments. That is,

$$SR \sum_{t=1}^{N} \text{notional amount} \times \frac{Days_t}{360} \times FDF_t = PV \text{ of floating-rate payments}$$

Exhibit 7: Calculating the Denominator for the Swap Rate Formula

(1)	(2)	(3)	(4)	(5)	(6)	(7)
Quarter starts	Quarter ends	Number of days in quarter	Period = End of quarter	Forward discount factor	Days/360	Forward discount factor × Days/360 × notional
Jan 1 year 1	Mar 31 year 1	90	1	0.98997649	0.25000000	24,749,412
Apr 1 year 1	June 30 year 1	91	2	0.97969917	0.25277778	24,764,618
July 1 year 1	Sept 30 year 1	92	3	0.96843839	0.25555556	24,748,981
Oct 1 year 1	Dec 31 year 1	92	4	0.95689609	0.25555556	24,454,011
Jan 1 year 2	Mar 31 year 2	90	5	0.94531597	0.25000000	23,632,899
Apr 1 year 2	June 30 year 2	91	6	0.93344745	0.25277778	23,595,477
July 1 year 2	Sept 30 year 2	92	7	0.92132183	0.25555556	23,544,891
Oct 1 year 2	Dec 31 year 2	92	8	0.90912441	0.25555556	23,233,179
Jan 1 year 3	Mar 31 year 3	90	9	0.89701471	0.25000000	22,425,368
Apr 1 year 3	June 30 year 3	91	10	0.88471472	0.25277778	22,363,622
July 1 year 3	Sept 30 year 3	92	11	0.87212224	0.25555556	22,287,568
Oct 1 year 3	Dec 31 year 3	92	12	0.85947083	0.25555556	21,964,255
					Total	281,764,282

Solving for the swap rate

$$SR = \frac{PV \text{ of floating-rate payments}}{\sum_{t=1}^{N} \text{notional amount} \times \frac{\text{Days}_t}{360} \times \text{FDF}_t}$$

All of the values to compute the swap rate are known.

Let's apply the formula to determine the swap rate for our 3-year swap. Exhibit 7 shows the calculation of the denominator of the formula. The forward discount factor for each period shown in Column (5) is obtained from Column (4) of Exhibit 6. The sum of the last column in Exhibit 7 shows that the denominator of the swap rate formula is $281,764,282. We know from Exhibit 6 that the present value of the floating-rate payments is $14,052,917. Therefore, the swap rate is

$$SR = \frac{\$14,052,917}{\$281,764,282} = 0.049875 = 4.9875\%$$

Given the swap rate, the *swap spread* can be determined. For example, since this is a 3-year swap, the convention is to use the 3-year on-the-run Treasury rate as the benchmark. If the yield on that issue is 4.5875%, the swap spread is 40 basis points (4.9875% − 4.5875%).

The calculation of the swap rate for all swaps follows the same principle: equating the present value of the fixed-rate payments to that of the floating-rate payments.

Exhibit 8: Rates and Floating-Rate Payments One Year Later if Rates Increase

(1)	(2)	(3)	(4)	(5)	(6)	(7)	(8)
Quarter starts	Quarter ends	Number of days in quarter	Current 3-month LIBOR	Eurodollar futures price	Forward rate	Period = End of quarter	Floating-rate payments at end of quarter
Jan 1 year 2	Mar 31 year 2	90	5.25%			1	1,312,500
Apr 1 year 2	June 30 year 2	91		94.27	5.73%	2	1,448,417
July 1 year 2	Sept 30 year 2	92		94.22	5.78%	3	1,477,111
Oct 1 year 2	Dec 31 year 2	92		94.00	6.00%	4	1,533,333
Jan 1 year 3	Mar 31 year 3	90		93.85	6.15%	5	1,537,500
Apr 1 year 3	June 30 year 3	91		93.75	6.25%	6	1,579,861
July 1 year 3	Sept 30 year 3	92		93.54	6.46%	7	1,650,889
Oct 1 year 3	Dec 31 year 3	92		93.25	6.75%	8	1,725,000

Valuing a Swap

Once the swap transaction is completed, changes in market interest rates will change the payments of the floating-rate side of the swap. The value of an interest rate swap is the difference between the present value of the payments of the two sides of the swap. The 3-month LIBOR forward rates from the current Eurodollar CD futures contracts are used to (1) calculate the floating-rate payments and (2) determine the discount factors at which to calculate the present value of the payments.

To illustrate this, consider the 3-year swap used to demonstrate how to calculate the swap rate. Suppose that one year later, interest rates change as shown in Columns (4) and (6) in Exhibit 8. In Column (4) shows the current 3-month LIBOR. In Column (5) are the Eurodollar CD futures price for each period. These rates are used to compute the forward rates in Column (6). Note that the interest rates have increased one year later since the rates in Exhibit 8 are greater than those in Exhibit 3. As in Exhibit 3, the current 3-month LIBOR and the forward rates are used to compute the floating-rate payments. These payments are shown in Column (8) of Exhibit 8.

In Exhibit 9, the forward discount factor is computed for each period. The calculation is the same as in Exhibit 5 to obtain the forward discount factor for each period. The forward discount factor for each period is shown in the last column of Exhibit 9.

In Exhibit 10 the forward discount factor (from Exhibit 9) and the floating-rate payments (from Exhibit 8) are shown. The fixed-rate payments need not be recomputed. They are the payments shown in Column (8) of Exhibit 4. This is the fixed-rate payments for the swap rate of 4.9875% and is reproduced in Exhibit 10. Now the two payment streams must be discounted using the new forward discount factors. As shown at the bottom of Exhibit 10, the two present values are as follows:

Present value of floating-rate payments $11,459,495

Present value of fixed-rate payments $9,473,390

Exhibit 9: Period Forward Rates and Forward Discount Factors One Year Later if Rates Increase

(1)	(2)	(3)	(4)	(5)	(6)	(7)
Quarter starts	Quarter ends	Number of days in quarter	Period = End of quarter	Forward rate	Period forward rate	Forward discount factor
Jan 1 year 2	Mar 31 year 2	90	1	5.25%	1.3125%	0.98704503
Apr 1 year 2	June 30 year 2	91	2	5.73%	1.4484%	0.97295263
July 1 year 2	Sept 30 year 2	92	3	5.78%	1.4771%	0.95879023
Oct 1 year 2	Dec 31 year 2	92	4	6.00%	1.5333%	0.94431080
Jan 1 year 3	Mar 31 year 3	90	5	6.15%	1.5375%	0.93001186
Apr 1 year 3	June 30 year 3	91	6	6.25%	1.5799%	0.91554749
July 1 year 3	Sept 30 year 3	92	7	6.46%	1.6509%	0.90067829
Oct 1 year 3	Dec 31 year 3	92	8	6.75%	1.7250%	0.88540505

Exhibit 10: Valuing the Swap One Year Later if Rates Increase

(1)	(2)	(3)	(4)	(5)	(6)	(7)
Quarter starts	Quarter ends	Forward discount factor	Floating cash flow at end of quarter	PV of floating cash flow	Fixed cash flow at end of quarter	PV of fixed cash flow
Jan 1 year 2	Mar 31 year 2	0.98704503	1,312,500	1,295,497	1,246,875	1,230,722
Apr 1 year 2	June 30 year 2	0.97295263	1,448,417	1,409,241	1,260,729	1,226,630
July 1 year 2	Sept 30 year 2	0.95879023	1,477,111	1,416,240	1,274,583	1,222,058
Oct 1 year 2	Dec 31 year 2	0.94431080	1,533,333	1,447,943	1,274,583	1,203,603
Jan 1 year 3	Mar 31 year 3	0.93001186	1,537,500	1,429,893	1,246,875	1,159,609
Apr 1 year 3	June 30 year 3	0.91554749	1,579,861	1,446,438	1,260,729	1,154,257
July 1 year 3	Sept 30 year 3	0.90067829	1,650,889	1,486,920	1,274,583	1,147,990
Oct 1 year 3	Dec 31 year 3	0.88540505	1,725,000	1,527,324	1,274,583	1,128,523
			Total	11,459,495		9,473,390

Summary	Fixed-rate payer	Fixed-rate receiver
PV of payments received	11,459,495	9,473,390
PV of payments made	9,473,390	11,459,495
Value of swap	1,986,105	−1,986,105

The two present values are not equal and therefore for one party the value of the swap increased and for the other party the value of the swap decreased. Let's look at which party gained and which party lost.

The fixed-rate payer will receive the floating-rate payments. And these payments have a present value of $11,459,495. The present value of the payments that must be made by the fixed-rate payer is $9,473,390. Thus, the swap has a positive value for the fixed-rate payer equal to the difference in the two present values of $1,986,105. This is the value of the swap to the fixed-rate payer. Notice, consistent with what we said in the previous chapter, when interest rates increase (as they did in the illustration analyzed), the fixed-rate payer benefits because the value of the swap increases.

In contrast, the fixed-rate receiver must make payments with a present value of $11,459,495 but will only receive fixed-rate payments with a present value equal to $9,473,390. Thus, the value of the swap for the fixed-rate receiver is − $1,986,105. Again, as explained earlier, the fixed-rate receiver is adversely affected by a rise in interest rates because it results in a decline in the value of a swap.

The same valuation principle applies to more complicated swaps. For example, there are swaps whose notional amount changes in a predetermined way over the life of the swap. These include amortizing swaps, accreting swaps, and roller coaster swaps. Once the payments are specified, the present value is calculated as described above by simply adjusting the payment amounts by the changing notional amounts — the methodology does *not* change.

Primary Determinants of Swap Spreads

As we have seen, interest rate swaps are valued using no-arbitrage relationships relative to instruments (funding or investment vehicles) that produce the same cash flows under the same circumstances. Earlier we provided two interpretations of a swap: (1) a package of futures/forward contracts and (2) a package of cash market instruments. The swap spread is defined as the difference between the swap's fixed rate and the rate on a Treasury whose maturity matches the swap's tenor.

Exhibit 11 displays interest rate swap spreads (in basis points) for all maturities out to 30 years on September 3, 1999. Current swap spreads can be obtained on Bloomberg using the functions ALLX $$SW or IRSB US. Bloomberg collects the spread information throughout the trading day and an average is calculated using the spreads from three market makers. The actual swap rates can be obtained simply by adding the swap spreads to the on-the-run U.S. Treasury yield curve. Exhibit 12 is a time series plot obtained from Bloomberg for daily values of the 5-year swap spread (in basis points) for the period March 3, 1999 to September 3, 1999. This plot can be obtained using the function $$SWAP5 Index GP.

The swap spread is determined by the same factors that drive the spread over Treasuries on instruments that replicate a swap's cash flows i.e., produce a similar return or funding profile. As discussed below, the swap spread's key determinant for swaps with tenors of five years or less is the cost of hedging in the Eurodollar CD futures market.[3] For longer tenor swaps, the swap spread is largely driven by credit spreads in the corporate bond market.[4] Specifically, longer-dated swaps are priced relative to rates paid by investment-grade credits in traditional fixed- and floating-rate markets.

---

[3] Naturally, this presupposes the reference rate used for the floating-rate cash flows is LIBOR. Furthermore, part of swap spread is attributable simply to the fact that LIBOR for a given maturity is higher than the rate on a comparable-maturity U.S. Treasury.

[4] The default risk component of a swap spread will be smaller than for a comparable bond credit spread. The reasons are straightforward. First, since only net interest payments are exchanged rather than both principal and coupon interest payments, the total cash flow at risk is lower. Second, the probability of default depends jointly on the probability of the counterparty defaulting and whether or not the swap has a positive value. See John C. Hull, *Introduction to Futures and Options Markets, Third Edition* (Upper Saddle River, NJ: Prentice Hall, 1998).

Exhibit 11: Swap Spreads for Various Maturities

```
<HELP> for explanation, <MENU> for similar functions.     P066 Index  A L L X
Press # <GO> to select an index or <TAB> to change # of periods to look back
D L R - D L R   S W A P   S P R E A D
```

Source: BLOOMBERG INDEX	<Indx> TICKER	CURRENT VALUE	DATE	PREVIOUS VALUE	DATE	PCT CHNG
1) SWAP DLR - DLR 2 YEARS	$$SWAP2	65	9/ 3	66	9/ 2	-1.52
2) SWAP DLR - DLR 3 YEARS	$$SWAP3	78	9/ 3	80	9/ 2	-2.50
3) SWAP DLR - DLR 4 YEARS	$$SWAP4	86	9/ 3	88	9/ 2	-2.27
4) SWAP DLR - DLR 5 YEARS	$$SWAP5	92	9/ 3	94	9/ 2	-2.13
5) SWAP DLR - DLR 6 YEARS	$$SWAP6	97	9/ 3	98	9/ 2	-1.02
6) SWAP DLR - DLR 7 YEARS	$$SWAP7	100	9/ 3	102	9/ 2	-1.96
7) SWAP DLR - DLR 8 YEARS	$$SWAP8	103	9/ 3	105	9/ 2	-1.90
8) SWAP DLR - DLR 9 YEARS	$$SWAP9	105	9/ 3	107	9/ 2	-1.87
9) SWAP DLR - DLR 10 YEARS	$$SWAP10	107	9/ 3	109	9/ 2	-1.83
10) SWAP DLR - DLR 15 YEARS	$$SWAP15	121	9/ 3	123	9/ 2	-1.63
11) SWAP DLR - DLR 20 YEARS	$$SWAP20	124	9/ 3	127	9/ 2	-2.36
12) SWAP DLR - DLR 30 YEARS	$$SWAP30	114	9/ 3	116	9/ 2	-1.72

```
Copyright 1999 BLOOMBERG L.P.  Frankfurt:69-920410  Hong Kong:2-977-6000  London:171-330-7500  New York:212-318-2000
Princeton:609-279-3000    Singapore:226-3000    Sydney:2-9777-8686    Tokyo:3-3201-8900    Sao Paulo:11-3048-4500
                                                                              G279-532-2 03-Sep-99 17:33:19
```

Source: Bloomberg Financial Markets

Exhibit 12: Time Series of the 5-Year Swap Spread

Given that a swap is a package of futures/forward contracts, the shorter-term swap spreads respond directly to fluctuations in Eurodollar CD futures prices. A Eurodollar CD futures contract is an instrument where a fixed dollar payment (i.e., the futures price) is exchanged for 3-month LIBOR. As noted, there is a liquid market for Eurodollar CD futures contracts with maturities every three months for five years. A market participant can create a synthetic fixed-rate security or a fixed-rate funding vehicle of up to five years by taking a position in a bundle of Eurodollar CD futures contracts (i.e., a position in every 3-month Eurodollar CD futures contract up to the desired maturity date).

For example, consider a financial institution that has fixed-rate assets and floating-rate liabilities. Both the assets and liabilities have a maturity of three years. The interest rate on the liabilities resets every three months based on 3-month LIBOR. This financial institution can hedge this mismatched asset/liability position by buying a 3-year bundle of Eurodollar CD futures contracts. By doing so, the financial institution is receiving LIBOR over the 3-year period and paying a fixed dollar amount (i.e., the futures price). The financial institution is now hedged because the assets are fixed rate and the bundle of long Eurodollar CD futures synthetically creates a fixed-rate funding arrangement. From the fixed dollar amount over the three years, an effective fixed rate that the financial institution pays can be computed. Alternatively, the financial institution can synthetically create a fixed-rate funding arrangement by entering into a 3-year swap in which it pays fixed and receives 3-month LIBOR. Other things equal, the financial institution will use the vehicle that delivers the lowest cost of hedging the mismatched position. That is, the financial institution will compare the synthetic fixed rate (expressed as a percentage over U.S. Treasuries) to the 3-year swap spread. The difference between the synthetic spread and the swap spread should be within a few basis points under normal circumstances.

For swaps with tenors greater than five years, we cannot rely on the Eurodollar CD futures since liquid markets do not exist for these contracts at longer maturities. Instead, longer-dated swaps are priced using rates available for investment-grade corporate borrowers in fixed-rate and floating-rate debt markets. Since a swap can be interpreted as a package of long and short positions in a fixed-rate bond and a floating-rate bond, it is the credit spreads in those two market sectors that will be the determinant of the swap spread. Empirically, the swap curve lies above the U.S. Treasury yield curve and below on-the-run yield curve for AA-rated banks.[5] Swap fixed rates are lower than AA-rated bond yields due to their lower credit due to netting and offsetting of swap positions.

In addition, there are a number of other technical factors that influence the level of swap spreads.[6] While the impact of some these factors is ephemeral, their influence can be considerable in the short run. Included among these factors are: (1) the level and shape of the Treasury yield curve; (2) the relative supply of fixed- and floating-rate payers in the interest rate swap market; (3) the level of asset-based swap activity; and (4) technical factors that affect swap dealers.

The level, slope, and curvature of the U.S. Treasury yield is an important influence of swap spreads at various maturities. The reason is that embedded in

---

[5] For a discussion of this point, see Andrew R. Young, *A Morgan Stanley Guide to Fixed Income Analysis* (New York: Morgan Stanley, 1997).

[6] See Ellen L. Evans and Gioia Parente Bales, "What Drives Interest Rate Swap Spreads," Chapter 13 in Carl R. Beidleman (ed.), *Interest Rate Swaps* (Burr Ridge, IL: Irwin Professional Publishing, 1991).

the yield curve are the market's expectations of the direction of future interest rates. While these expectations are sometimes challenging to extract, the decision to borrow at a fixed-rate or a floating-rate will be based, in part, on these expectations. The relative supply of fixed- and floating-rate payers in the interest rate swap market should also be influenced by these expectations. For example, many corporate issuers — financial institutions and federal agencies in particular — swap their newly issued fixed-rate debt into floating using the swap market. Consequently, swap spreads will be affected by the corporate debt issuance calendar. In addition, swap spreads are more (less) volatile on the short-end (long-end) of the curve. These movements correspond to the Treasury volatility curve (the relationship between the standard deviation of Treasury yields and term to maturity) which is typically downward sloping. Simply put, this means that short-rates are usually more volatile than long rates. For example, as on-the-run Treasuries go "on special," it is correspondingly more expensive to use these Treasuries as a hedge. This increase in hedging costs engenders wider swap spreads.[7]

Another influence on the level of swap spreads is the volume of asset-based swap transactions. An asset-based swap transaction involves the creation of a synthetic security via the purchase of an existing security and the simultaneous execution of a swap. For example, after the Russian debt default and ruble devaluation in August 1998, risk-averse investors sold corporate bonds and fled to the relative safety of U.S. Treasuries. Credit spreads widened considerably and liquidity diminished. A contrary-minded floating-rate investor like a financial institution could have taken advantage of these circumstances by buying newly issued investment grade corporate bonds with relatively attractive coupon rates and simultaneously taking a long position in an interest rate swap (pay fixed/receive floating). Because of the higher credit spreads, the coupon rate that the financial institution receives is higher than the fixed-rate paid in the swap. Accordingly, the financial institution ends up with a synthetic floating-rate asset with a sizeable spread above LIBOR.

By similar reasoning, investors can use swaps to create a synthetic fixed-rate security. For example, during the mid-1980s, many banks issued perpetual floating-rate notes in the Eurobond market. A perpetual floating-rate note is a security that delivers floating-rate cash flows forever. The coupon is reset and paid usually every three months with a coupon formula equal to the reference rate (e.g., 3-month LIBOR) plus a spread. When the perpetual floating-rate note market collapsed in late 1986, the contagion spread into other sectors of the floaters market.[8] Many floaters cheapened considerably. As before, contrary-minded fixed-rate investors could exploit this situation through the purchase of a relatively cheap (from the investor's perspective) floater while simultaneously taking a short posi-

---

[7] Traders often use the repo market to obtain specific securities to cover short positions. If a security is in short supply relative to demand, the repo rate on a specific security used as collateral in repo transaction will be below the general (i.e., generic) collateral repo rate. When a particular security's repo rate falls markedly, that security is said to be "on special." Investors who own these securities are able to lend them out as collateral and borrow at bargain basement rates.

[8] Suresh E. Krishman, "Asset-Based Interest Rate Swaps," Chapter 8 in *Interest Rate Swaps*.

tion in an interest rate swap (pay floating/receive fixed) and create a synthetic fixed-rate investment. The investor makes floating-rate payments (say based on LIBOR) to their counterparty and receives fixed-rate payments equal to the Treasury yield plus the swap spread. Accordingly, the fixed rate on this synthetic security is equal to the sum of the following: (1) the Treasury bond yield that matches the swap's tenor; (2) the swap spread; and (3) the floater's index spread.

Finally, swap spreads are also affected by the hedging costs faced by swap dealers. Dealers hedge the interest rate risk of long (short) swap positions by taking a long (short) position in a Treasury security with the same maturity as the swap's tenor and borrowing funds (lending funds) in the repo market. As a result, the spread between LIBOR and the appropriate repo rate will be a critical determinant of the hedging costs.

FIXED EQUIVALENT COUPON

As will be discussed in several chapters of this book, investors employ a variety of approaches to evaluate floaters. Every approach has some merit as well as some attending limitations. The purpose of this section is to describe how swap markets are used as a tool to gauge the relative value of floaters. Simply put, the swap market is used to convert a floater into a fixed-rate bond (effectively swapping out the implied LIBOR financing).

The coupon on this hypothetical fixed-rate security with the same maturity and coupon frequency as the floater is called the *fixed-equivalent coupon*.[9] Once computed, a floater's fixed-equivalent coupon rate can then be compared to the yields on instruments in liquid fixed-rate markets.

We will illustrate the calculation of a fixed-equivalent coupon with a floating-rate note issued by Enron Corp. (ticker symbol "ENE 03/00") that matures March 30, 2000. The Security Description screen (DES) from Bloomberg is presented in Exhibit 13. This issue contains no embedded options (e.g., caps, floors, call feature, etc.). As can be seen from the description screen, this floater delivers cash flows quarterly and has a coupon formula equal to 3-month LIBOR plus 45 basis points. The day count convention is ACT/360.

Floater valuation analysis is carried out using Bloomberg's *YAF function*. The YAF screen is displayed in Exhibit 14. Recall that a floater's value can decomposed into three parts: (1) the value of a pure floater whose coupon formula is equal to the floater's reference rate flat; (2) the value of any quoted margin (the amount added/subtracted to the reference rate in the coupon formula); and (3) the value of any embedded options. Let's partition the Enron floater's market price of 99.99 into these first two components parts since this floater does not contain an embedded cap and/or floor.[10]

---

[9] The fixed rate is also referred to as *yield-to-forward LIBOR*.

[10] Although there is no current market price available for this floater as indicated by the words "NOT PRICED" at the top center of the screen, we will use the Bloomberg default price for a floater of 99.99 in our analysis.

Exhibit 13: Description of Enron Corp. Floater

```
Menu                                              DG41 Corp   D E S

S E C U R I T Y   D E S C R I P T I O N
ENRON CORP           ENE Float 03/00    N O T    P R I C E D
┌─────────────────────────────┬─────────────────────────┬──────────────────────┐
│ ISSUER INFORMATION          │ IDENTIFIERS             │ 1) Additional Sec Info│
│ Name ENRON CORP             │ ISIN     US293561BV79   │ 2) Floating Rates     │
│ Type Pipelines              │ CUSIP      293561BV7    │ 3) Identifiers        │
│ Market of Issue US DOMESTIC │ BB number  EC0486471    │ 4) Ratings            │
│ SECURITY INFORMATION        │ RATINGS                 │ 5) Prospectus         │
│ Country USA    Currency USD │ Moody's      Baa2       │ 6) Sec. Specific News │
│ Collateral Type NOTES       │ S&P          BBB+       │ 7) Involved Parties   │
│ Calc Typ ( 21)FLOAT RATE NOTE│ FI          BBB+       │ 8) Custom Notes       │
│  Maturity  3/30/2000 Series │ ISSUE SIZE              │ 9) Issuer Information  │
│ NORMAL                      │ Amt Issued              │ 10) Pricing Sources   │
│ Coupon5.45      FLOATING QUARTLY│ USD 250,000.00   (M)│                       │
│ QUARTL US LIB +45    ACT/360│ Amt Outstanding         │                       │
│ Announcement Dt   9/24/98   │ USD 250,000.00   (M)    │                       │
│ Int. Accrual Dt   9/30/98   │ Min Piece/Increment     │                       │
│ 1st Settle Date   9/30/98   │   1,000.00/  1,000.00   │                       │
│ 1st Coupon Date  12/30/98   │ Par Amount   1,000.00   │                       │
│ Iss Pr 100                  │ LEAD MANAGER/EXCHANGE   │                       │
│                             │ ML,SSB                  │ 65) Old DES           │
│ HAVE PROSPECTUS             │                         │ 66) Send as Attachment│
└─────────────────────────────┴─────────────────────────┴──────────────────────┘
CPN RATE=3MO US$LIBOR +45BP. UNSEC'D.
```

Source: Bloomberg Financial Markets

Exhibit 14: Analysis of Enron Corp. Floater

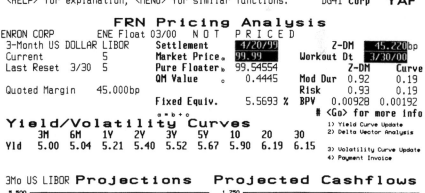

```
<HELP> for explanation, <MENU> for similar functions.    DG41 Corp   YAF

                FRN  Pricing  Analysis
ENRON CORP           ENE Float 03/00   N O T    P R I C E D
3-Month US DOLLAR LIBOR      Settlement    4/20/99      Z-DM    45.220bp
Current           5          Market Price. 99.99        Workout Dt  3/30/00
Last Reset  3/30 5          Pure Floater. 99.54554                 Z-DM    Curve
                            QM Value   .   0.4445       Mod Dur  0.92    0.19
Quoted Margin   45.000bp                                Risk     0.93    0.19
                            Fixed Equiv.   5.5693 %     BPV    0.00928  0.00192
                                a = b + o               # <Go> for more info
Yield/Volatility  Curves                                1) Yield Curve Update
     3M   6M   1Y   2Y   3Y   5Y   10   20   30         2) Delta Vector Analysis
Yld  5.00 5.04 5.21 5.40 5.52 5.67 5.90 6.19 6.15       3) Volatility Curve Update
                                                        4) Payment Invoice
```

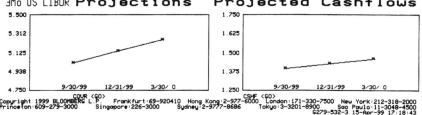

Source: Bloomberg Financial Markets

Exhibit 15: Description of Economic Development Corp. Floater

```
65                                                      DG41 Corp    O D E 5
<Page> For More Information On This Security.
              S E C U R I T Y   D I S P L A Y              PAGE    1/ 4
EXPORT DEV CORP   EDC Float 02/03    N O T    P R I C E D
```

		ISSUER INFORMATION		
SECURITY INFORMATION		SERIES: EMTN	NAME	EXPORT DEVELOPMENT CORP
CPN FREQ	SEMI-AN	SEASONED	TYPE	GOVT AGENCY
CPN TYPE	FLOATING	IDENTIFICATION #'s		REDEMPTION INFO
MTY/REFUND TYP	NORMAL	ISIN	XS0041640672	MATURITY DT	2/ 5/03
CALC TYP (21)	FLOAT RATE NOTE	MLNUM FCCP9		REFUNDING DT
DAY COUNT(2)	ACT/360			NEXT CALL DT
MARKET ISS	EURO MTN	COMMON	004164067	WORKOUT DT	2/ 5/03
COUNTRY/CURR	CAN /USD			RISK FACTOR
COLLATERAL TYP	DEBENTURES	ISSUANCE INFO		
AMT ISSUED	100,000(M)	ANNOUNCE DT	1/ 5/93	RATINGS
AMT OUTSTAND	100,000(M)	1ST SETTLE DT	2/ 5/93	MOODY	Aa2
MIN PC/INC	1,000/ 1,000	1ST CPN DT	8/ 5/93	S & P	AA+
PAR AMT	1,000.00	INT ACCRUE DT	2/ 5/93	COMP	AA2
LEADMGR/UWRTR	ML INTL	PRICE @ ISSUE	100	CBRS	NR
EXCHANGE	UNKNOWN			DOMINION	NR

```
NOTES  NO PROSPECTUS
CPN RATE=6MO $LIBOR -25BP. SR, UNSEC'D. SEASONED EFF 3/17/93.
```

```
Copyright 1999 BLOOMBERG L.P.   Frankfurt:69-920410  Hong Kong:2-977-6000  London:171-330-7500  New York:212-318-2000
Princeton:609-279-3000    Singapore:226-3000    Sydney:2-9777-8686    Tokyo:3-3201-8900    Sao Paulo:11-3048-4500
                                                                        G279-532-3 29-Apr-99 17:19:07
```

Source: Bloomberg Financial Markets

The *QM Value* is the quoted margin value. It represents the present value of any payments paid (received) attributable to the quoted margin above (below) the floater's reference rate.[11] In our example, the quoted margin is 45 basis points so the cash flows attributable to the quoted margins are 45 basis points multiplied by 100 (i.e., the floater's maturity value) divided by 4 to reflect the quarterly payments. The discount rates for these cash flows are the swap curve's implied zero rates derived from Bloomberg's dealer-contributed swap curves.[12] The QM value for this floater is 0.4445 (per $100 of par value).

The value of a pure floater is determined by subtracting the QM value from the market price. In our example, the pure floater value is 99.54554 (99.99 − 0.4445). The pure floater can then be used to determine the fixed-equivalent coupon (*Fixed Equiv.* in the center of the screen). The fixed-equivalent coupon is simply the coupon rate (annualized) that would be required of a hypothetical fixed-rate bond (with the same maturity and coupon frequency) that would generate the same present value as the pure floater given the projected cash flows. For the Enron floater, the fixed-equivalent coupon rate is 5.5693%. Once again, the discount rates are derived from the dealer-contributed swap curves.

Now that the basic concept is in place, let's illustrate the fixed-equivalent coupon calculation with a floater that contains an embedded option. Consider a floater issued by the Economic Development Corp (ticker symbol "EDC 02/3") that matures February 5, 2003. The *Security Description* screen from Bloomberg is presented in Exhibit 15. This floater delivers cash flows semiannually with a

---

[11] If the quoted margin is negative, the QM value will be negative.

[12] The swap curve can be accessed under yield curve update at the center-right edge of the screen.

coupon formula of 6-month LIBOR minus 25 basis points. Moreover, the floater has an embedded collar such that minimum coupon rate is 5% and the maximum coupon rate is 8% regardless of the level of the underlying reference rate. The day count convention is ACT/360.

As before, floater valuation analysis in Bloomberg is accomplished using the YAF function. The YAF screen is displayed in Exhibit 16. The floater value is partitioned into its three components parts. The value of the pure LIBOR floater is 100.1187 while the QM value is −0.9121. Note the QM value is negative because the quoted margin is negative (i.e., minus 25 basis points). The collar premium represents the value of the embedded collar. An investor's position in a collared floater can be described as a combination of three positions, namely: (1) a long position in a pure floater plus/minus the quoted margin; (2) a short position in a call option with an exercise price equal to the cap rate; and (3) a long position in a put option with an exercise price equal to the floor rate. Accordingly, the collar premium represents the net value of these two options positions. In our illustration, the collar premium is 0.7834 (per $100 of par value).

Bloomberg's YAF function values caps, floor, and collars using a modified Black-Scholes model. The volatility assumptions used in the calculation are derived from Bloomberg's dealer-contributed volatility curves. This Volatility Curve Update screen is accessed from the YAF function located in center-right part of the screen. The *Volatility Curve Update* screen is presented in Exhibit 17.

Exhibit 16: Analysis of Export Development Corp. Floater

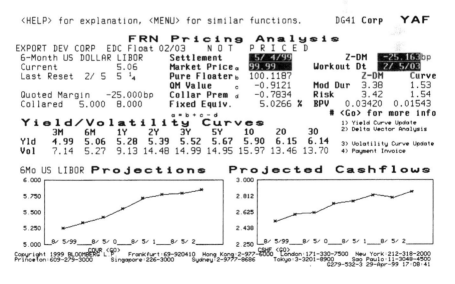

Exhibit 17: Bloomberg's Volatility Curve Update

```
<HELP> for explanation.                          DG41 Corp   Y A F

     V O L A T I L I T Y   C U R V E   U P D A T E   S C R E E N
```

Mty/Term	VOL	Mty/Term	VOL	Mty/Term	VOL
8/ 3/99	7.16				
11/ 3/99	5.25				
5/ 6/00	9.17				
5/ 5/01	14.50				
5/ 4/02	15.00				
5/ 4/03	14.21				
5/ 4/04	14.95				
5/ 4/05	15.43				
5/ 6/06	15.22				
5/ 5/07	15.63				
5/ 4/08	15.79				
5/ 4/09	15.97				
5/ 4/14	14.78				
5/ 4/19	13.46				
5/ 5/29	13.70				

```
                                   Legend
   Shift all        Vol Curve#:  23
 Volatilities       Type: Swap    90-Day              X3    to return to
    0.00%           ccy:   US   Date: 4/29/99                calculator
Copyright 1999 BLOOMBERG L.P.   Frankfurt:69-920410  Hong Kong:2-977-6000  London:171-330-7500  New York:212-318-2000
Princeton:609-279-3000    Singapore:226-3000    Sydney:2-9777-8686    Tokyo:3-3201-8900    Sao Paulo:11-3048-4500
                                                            G279-532-3 29-Apr-99 17:10:52
```

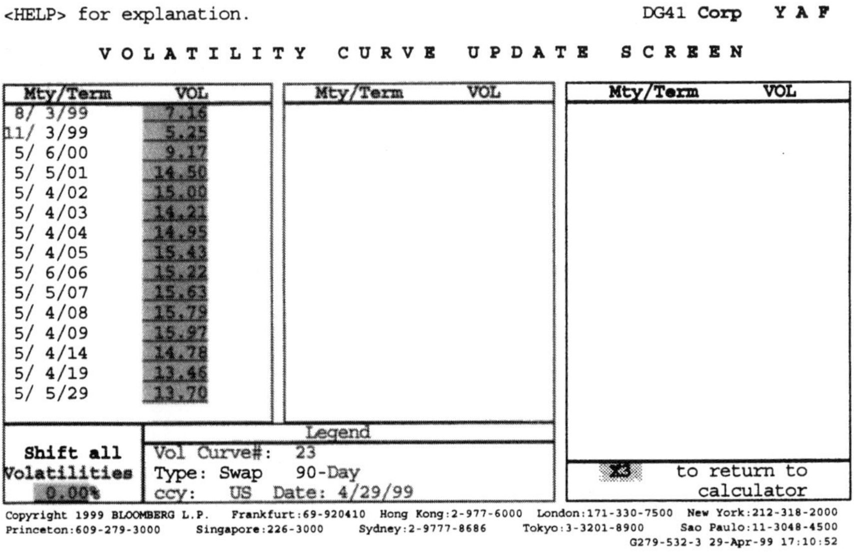

Source: Bloomberg Financial Markets

The pure floater value for this security is determined by adding the QM value to the market price and then subtracting the collar premium. In our example, the pure floater value of 100.1187 is determined as follows: 99.99 (market price) + 0.9121 (QM value) − 0.7834 (collar premium). Once the pure floater value is determined, the fixed-equivalent coupon can be computed in the same manner as above. For the Economic Development Corporation floater, the fixed-equivalent coupon is 5.0266%.

SUMMARY

Swap contracts are invaluable tools for transforming the nature of cash flows. Increasingly, swaps are used as a vehicle to gauge the relative value of floaters. After reviewing some swap market basics including how swaps are valued, we described how the cash flows of a floater can effectively be converted using swaps into a fixed-rate security. Once transformed, a floater's fixed-equivalent coupon rate can then be compared to the yields on comparable fixed-rate securities. Thus, using the swap market an investor can turn a floater into an equivalent fixed-rate security or vice versa. Our discussion highlights an essential function of the swap market, namely, the swap market ties both fixed and floating-rate markets together.

Chapter 7

Adjustable-Rate Mortgage Passthrough Securities

A n asset-backed security (ABS) is a security created by pooling together loans or receivables. The cash flow to pay the holders of the security comes from the cash flow of the underlying loans or receivables. A mortgage-backed security (MBS) refers to an ABS created by pooling mortgage loans on real estate property. While technically the MBS market is part of the ABS market, in the United States the two markets are viewed as being separate.

In this chapter and the two that follow we will describe the floating-rate securities that are available in the MBS and ABS markets. Our focus in this chapter is on mortgage passthrough securities and, in particular, securities in which the underlying pool of loans is adjustable-rate mortgages. We will also describe mortgage passthrough securities in which the underlying mortgage loans have a fixed rate because these securities have been pooled to create collateralized mortgage obligations (CMOs). As part of a CMO structure, bond classes or "tranches" have been created with a floating rate despite the fact that the underlying loans pay a fixed rate. We will refer to such floaters as *CMO floaters*. In Chapter 8, we describe the various types of CMO floaters. In Chapter 9, we look at floaters available in the ABS market.

MORTGAGE LOANS

While any type of mortgage loans — residential or commercial — can be used as collateral for an MBS, most are backed by residential mortgages. We begin our coverage of MBSs with a description of the raw product — the mortgage loan.

Mortgage Designs

A mortgage loan, or simply mortgage, is a loan secured by the collateral of some specified real estate property which obliges the borrower to make a predetermined series of payments. The mortgage gives the lender the right if the borrower defaults to "foreclose" on the loan and seize the property in order to ensure that the debt is paid off. The interest rate on the mortgage loan is called the *mortgage rate* or *contract rate*.

There are many types of mortgage designs. By a mortgage design we mean the specification of the interest rate (fixed or floating), the term of the mortgage, and the manner in which the principal is repaid. We summarize the major mortgage designs below.

Fixed-Rate, Level-Payment, Fully Amortized Mortgage

The basic idea behind the design of the fixed-rate, level payment, fully amortized mortgage is that the borrower pays interest and repays principal in equal installments over an agreed-upon period of time, called the maturity or term of the mortgage. The frequency of payment is typically monthly. Each monthly mortgage payment for this mortgage design is due on the first of each month and consists of:

1. interest of $\frac{1}{12}$th of the annual interest rate times the amount of the outstanding mortgage balance at the beginning of the previous month, and
2. a repayment of a portion of the outstanding mortgage balance (principal).

The difference between the monthly mortgage payment and the portion of the payment that represents interest equals the amount that is applied to reduce the outstanding mortgage balance. The portion of the monthly mortgage payment applied to interest declines each month and the portion applied to reducing the mortgage balance increases each month. The reason for this is that as the mortgage balance is reduced with each monthly mortgage payment, the interest on the mortgage balance declines. Since the monthly mortgage payment is fixed, an increasingly larger portion of the monthly payment is applied to reduce the outstanding principal in each subsequent month. The monthly mortgage payment is designed so that after the last scheduled monthly payment of the loan is made, the amount of the outstanding mortgage balance is zero (i.e., the mortgage is fully repaid or amortized).

The cash flow from this mortgage loan, as well as all mortgage designs, is not simply the interest payment and the scheduled principal repayments. There are two additional factors — servicing fees and prepayments.

Servicing Fee and Net Interest Every mortgage loan must be serviced.[1] The servicing fee is a portion of the mortgage rate. If the mortgage rate is 8.125% and the servicing fee is 50 basis points, then the investor receives interest of 7.625%. The interest rate that the investor receives is said to be the *net interest* or *net coupon*. The servicing fee is commonly called the *servicing spread*. The dollar amount of the servicing fee declines over time as the mortgage amortizes. This is true for not only the mortgage design that we have just described, but for all mortgage designs.

Prepayments The second modification to the cash flow is that the borrower typically has that the right to pay off any portion of the mortgage balance prior to the scheduled due date without a penalty.[2] Payments made in excess of the scheduled

---

[1] Servicing of a mortgage loan involves collecting monthly payments and forwarding proceeds to owners of the loan; sending payment notices to mortgagors; reminding mortgagors when payments are overdue; maintaining records of principal balances; administering an escrow balance for real estate taxes and insurance purposes; initiating foreclosure proceedings if necessary; and, furnishing tax information to mortgagors when applicable.

[2] In recent years, prepayment penalty mortgage loans have been originated

principal repayments are called *prepayments*. When less than the entire amount of the outstanding mortgage balance is prepaid in a month, this type of prepayment is called a *curtailment* because it shortens or curtails the life of the loan.

The effect of prepayments is that the amount and timing of the cash flows from a mortgage are not known with certainty. This risk is referred to as *prepayment risk*. For example, assuming that the borrower does not default, all that the investor in a $100,000, 8.125% 30-year mortgage knows is, that as long as the loan is outstanding, interest will be received and the principal will be repaid at the scheduled date each month; then at the end of the 30 years, the investor would have received $100,000 in principal payments. What the investor does not know — the uncertainty — is for how long the loan will be outstanding because of prepayments, and therefore what the timing of the principal payments will be. This is true for all mortgage loans, not just fixed-rate, level-payment, fully amortized mortgages.

Balloon Mortgages

In a *balloon mortgage*, the borrower is given long-term financing by the lender but at specified future dates the contract rate is renegotiated. Thus, the lender is providing long-term funds for what is effectively a short-term borrowing, how short depending on the frequency of the renegotiation period. Effectively it is a short-term balloon loan in which the lender agrees to provide financing for the remainder of the term of the mortgage if certain conditions are met. The balloon payment is the original amount borrowed less the amount amortized. Thus, in a balloon mortgage, the actual maturity is shorter than the stated maturity.

Adjustable-Rate Mortgages

As the name implies, an *adjustable-rate mortgage* (ARM) has an adjustable or floating coupon instead of a fixed one. The coupon adjusts periodically — monthly, semiannually or annually. Some ARMs even have coupons that adjust every three years or five years. The coupon formula for an ARM is specified in terms of an index level plus a margin.

At origination, the mortgage usually has an initial rate for an initial period (*teaser period*) which is slightly below the rate specified by the coupon formula. This is called a *teaser rate* and makes it easier for first time home buyers to qualify for the loan. At the end of the teaser period, the loan rate is reset based on the coupon formula. Once the loan comes out of its teaser period and resets based on the coupon formula, it is said to be fully indexed.

To protect the homeowner from interest rate shock, there are caps imposed on the coupon adjustment level. There are periodic caps and lifetime caps. The *periodic cap* limits the amount of coupon reset upward from one reset date to another. The *lifetime cap* is the maximum absolute level for the coupon rate that the loan can reset to for the life of the mortgage.

Since the borrower prefers to be warned in advance of any interest rate adjustment, the coupon determination actually has to take place prior to the coupon reset. This is called the *lookback period*. A typical lookback period for constant maturity Treasury (CMT) ARMs is 45 days, meaning that the CMT rate 45 days before the anniversary date is being used to reset the coupon for the next period.

There are ARMs that can be converted into fixed-rate mortgages at the option of the borrower. These ARMS, called *convertible ARMs*, reduce the cost of refinancing. When converted, the new loan rate may be either (1) a rate determined by the lender or (2) a market-determined rate.

Due to the caps and conversion feature, the value of an ARM and securities backed by ARMs must be valued using the methodology described in Chapter 10. This is because the methodology described considers the potential path of interest rates over the life of the ARM and how that path affects the coupon rate after adjusting for periodic and lifetime caps and whether the borrower will exercise the conversion option.

Two categories of indices have been used in ARMs: (1) market determined rates and (2) calculated cost of funds for thrifts. The most common market determined rates used are the 1-year, 3-year or 5-year CMT and 3-month or 6-month London interbank offered rate (LIBOR). The most popular cost of funds for thrift index used is the Eleventh Federal Home Loan Bank Board District Cost of Funds Index (COFI). We described these reference rates in Chapter 2.

Describing ARMs The attributes needed to describe an ARM are the teaser rate, teaser period, index, margin, reset frequency, periodic cap, and lifetime cap. Of course, maturity is important too but almost all ARMs are 30-year loans, unlike 5-year, 7-year, 15-year, and 20-year fixed-rate loans.

For example, a "6% 1-year CMT + 3% ARM with 2/12 caps" means the loan has a 6% coupon for the first year. It will reset the second year coupon to the then 1-year CMT index rate plus 3% on the anniversary date subject to the 2% periodic cap and 12% lifetime cap constraints. If the prevailing CMT rate is 4.8%, the coupon will simply reset to 7.8% (4.8% + 3%). If the prevailing CMT rate is 5.5%, the coupon can only reset to 8% (not 5.5% + 3%) because the 2% periodic cap only allows a maximum of 2% movement (plus or minus) in the coupon rate from one period to another. The 12% lifetime cap limits the coupon to 12% during the life of the loan.

MORTGAGE PASSTHROUGH SECURITIES

A mortgage passthrough is an MBS where the cash flows from the underlying pool of mortgage loans is distributed to the security holders on a *pro rata* basis. That is, if there are X certificates issued against a pool of mortgage loans, then a certificate holder is entitled to $1/X$ of the cash flow from the pool of mortgage loans. The cash flow depends on the cash flow of the underlying mortgages: monthly mortgage payments representing interest, the scheduled repayment of principal, and any prepayments.

Payments are made to security holders each month. Neither the amount nor the timing, however, of the cash flows from the pool of mortgages are identical to that of the cash flows passed through to investors. The monthly cash flows for a passthrough are less than the monthly cash flows of the underlying mortgages by an amount equal to servicing fee and other fees. The other fees are those charged by the issuer or guarantor of the passthrough for guaranteeing the issue. The coupon rate on a passthrough, called the *passthrough coupon rate*, is less than the mortgage rate on the underlying pool of mortgage loans by an amount equal to the servicing fee and guarantee fee. The latter is a fee charged by an agency for providing one of the guarantees discussed later.

The timing of the cash flows is also different. The monthly mortgage payment is due from each mortgagor on the first day of each month, but there is a delay in passing through the corresponding monthly cash flow to the security holders. The length of the delay varies by the type of passthrough security.

Not all of the mortgages that are included in a pool of mortgages that are securitized have the same mortgage rate and the same maturity. Consequently, when describing a passthrough security, a *weighted average coupon rate* and a *weighted average maturity* are determined. A weighted average coupon rate, or WAC, is found by weighting the mortgage rate of each mortgage loan in the pool by the amount of the mortgage balance outstanding. A weighted average maturity, or WAM, is found by weighting the remaining number of months to maturity for each mortgage loan in the pool by the amount of the mortgage balance outstanding.

Agency Mortgage Passthrough Securities

There are three government agencies that issue passthrough securities: Government National Mortgage Association, Federal National Mortgage Association, and Federal Home Loan Mortgage Corporation. The first is a federally related government agency. The last two are government sponsored enterprises. There are also MBS issued by nonagencies. We will postpone discussion of nonagency MBS until the next chapter.

The *Government National Mortgage Association* (nicknamed "Ginnie Mae") passthroughs are guaranteed by the full faith and credit of the U.S. government. For this reason, Ginnie Mae passthroughs are viewed as risk-free in terms of default risk, just like Treasury securities. The security guaranteed by Ginnie Mae is called a *mortgage-backed security* (MBS). All Ginnie Mae MBS are guaranteed with respect to the timely payment of interest and principal, meaning the interest and principal will be paid when due, even if any of the mortgagors fail to make their monthly mortgage payments.

Only mortgage loans insured or guaranteed by either the Federal Housing Administration, the Veterans Administration, or the Rural Housing Service can be included in a mortgage pool guaranteed by Ginnie Mae. The maximum loan size is set by Congress, based on the maximum amount that the FHA, VA, or RHS may guarantee. The maximum for a given loan varies with the region of the country and type of residential property.

Exhibit 1: Agency ARM Programs

	Ginnie ARM	CMT ARM	COFI ARM	LIBOR ARM
Agency	GNMA	FNMA FHLMC	FNMA FHLMC	FNMA FHLMC
Teaser Period	1 year	1 year	6 months	6 months
Reset Frequency	annually	annually	monthly	semi-annually
Index	1-year CMT	1-year CMT	11th COFI	6-month LIBOR
Margin	2%	2% to 4%	2% to 4%	2% to 4%
Periodic Cap	1%	2%	none	1%
Lifetime Cap	teaser rate +5%	teaser rate +6%	teaser rate +6%	teaser rate +6%
Lookback	45 days	45 days	3 months	45 days
Convertability	No	Yes/No	No	Yes/No

The passthroughs issued by the *Federal National Mortgage Association* (nicknamed "Fannie Mae") are called mortgage-backed securities (MBSs). Although a guarantee of Fannie Mae is not a guarantee by the U.S. government, most market participants view Fannie Mae MBSs as similar, although not identical, in credit worthiness to Ginnie Mae passthroughs. All Fannie Mae MBSs carry its guarantee of timely payment of both interest and principal.

The *Federal Home Loan Mortgage Corporation* (nicknamed "Freddie Mac") is a government sponsored enterprise that issues a passthrough security that is called a *participation certificate* (PC). As with Fannie Mae MBS, a guarantee of Freddie Mac is not a guarantee by the U.S. government, but most market participants view Freddie Mac PCs as similar, although not identical, in credit worthiness to Ginnie Mae passthroughs. Freddie Mac has issued PCs with different types of guarantee. The old PCs issued by Freddie Mac guarantee the timely payment of interest; the scheduled principal is passed through as it is collected, with Freddie Mac only guaranteeing that the scheduled payment will be made no later than one year after it is due. Today, Freddie Mac issues PCs under its "Gold Program" in which both the timely payment of interest and principal are guaranteed.

Agency ARM Programs

Ginnie Mae, Fannie Mae, and Freddie Mac, have several standardized ARM programs to promote uniformity and liquidity in the trading of passthrough securities backed by a pool of ARMs. The most common programs are summarized in Exhibit 1.

While the programs in Exhibit 1 are the most common standardized ARM programs sponsored by the agencies, there are many variations. For instance, there are 3-year CMT ARMs that reset every three years off the 3-year CMT index and 5-year CMT ARMs that reset every five years off the 5-year CMT index. There are also 6-month Treasury bill ARMs that reset off the 6-month Treasury bill rate semiannually with a 1% periodic cap. There are semiannual and annual COFI ARMs that work exactly like CMT ARMs. There are also quarterly reset LIBOR ARMs that reset off the 3-month moving average LIBOR.

There exists another group of hybrid fixed/ARM loans that look like both fixed- and adjustable-rate mortgages. For instance, a "10/1 loan" has a fixed coupon for 10 years, then it will convert to a 1-year CMT ARM starting the 11th year. A "7/23 loan" is a fixed-rate loan that will reset only once for the life of the loan at the end of the 7th year to the prevailing market rate which will then be fixed for the remaining 23 years.

Price Quotes and Trading Procedures

Passthroughs are quoted in the same manner as U.S. Treasury coupon securities. A quote of 94-05 means 94 and 5/32nds of par value, or 94.15625% of par value. The price that the buyer pays the seller is the agreed upon sale price plus accrued interest. Given the par value, the dollar price (excluding accrued interest) is affected by the amount of the mortgage pool balance outstanding. The *pool factor* indicates the percentage of the initial mortgage balance still outstanding. So, a pool factor of 90 means that 90% of the original mortgage pool balance is outstanding. The pool factor is reported by the agency each month.

The dollar price paid for just the principal is found as follows given the agreed upon price, par value, and the month's pool factor provided by the agency:

Price × Par value × Pool factor

For example, if the parties agree to a price of 92 for $1 million par value for an ARM passthrough with a pool factor of 85, then the dollar price paid by the buyer in addition to accrued interest is:

0.92 × $1,000,000 × 0.85 = $782,000

Agency passthroughs are identified by a pool prefix and pool number provided by the agency. The prefix indicates the type of passthrough. For example, a pool prefix of "AR" for a Ginnie Mae MBS means that the underlying pool consists of adjustable-rate mortgages. The pool number indicates the specific mortgages underlying the passthrough.

Many trades occur while a pool is still unspecified, and therefore no pool information is known at the time of the trade. This kind of trade is known as a "*TBA*" (*to be announced*) *trade*. In a TBA trade for a fixed-rate passthrough, the two parties agree on the agency type, the agency program, the coupon rate, the face value, the price, and the settlement date. The actual pools underlying the agency passthrough are not specified in a TBA trade. However, this information is provided by the seller to the buyer before delivery. In contrast to a TBA trade, there are *specified pool trades* wherein the actual pool numbers to be delivered are specified.

For Ginnie Mae ARMs, new production ARMs are traded on a TBA basis while seasoned issues are traded on a specified pool basis. With one exception, the ARMs issued by Freddie Mac and Fannie Mae trade on a specified pool basis. The exception is an ARM by these two government sponsored enterprises that are indexed to COFI. These ARMs trade on a TBA basis.[3]

Prepayment Conventions and Cash Flows

As explained in Chapter 3, to value a security it is necessary to project its cash flows. The difficulty for an MBS is that the cash flows are unknown because of prepayments. The only way to project cash flows is to make some assumption about the prepayment rate over the life of the underlying mortgage pool. The prepayment rate is sometimes referred to as the *prepayment speed*, or simply *speed*. Two conventions have been used as a benchmark for prepayment rates — conditional prepayment rate and Public Securities Association prepayment benchmark.

Conditional Prepayment Rate

One convention for projecting prepayments and the cash flows of a passthrough assumes that some fraction of the remaining principal in the pool is prepaid each month for the remaining term of the mortgage. The prepayment rate assumed for a pool, called the *conditional prepayment rate* (CPR), is based on the characteristics of the pool (including its historical prepayment experience) and the current and expected future economic environment.

The CPR is an annual prepayment rate. To estimate monthly prepayments, the CPR must be converted into a monthly prepayment rate, commonly referred to as the *single-monthly mortality rate* (SMM). The formula can be used to determine the SMM for a given CPR:

$$SMM = 1 - (1 - CPR)^{1/12}$$

Suppose that the CPR used to estimate prepayments is 6%. The corresponding SMM is:

$$SMM = 1 - (1 - 0.06)^{1/12}$$
$$= 1 - (0.94)^{0.08333} = 0.005143$$

An SMM of $w\%$ means that approximately $w\%$ of the remaining mortgage balance at the beginning of the month, less the scheduled principal payment, will prepay that month. That is,

Prepayment for month t = SMM
    × (Beginning mortgage balance for month t
    − Scheduled principal payment for month t)

---

[3] Satish M. Mansukhani, "Valuation and Analysis of ARMS," Chapter 10 in Frank J. Fabozzi (ed.), *Advances in Fixed Income Valuation Modeling and Risk Management* (New Hope, PA: Frank J. Fabozzi Associates, 1997), pp. 172-173.

Exhibit 2: Graphical Depiction of 100 PSA

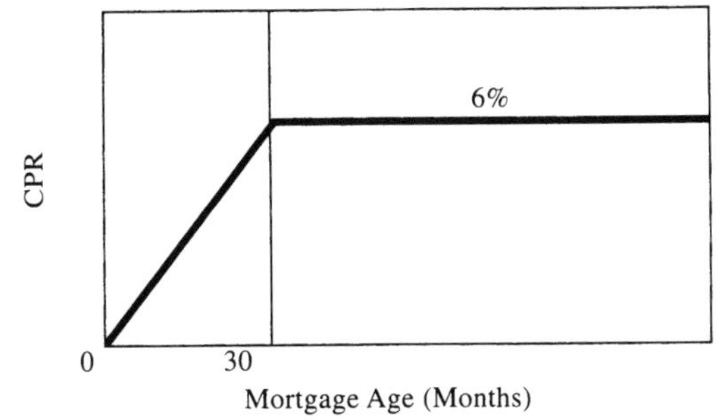

For example, suppose that an investor owns a passthrough in which the remaining mortgage balance at the beginning of some month is $290 million. Assuming that the SMM is 0.5143% and the scheduled principal payment is $3 million, the estimated prepayment for the month is:

$$0.005143 \times (\$290,000,000 - \$3,000,000) = \$1,476,041$$

PSA Prepayment Benchmark

The Public Securities Association (PSA) prepayment benchmark is expressed as a monthly series of CPRs. The PSA benchmark assumes that prepayment rates are low for newly originated mortgages and then will speed up as the mortgages become seasoned.

The PSA prepayment benchmark assumes the following prepayment rates for 30-year mortgages:

(1) a CPR of 0.2% for the first month, increased by 0.2% per year per month for the next 30 months when it reaches 6% per year, and
(2) a 6% CPR for the remaining years.

This benchmark, referred to as "100% PSA" or simply "100 PSA," is graphically depicted in Exhibit 2. Mathematically, 100 PSA can be expressed as follows:

if $t \le 30$ then CPR $= \dfrac{6\% \, t}{30}$

if $t > 30$ then CPR = 6%

where t is the number of months since the mortgage originated.

Slower or faster speeds are then referred to as some percentage of PSA. For example, 50 PSA means one-half the CPR of the PSA benchmark prepayment rate; 150 PSA means 1.5 times the CPR of the PSA benchmark prepayment rate; 300 PSA means three times the CPR of the benchmark prepayment rate. A prepayment rate of 0 PSA means that no prepayments are assumed.

The CPR is converted to an SMM using the formula given above. For example, the SMMs for month 5 and month 20 assuming 100 PSA are calculated as follows:

for month 5:

$$CPR = 6\% \ (5/30) = 1\% = 0.01$$
$$SMM = 1 - (1 - 0.01)^{1/12} = 0.000837$$

for month 20:

$$CPR = 6\% \ (20/30) = 4\% = 0.04$$
$$SMM = 1 - (1 - 0.04)^{1/12} = 0.003396$$

The SMMs for month 5, month 20, and months 31 through 360 assuming 165 PSA are computed as follows:

for month 5:

$$CPR = 6\% \ (5/30) = 1\% = 0.01$$
$$165 \ PSA = 1.65 \ (0.01) = 0.0165$$
$$SMM = 1 - (1 - 0.0165)^{1/12} = 0.001386$$

for month 20:

$$CPR = 6\% \ (20/30) = 4\% = 0.04$$
$$165 \ PSA = 1.65 \ (.04) = 0.066$$
$$SMM = 1 - (1 - 0.066)^{1/12} = 0.005674$$

for months 31-360:

$$CPR = 6\%$$
$$165 \ PSA = 1.65 \ (0.06) = 0.099$$
$$SMM = 1 - (1 - 0.099)^{1/12} = 0.007828$$

Notice that the SMM assuming 165 PSA is not just 1.65 times the SMM assuming 100 PSA. It is the CPR that is a multiple of the CPR assuming 100 PSA.

It is important to understand the PSA benchmark is commonly referred to as a prepayment model, suggesting that it can be used to estimate prepayments. Characterization of this benchmark as a prepayment model is incorrect. It is simply a market convention describing what the PSA believes the pattern will be for prepayments.

It is worthwhile to see a monthly cash flow for a hypothetical passthrough given a PSA assumption since we can use the information later in our discussion of CMOs in the next chapter. Exhibit 3 shows the cash flow for selected months assuming 165 PSA for a passthrough security in which the underlying loans are assumed to be fixed-rate, level-payment, fully amortized mortgages with a WAC of 8.125%. It is assumed that the passthrough rate is 7.5% with a WAM of 357 months. The cash flow in Exhibit 3 is broken down into three components: (1) interest (based on the passthrough rate), (2) the regularly scheduled principal repayment, and (3) prepayments based on 165 PSA.

Since the WAM is 357 months, the underlying mortgage pool is seasoned an average of three months. Therefore, the CPR for month 27 is 1.65 times 6%.[4]

Average Life Measure

Because an MBS is an amortizing security, market participants do not talk in terms of an issues maturity. Instead, the *average life* of an MBS. The average life is the average time to receipt of principal payments (scheduled principal payments and projected prepayments), weighted by the amount of principal expected. Specifically, the average life is found by first calculating:

$1 \times$ (Projected principal received in month 1)
$2 \times$ (Projected principal received in month 2)
$3 \times$ (Projected principal received in month 3)

...

$+ \; T \times$ (Projected principal received in month T)

Weighted monthly average of principal received

where T is the last month that principal is expected to be received. Then the average life is found as follows:

$$\text{Average life} = \frac{\text{Weighted monthly average of principal received}}{12(\text{Total principal to be received})}$$

The average life of a passthrough depends on the PSA prepayment assumption. To see this, the average life is shown below for different prepayment speeds for the passthrough we used to illustrate the cash flows for 165 PSA in Exhibits 3:

PSA speed	50	100	165	200	300	400	500	600	700
Average life	15.11	11.66	8.76	7.68	5.63	4.44	3.68	3.16	2.78

A CLOSER LOOK AT PREPAYMENT RISK: CONTRACTION RISK AND EXTENSION RISK

Just like the owner of any security that contains an embedded option, investors in passthrough securities do not know what their cash flows will be because of pre-payments — the borrower's option to alter the mortgage's cash flows. As we noted earlier, this risk is called prepayment risk. To understand the significance of prepayment risk, suppose an investor buys a 8.5% coupon Ginnie Mae at a time when mortgage rates are 8.5%. Let's consider what will happen to prepayments if

---

[4] The details for the construction of the exhibit are provided in Chapter 3 in Frank J. Fabozzi and Chuck Ramsey, *Collateralized Mortgage Obligations: Structures and Analysis Third Edition* (New Hope, PA: Frank J. Fabozzi Association, 1999).

mortgage rates decline to, say, 6.5%. There will be two adverse consequences. First, a basic property of fixed-income securities is that the price of an option-free bond increases at an increasing rate as interest rates decline. However, for a passthrough security with an embedded prepayment option, the rise in price will not be as large as that of an option-free bond because a drop in interest rates will give the borrower an incentive to prepay the loan and refinance the debt at a lower rate. In other words, the borrower is altering the mortgage's flows (i.e., exercising the prepayment option) when this action enhances his/her economic value. Thus, the upside price potential of a passthrough security is truncated because of prepayments in a manner similar to that of a callable bond. The second adverse consequence is that the cash flows must be reinvested at a lower rate. These two adverse consequences when mortgage rates decline are referred to as *contraction risk*. In essence, contraction risk is all the consequences resulting from borrowers prepaying at a faster rate than anticipated.

Exhibit 3: Monthly Cash Flow for a $400 Million Passthrough with a 7.5% Passthrough Rate, a WAC of 8.125%, and a WAM of 357 Months Assuming 165 PSA

(1)	(2)	(3)	(4)	(5)	(6)	(7)	(8)	(9)
Month	Outstanding Balance	SMM	Mortgage Payment	Net Interest	Scheduled Principal	Prepayment	Total Principal	Cash Flow
1	$400,000,000	0.00111	$2,975,868	$2,500,000	$267,535	$442,389	$709,923	$3,209,923
2	399,290,077	0.00139	2,972,575	2,495,563	269,048	552,847	821,896	3,317,459
3	398,468,181	0.00167	2,968,456	2,490,426	270,495	663,065	933,560	3,423,986
4	397,534,621	0.00195	2,963,513	2,484,591	271,873	772,949	1,044,822	3,529,413
5	396,489,799	0.00223	2,957,747	2,478,061	273,181	882,405	1,155,586	3,633,647
6	395,334,213	0.00251	2,951,160	2,470,839	274,418	991,341	1,265,759	3,736,598
7	394,068,454	0.00279	2,943,755	2,462,928	275,583	1,099,664	1,375,246	3,838,174
8	392,693,208	0.00308	2,935,534	2,454,333	276,674	1,207,280	1,483,954	3,938,287
9	391,209,254	0.00336	2,926,503	2,445,058	277,690	1,314,099	1,591,789	4,036,847
10	389,617,464	0.00365	2,916,666	2,435,109	278,631	1,420,029	1,698,659	4,133,769
11	387,918,805	0.00393	2,906,028	2,424,493	279,494	1,524,979	1,804,473	4,228,965
24	356,711,789	0.00775	2,698,575	2,229,449	283,338	2,761,139	3,044,477	5,273,926
25	353,667,312	0.00805	2,677,670	2,210,421	283,047	2,843,593	3,126,640	5,337,061
26	350,540,672	0.00835	2,656,123	2,190,879	282,671	2,923,885	3,206,556	5,397,435
27	347,334,116	0.00865	2,633,950	2,170,838	282,209	3,001,955	3,284,164	5,455,002
28	344,049,952	0.00865	2,611,167	2,150,312	281,662	2,973,553	3,255,215	5,405,527
29	340,794,737	0.00865	2,588,581	2,129,967	281,116	2,945,400	3,226,516	5,356,483
30	337,568,221	0.00865	2,566,190	2,109,801	280,572	2,917,496	3,198,067	5,307,869
100	170,142,350	0.00865	1,396,958	1,063,390	244,953	1,469,591	1,714,544	2,777,933
101	168,427,806	0.00865	1,384,875	1,052,674	244,478	1,454,765	1,699,243	2,751,916
102	166,728,563	0.00865	1,372,896	1,042,054	244,004	1,440,071	1,684,075	2,726,128
103	165,044,489	0.00865	1,361,020	1,031,528	243,531	1,425,508	1,669,039	2,700,567

Exhibit 3 *(Continued)*

(1)	(2)	(3)	(4)	(5)	(6)	(7)	(8)	(9)
Month	Outstanding Balance	SMM	Mortgage Payment	Net Interest	Scheduled Principal	Prepayment	Total Principal	Cash Flow
200	56,746,664	0.00865	585,990	354,667	201,767	489,106	690,874	1,045,540
201	56,055,790	0.00865	580,921	350,349	201,377	483,134	684,510	1,034,859
202	55,371,280	0.00865	575,896	346,070	200,986	477,216	678,202	1,024,273
203	54,693,077	0.00865	570,915	341,832	200,597	471,353	671,950	1,013,782
300	11,758,141	0.00865	245,808	73,488	166,196	100,269	266,465	339,953
301	11,491,677	0.00865	243,682	71,823	165,874	97,967	263,841	335,664
302	11,227,836	0.00865	241,574	70,174	165,552	95,687	261,240	331,414
303	10,966,596	0.00865	239,485	68,541	165,232	93,430	258,662	327,203
353	760,027	0.00865	155,107	4,750	149,961	5,277	155,238	159,988
354	604,789	0.00865	153,765	3,780	149,670	3,937	153,607	157,387
355	451,182	0.00865	152,435	2,820	149,380	2,611	151,991	154,811
356	299,191	0.00865	151,117	1,870	149,091	1,298	150,389	152,259
357	148,802	0.00865	149,809	930	148,802	0	148,802	149,732

Note: Since the WAM is 357 months, the underlying mortgage pool is seasoned an average of three months. Therefore, the CPR for month 27 is $1.65 \times 6\%$.

Now let's look at what happens if mortgage rates rise to 10.5%. The price of the passthrough, like the price of any bond, will decline. But again it will decline more because the higher rates will tend to slow down the rate of prepayment, in effect increasing the amount invested at the coupon rate, which is lower than the market rate. Prepayments will slow down because homeowners will not refinance or partially prepay their mortgages when mortgage rates are higher than the contract rate of 8.5%. Of course, this is just the time when investors want prepayments to speed up so that they can reinvest the prepayments at the higher market interest rate. This adverse consequence of rising mortgage rates is called *extension risk* and results from borrowers prepaying at a slower rate than anticipated.

Therefore, prepayment risk encompasses contraction risk and extension risk. Prepayment risk makes passthrough securities unattractive for certain individuals and financial institutions to hold for purposes of accomplishing their investment objectives. Some individuals and institutional investors are concerned with extension risk and others with contraction risk when they purchase a passthrough security. Is it possible to alter the cash flows of a mortgage passthrough security so as to reduce the contraction risk and extension risk for institutional investors? This can be done as we will see in the next chapter where we cover CMOs.

Chapter 8
CMO Floaters

In the previous chapter, we discussed one type of mortgage-backed securities, a mortgage passthrough security. Investors in floaters who are interested in passthrough securities purchase those backed by adjustable-rate mortgages. In this chapter, we will see how mortgage passthroughs securities backed by fixed-rate mortgage loans can be used to create a structure called a *collateralized mortgage obligation* (CMO). One type of bond class that can be created within the structure is a floating-rate bond class. We will refer to this type of CMO bond class as a CMO floater and it will be the main focus of attention.

We will discuss CMOs issued by the three agencies that issue mortgage passthrough securities and CMOs issued by private entities. CMOs are also referred to as paythroughs or multi-class passthroughs. Because they are created so as to comply with a provision in the tax law called the Real Estate Mortgage Investment Conduit, or REMIC, they are also referred to as "REMICs." Throughout this chapter we refer to these structures as simply CMOs. A security structure in which collateral is carved into different bond classes is not uncommon. We will see similar paythrough or multi-class passthrough structures when we cover other asset-backed security structures in the next chapter.

BASIC PRINCIPLES

By investing in a mortgage passthrough security an investor is exposed to prepayment risk. Furthermore, as explained at the end of the previous chapter, prepayment risk can be divided into extension risk and contraction risk. Some investors are concerned with extension risk and others with contraction risk when they invest in a passthrough. An investor may be willing to accept one form of prepayment risk but seek to avoid the other. For example, a portfolio manager who seeks a short-term security is concerned with extension risk. A portfolio manager who seeks a long-term security, and wants to avoid reinvesting unexpected principal prepayments due to refinancing of mortgages should interest rates drop, is concerned with contraction risk.

By redirecting how the cash flows of passthrough securities are paid to different bond classes that are created, securities can be created that have different exposure to prepayment risk. When the cash flows of mortgage-related products are redistributed to different bond classes, the resulting securities are called CMOs. Simply put, CMOs are rules for dividing up cash flows among bond classes.

The basic principle is that redirecting cash flows (interest and principal) to different bond classes, called tranches, mitigates different forms of prepayment risk. It is never possible to eliminate prepayment risk. If one tranche in a CMO structure has less prepayment risk than the mortgage passthrough securities that are collateral for the structure, then another tranche in the same structure has greater prepayment risk than the collateral.

AGENCY COLLATERALIZED MORTGAGE OBLIGATIONS

Issuers of CMOs are the same three entities that issue agency passthrough securities: Freddie Mac, Fannie Mae, and Ginnie Mae. There has been little issuance of Ginnie Mae CMOs. However, Freddie Mac and Fannie Mae have used Ginnie Mae passthroughs as collateral for their own CMOs. CMOs issued by any of these entities are referred to as *agency CMOs*.

When an agency CMO is created it is structured so that even under the worst circumstances regarding prepayments, the interest and principal payments from the collateral will be sufficient to meet the interest obligation of each tranche and pay off the par value of each tranche. Defaults are ignored because the agency that has issued the passthroughs used as collateral is expected to make up any deficiency. Thus, the credit risk of agency CMOs is minimal. However, as we noted previously in this chapter, the guarantee of a government sponsored enterprise does not carry the full faith and credit of the U.S. government. Fannie Mae and Freddie Mac CMOs created from Ginnie Mae passthroughs effectively carry the full faith and credit of the U.S. government.

Sequential-Pay Tranches

The first CMO was structured so that each tranche would be retired sequentially. Such structures are referred to as *sequential-pay CMOs*. To illustrate a sequential-pay CMO, we will use a hypothetical deal that we will refer to as Deal 1. The collateral for Deal 1 is a hypothetical passthrough with a total par value of $400 million and the following characteristics: (1) the passthrough coupon rate is 7.5%, (2) the weighted average coupon (WAC) is 8.125%, and (3) the weighted average maturity (WAM) is 357 months. This is the same passthrough that we used in the previous chapter to describe the cash flows of a passthrough based on an assumed 165 PSA prepayment speed.

From this $400 million of collateral, four tranches are created. Their characteristics are summarized in Exhibit 1. The total par value of the four tranches is equal to the par value of the collateral (i.e., the passthrough security). In this simple structure, the coupon rate is the same for each tranche and also the same as the collateral's coupon rate. There is no reason why this must be so, and, in fact, typically the coupon rate varies by tranche. For example, if the yield curve is upward-sloping, the coupon rates of the tranches will usually increase with average life.

Exhibit 1: Deal 1: A Hypothetical Four-Tranche Sequential-Pay Structure

Tranche	Par Amount	Coupon Rate (%)
A	$194,500,000	7.5
B	36,000,000	7.5
C	96,500,000	7.5
D	73,000,000	7.5
Total	$400,000,000	

Payment rules:
1. *For payment of periodic coupon interest:* Disburse periodic coupon interest to each tranche on the basis of the amount of principal outstanding at the beginning of the period.
2. *For disbursement of principal payments:* Disburse principal payments to tranche A until it is completely paid off. After tranche A is completely paid off, disburse principal payments to tranche B until it is completely paid off. After tranche B is completely paid off, disburse principal payments to tranche C until it is completely paid off. After tranche C is completely paid off, disburse principal payments to tranche D until it is completely paid off.

Now remember that a CMO is created by redistributing the cash flow — interest and principal — to the different tranches based on a set of payment rules. The payment rules at the bottom of Exhibit 1 set forth how the monthly cash flow from the passthrough (i.e., collateral) is to be distributed among the four tranches. There are separate rules for the payment of the coupon interest and the payment of principal, the principal being the total of the regularly scheduled principal payment and any prepayments.

In Deal 1, each tranche receives periodic coupon interest payments based on the amount of the outstanding balance. The disbursement of the principal, however, is made in a special way. A tranche is not entitled to receive principal until the entire principal of the tranche before it has been paid off. More specifically, tranche A receives all the principal payments until the entire principal amount owed to that tranche, $194,500,000, is paid off; then tranche B begins to receive principal and continues to do so until it is paid the entire $36,000,000. Tranche C then receives principal, and when it is paid off, tranche D starts receiving principal payments.

While the payment rules for the disbursement of the principal payments are known, the precise amount of the principal in each period is not. This will depend on the cash flow, and therefore principal payments, of the collateral, which depends on the actual prepayment rate of the collateral. An assumed PSA speed allows the monthly cash flow to be projected. Exhibit 3 of the previous chapter shows the monthly cash flow (interest, regularly scheduled principal repayment, and prepayments) assuming 165 PSA. Assuming that the collateral does prepay at 165 PSA, the cash flows available to all four tranches of Deal 1 will be precisely the cash flows shown in Exhibit 3 of the previous chapter.

Exhibit 2: Monthly Cash Flow for Selected Months for Deal 1 Assuming 165 PSA

Month	Tranche A Balance	Principal	Interest	Tranche B Balance	Principal	Interest
1	194,500,000	709,923	1,215,625	36,000,000	0	225,000
2	193,790,077	821,896	1,211,188	36,000,000	0	225,000
3	192,968,181	933,560	1,206,051	36,000,000	0	225,000
4	192,034,621	1,044,822	1,200,216	36,000,000	0	225,000
5	190,989,799	1,155,586	1,193,686	36,000,000	0	225,000
6	189,834,213	1,265,759	1,186,464	36,000,000	0	225,000
7	188,568,454	1,375,246	1,178,553	36,000,000	0	225,000
8	187,193,208	1,483,954	1,169,958	36,000,000	0	225,000
9	185,709,254	1,591,789	1,160,683	36,000,000	0	225,000
10	184,117,464	1,698,659	1,150,734	36,000,000	0	225,000
11	182,418,805	1,804,473	1,140,118	36,000,000	0	225,000
12	180,614,332	1,909,139	1,128,840	36,000,000	0	225,000
75	12,893,479	2,143,974	80,584	36,000,000	0	225,000
76	10,749,504	2,124,935	67,184	36,000,000	0	225,000
77	8,624,569	2,106,062	53,904	36,000,000	0	225,000
78	6,518,507	2,087,353	40,741	36,000,000	0	225,000
79	4,431,154	2,068,807	27,695	36,000,000	0	225,000
80	2,362,347	2,050,422	14,765	36,000,000	0	225,000
81	311,926	311,926	1,950	36,000,000	1,720,271	225,000
82	0	0	0	34,279,729	2,014,130	214,248
83	0	0	0	32,265,599	1,996,221	201,660
84	0	0	0	30,269,378	1,978,468	189,184
85	0	0	0	28,290,911	1,960,869	176,818
95	0	0	0	9,449,331	1,793,089	59,058
96	0	0	0	7,656,242	1,777,104	47,852
97	0	0	0	5,879,138	1,761,258	36,745
98	0	0	0	4,117,880	1,745,550	25,737
99	0	0	0	2,372,329	1,729,979	14,827
100	0	0	0	642,350	642,350	4,015
101	0	0	0	0	0	0
102	0	0	0	0	0	0
103	0	0	0	0	0	0
104	0	0	0	0	0	0
105	0	0	0	0	0	0

To demonstrate how the payment rules for Deal 1 work, Exhibit 2 shows the cash flow for selected months assuming the collateral prepays at 165 PSA. For each tranche, the exhibit shows: (1) the balance at the end of the month, (2) the principal paid down (regularly scheduled principal repayment plus prepayments), and (3) interest. In month 1, the cash flow for the collateral consists of a principal payment of $709,923 and interest of $2.5 million (0.075 times $400 million divided by 12). The interest payment is distributed to the four tranches based on the amount of the par value outstanding. So, for example, tranche A receives $1,215,625 (0.075 times $194,500,000 divided by 12) of the $2.5 million. The principal, however, is all distributed to tranche A. Therefore, the cash flow for tranche A in month 1 is $1,925,548.

The principal balance at the end of month 1 for tranche A is $193,790,076 (the original principal balance of $194,500,000 less the principal payment of $709,923). No principal payment is distributed to the three other tranches because there is still a principal balance outstanding for tranche A. This will be true for months 2 through 80.

Exhibit 2 (Concluded)

Month	Tranche C Balance	Principal	Interest	Tranche D Balance	Principal	Interest
1	96,500,000	0	603,125	73,000,000	0	456,250
2	96,500,000	0	603,125	73,000,000	0	456,250
3	96,500,000	0	603,125	73,000,000	0	456,250
4	96,500,000	0	603,125	73,000,000	0	456,250
5	96,500,000	0	603,125	73,000,000	0	456,250
6	96,500,000	0	603,125	73,000,000	0	456,250
7	96,500,000	0	603,125	73,000,000	0	456,250
8	96,500,000	0	603,125	73,000,000	0	456,250
9	96,500,000	0	603,125	73,000,000	0	456,250
10	96,500,000	0	603,125	73,000,000	0	456,250
11	96,500,000	0	603,125	73,000,000	0	456,250
12	96,500,000	0	603,125	73,000,000	0	456,250
95	96,500,000	0	603,125	73,000,000	0	456,250
96	96,500,000	0	603,125	73,000,000	0	456,250
97	96,500,000	0	603,125	73,000,000	0	456,250
98	96,500,000	0	603,125	73,000,000	0	456,250
99	96,500,000	0	603,125	73,000,000	0	456,250
100	96,500,000	1,072,194	603,125	73,000,000	0	456,250
101	95,427,806	1,699,243	596,424	73,000,000	0	456,250
102	93,728,563	1,684,075	585,804	73,000,000	0	456,250
103	92,044,489	1,669,039	575,278	73,000,000	0	456,250
104	90,375,450	1,654,134	564,847	73,000,000	0	456,250
105	88,721,315	1,639,359	554,508	73,000,000	0	456,250
175	3,260,287	869,602	20,377	73,000,000	0	456,250
176	2,390,685	861,673	14,942	73,000,000	0	456,250
177	1,529,013	853,813	9,556	73,000,000	0	456,250
178	675,199	675,199	4,220	73,000,000	170,824	456,250
179	0	0	0	72,829,176	838,300	455,182
180	0	0	0	71,990,876	830,646	449,943
181	0	0	0	71,160,230	823,058	444,751
182	0	0	0	70,337,173	815,536	439,607
183	0	0	0	69,521,637	808,081	434,510
184	0	0	0	68,713,556	800,690	429,460
185	0	0	0	67,912,866	793,365	424,455
350	0	0	0	1,235,674	160,220	7,723
351	0	0	0	1,075,454	158,544	6,722
352	0	0	0	916,910	156,883	5,731
353	0	0	0	760,027	155,238	4,750
354	0	0	0	604,789	153,607	3,780
355	0	0	0	451,182	151,991	2,820
356	0	0	0	299,191	150,389	1,870
357	0	0	0	148,802	148,802	930

Exhibit 3: Average Life for the Collateral and the Four Tranches of Deal 1

Prepayment speed (PSA)	Average life for				
	Collateral	Tranche A	Tranche B	Tranche C	Tranche D
50	15.11	7.48	15.98	21.02	27.24
100	11.66	4.90	10.86	15.78	24.58
165	8.76	3.48	7.49	11.19	20.27
200	7.68	3.05	6.42	9.60	18.11
300	5.63	2.32	4.64	6.81	13.36
400	4.44	1.94	3.70	5.31	10.34
500	3.68	1.69	3.12	4.38	8.35
600	3.16	1.51	2.74	3.75	6.96
700	2.78	1.38	2.47	3.30	5.95

After month 81, the principal balance will be zero for tranche A. For the collateral the cash flow in month 81 is $3,318,521, consisting of a principal payment of $2,032,196 and interest of $1,286,325. At the beginning of month 81 (end of month 80), the principal balance for tranche A is $311,926. Therefore, $311,926 of the $2,032,196 of the principal payment from the collateral will be disbursed to tranche A. After this payment is made, no additional principal payments are made to this tranche as the principal balance is zero. The remaining principal payment from the collateral, $1,720,271, is disbursed to tranche B. According to the assumed prepayment speed of 165 PSA, tranche B then begins receiving principal payments in month 81.

Exhibit 2 shows that tranche B is fully paid off by month 100, when tranche C begins to receive principal payments. Tranche C is not fully paid off until month 178, at which time tranche D begins receiving the remaining principal payments. The maturity (i.e., the time until the principal is fully paid off) for these four tranches assuming 165 PSA is 81 months for tranche A, 100 months for tranche B, 178 months for tranche C, and 357 months for tranche D.

The *principal pay down window* for a tranche is the time period between the beginning and the ending of the principal payments to that tranche. So, for example, for tranche A, the principal pay down window would be month 1 to month 81 assuming 165 PSA. For tranche B it is from month 81 to month 100. In confirmation of trades involving CMOs, the principal pay down window is specified in terms of the initial month that principal is expected to be received based on an assumed PSA speed to the final month that principal is expected to be received.

Let's look at what has been accomplished by creating the CMO. First, in the previous chapter we saw that the average life of the passthrough is 8.76 years, assuming a prepayment speed of 165 PSA. Exhibit 3 reports the average life of the collateral and the four tranches assuming different prepayment speeds. Notice that the four tranches have average lives that are both shorter and longer than the collateral thereby attracting investors who have a preference for an average life different from that of the collateral.

Exhibit 4: Deal 2: A Hypothetical Four-Tranche Sequential-Pay Structure with an Accrual Bond Class

Tranche	Par Amount	Coupon rate (%)
A	$194,500,000	7.5
B	36,000,000	7.5
C	96,500,000	7.5
Z (Accrual)	73,000,000	7.5
Total	$400,000,000	

Payment rules:
1. *For payment of periodic coupon interest:* Disburse periodic coupon interest to tranches A, B, and C on the basis of the amount of principal outstanding at the beginning of the period. For tranche Z, accrue the interest based on the principal plus accrued interest in the previous period. The interest for tranche Z is to be paid to the earlier tranches as a principal paydown.
2. *For disbursement of principal payments:* Disburse principal payments to tranche A until it is completely paid off. After tranche A is completely paid off, disburse principal payments to tranche B until it is completely paid off. After tranche B is completely paid off, disburse principal payments to tranche C until it is completely paid off. After tranche C is completely paid off, disburse principal payments to tranche Z until the original principal balance plus accrued interest is completely paid off.

There is still a major problem: there is considerable variability of the average life for the tranches. We'll see how this can be tackled later on. However, there is some protection provided for each tranche against prepayment risk. This is because prioritizing the distribution of principal (i.e., establishing the payment rules for principal) effectively protects the shorter-term tranche A in this structure against extension risk. This protection must come from somewhere — it comes from the three other tranches. Similarly, tranches C and D provide protection against extension risk for tranche B. At the same time, tranches C and D benefit because they are provided protection against contraction risk, the protection coming from tranches A and B.

Accrual Tranches

In Deal 1, the payment rules for interest provide for all tranches to be paid interest each month. In many sequential-pay CMO structures, at least one tranche does not receive current interest. Instead, the interest for that tranche would accrue and be added to the principal balance. Such a bond class is commonly referred to as an *accrual tranche* or a *Z bond* (because the bond is similar to a zero-coupon bond). The interest that would have been paid to the accrual tranche is then used to speed up pay down of the principal balance of earlier tranches.

To see this, consider Deal 2, a hypothetical CMO structure with the same collateral as Deal 1 and with four tranches, each with a coupon rate of 7.5%. The difference is in the last tranche, Z, which is an accrual tranche. The structure for Deal 2 is shown in Exhibit 4.

It can be shown that the expected final maturity for tranches A, B, and C will shorten as a result of the inclusion of tranche Z. The final payout for tranche A is 64 months rather than 81 months; for tranche B it is 77 months rather than 100 months;

and for tranche C it is 112 months rather than 178 months. The average lives for tranches A, B, and C are shorter in Deal 2 compared to Deal 1 because of the inclusion of the accrual tranche. For example, at 165 PSA, the average lives are as follows:

Structure	Tranche A	Tranche B	Tranche C
Deal 1	3.48	7.49	11.19
Deal 2	2.90	5.86	7.87

The reason for the shortening of the non-accrual tranches is that the interest that would be paid to the accrual tranche is being allocated to the other tranches. Tranche Z in Deal 2 will have a longer average life than tranche D in Deal 1.

Thus, shorter-term tranches and a longer term tranche are created by including an accrual tranche, a tranche that has appeal to investors who are concerned with reinvestment risk. Since there are no coupon payments to reinvest, reinvestment risk is eliminated until all the other tranches are paid off. On the other hand, the accrual tranche will have a higher effective duration.

Floating-Rate Tranches

Now let's see how a floating-rate tranche can be created from a fixed-rate tranche. This is done by creating a floater and an inverse floater. We will illustrate the creation of a floater and an inverse floater tranche using the hypothetical CMO structure Deal 2, which is a four tranche sequential-pay structure with an accrual tranche. We can select any of the tranches from which to create a floater tranche and an inverse floater tranche. In fact, we can create these two securities for more than one of the four tranches or for only a portion of one tranche.

In this case, we created a floater and an inverse floater from tranche C. The par value for this tranche is $96.5 million, and we create two tranches that have a combined par value of $96.5 million. We refer to this CMO structure with a floater and an inverse floater as Deal 3. It has five tranches, designated A, B, FL, IFL, and Z, where FL is the floating-rate tranche and IFL is the inverse floating-rate tranche. Exhibit 5 describes Deal 3. Any reference rate can be used to create a floater and the corresponding inverse floater. The reference rate selected for setting the coupon rate for FL and IFL in Deal 3 is 1-month LIBOR. The principal paydown for the floater and inverse floater is proportionate to the amount of the principal paydown of tranche C.

The amount of the par value of the floater tranche will be some portion of the $96.5 million. There are an infinite number of ways to cut up the $96.5 million between the floater and inverse floater, and final partitioning will be driven by the demands of investors. In Deal 3, we made the floater from $72,375,000 or 75% of the $96.5 million. Therefore, for every $100 of principal received in a month, the floater receives $75 and the inverse floater receives $25. The coupon rate on the floater is set at 1-month LIBOR plus 50 basis points. So, for example, if LIBOR is 3.75% at the coupon reset date, the coupon rate on the floater is 3.75% + 0.5%, or 4.25%. There is a cap on the coupon rate for the floater (discussed later).

Exhibit 5: Deal 3: A Hypothetical Five-Tranche Sequential-Pay Structure with Floater, Inverse Floater, and Accrual Tranches

Tranche	Par amount	Coupon rate
A	$194,500,000	7.50%
B	36,000,000	7.50%
FL	72,375,000	1-mo. LIBOR + 0.50
IFL	24,125,000	28.50 – 3 × (1-mo. LIBOR)
Z (Accrual)	73,000,000	7.50%
Total	$400,000,000	

Payment rules:

1. *For payment of periodic coupon interest:* Disburse periodic coupon interest to tranches A, B, FL, and IFL on the basis of the amount of principal outstanding at the beginning of the period. For tranche Z, accrue the interest based on the principal plus accrued interest in the previous period. The interest for tranche Z is to be paid to the earlier tranches as a principal paydown. The maximum coupon rate for FL is 10%; the minimum coupon rate for IFL is 0%.

2. *For disbursement of principal payments:* Disburse principal payments to tranche A until it is completely paid off. After tranche A is completely paid off, disburse principal payments to tranche B until it is completely paid off. After tranche B is completely paid off, disburse principal payments to tranches FL and IFL until they are completely paid off. The principal payments between tranches FL and IFL should be made in the following way: 75% to tranche FL and 25% to tranche IFL. After tranches FL and IFL are completely paid off, disburse principal payments to tranche Z until the original principal balance plus accrued interest is completely paid off.

Unlike the floaters discussed earlier in this book whose principal is unchanged over the life of the instrument (except for the index amortizing note), the floater's principal balance declines over time as principal repayments are made. The principal payments to the floater are determined by the principal payments from the tranche from which the floater is created. In Deal 3, this is tranche C.

Since the floater's par value is $72,375,000 of the $96.5 million, the balance is the inverse floater. Assuming that 1-month LIBOR is the reference rate, the coupon reset formula for an inverse floater takes the following form:

$$K - L \times (1\text{-month LIBOR})$$

In Deal 3, K is set at 28.50% and L at 3. Thus, if 1-month LIBOR is 3.75%, the coupon rate for the month is:

$$28.50\% - 3 \times (3.75\%) = 17.25\%$$

K is the cap or maximum coupon rate for the inverse floater. In Deal 3, the cap for the inverse floater is 28.50%.

The L or multiple in the coupon reset formula for the inverse floater is called the *coupon leverage*. The higher the coupon leverage, the more the inverse floater's coupon rate changes for a given change in 1-month LIBOR. For example, a coupon leverage of 3 means that a 1-basis point change in 1-month LIBOR will change the coupon rate on the inverse floater by 3 basis points.

Because 1-month LIBOR is always positive, the coupon rate paid to the floating-rate tranche cannot be negative. If there are no restrictions placed on the coupon rate for the inverse floater, however, it is possible for the coupon rate for that tranche to be negative. To prevent this, a floor, or minimum, is placed on the coupon rate. In many structures, the floor is set at zero. Once a floor is set for the inverse floater, a cap is imposed on the floater. In Deal 3, a floor of zero is set for the inverse floater. The floor results in a cap for the floater of 10%.

Superfloaters

A *superfloater* is a CMO floater whose coupon rate is a multiple of a reference rate. A superfloater takes the same form as an inverse floater, except that the superfloater's coupon rate increases with the reference rate. The formula is as follows, assuming that the reference rate is 1-month LIBOR:

$$C \times (\text{1-month LIBOR}) - M$$

where C is the coupon leverage and M is a constant.

For example, if C is 3 and M is 16.5%, then the formula for the coupon rate for the superfloater is:

$$3 \times (\text{1-month LIBOR}) - 16.5\%$$

If 1-month LIBOR is 8%, for example, then the superfloater's coupon rate for the month is

$$3 \times 8\% - 16.5\% = 7.5\%$$

There must be a floor on the coupon rate to prevent it from becoming negative. As with the conventional floater, an inverse floater is needed so that the collateral can support the interest payments regardless of the level of 1-month LIBOR.

To illustrate a superfloater, let's consider once again Deal 2. From tranche C, we created a floater and an inverse floater, described as Deal 3. In Deal 4 we create a superfloater and inverse superfloater from tranche C. Exhibit 6 summarizes this CMO structure. The superfloater (labeled tranche SFL in the structure) is created from 62.5% of the $96.5 million of tranche C, and the inverse superfloater (labeled tranche ISFL) is created from the balance. The coupon rate and restrictions on the superfloater and inverse superfloater are summarized below:

Tranche	Coupon	Floor	Cap
Superfloater	$3 \times$ (1-mo. LIBOR) $- 16.5$	6%	12%
Inverse superfloater	$47.5 - 5 \times$ (1-mo. LIBOR)	0%	10%

Exhibit 6: Deal 4: A Hypothetical Five-Tranche Sequential-Pay Structure with Superfloater, Inverse Superfloater, and Accrual Tranches

Tranche	Par amount	Coupon rate (%)
A	$194,500,000	7.50
B	36,000,000	7.50
SFL	60,312,500	3 × (1-month LIBOR) – 16.5
ISFL	36,187,500	47.5 – 5 × (1-month LIBOR)
Z (Accrual)	73,000,000	7.50
Total	$400,000,000	

Payment rules:

1. *For payment of periodic coupon interest:* Disburse periodic coupon interest to tranches A, B, SFL, and ISFL on the basis of the amount of principal outstanding at the beginning of the period. For tranche Z, accrue the interest based on the principal plus accrued interest in the previous period. The interest for tranche Z is to be paid to the earlier tranches as a principal paydown. The minimum (floor) coupon rate for SFL is 6%, and the maximum (cap) is 12%. The minimum (floor) coupon rate for ISFL is 0%, and the maximum (cap) is 10%.

2. *For disbursement of principal payments:* Disburse principal payments to tranche A until it is completely paid off. After tranche A is completely paid off, disburse principal payments to tranche B until it is completely paid off. After tranche B is completely paid off, disburse principal payments to tranches SFL and ISFL until they are completely paid off. The principal payments between tranches SFL and ISFL should be made in the following way: 62.5% to tranche SFL and 37.5% to tranche ISFL. After tranches SFL and ISFL are completely paid off, disburse principal payments to tranche Z until the original principal balance plus accrued interest is completely paid off.

Exhibit 7 gives the coupon rate for the superfloater and inverse superfloater for a range of rates for 1-month LIBOR. Notice that there are two critical levels for LIBOR where the restrictions on the superfloater and inverse superfloater will take effect. If LIBOR is 7.5% or less, the superfloater's coupon rate reaches its floor (6%) while the inverse superfloater's coupon rate realizes its cap (10%). Thus, LIBOR of 7.5% is referred to as the *strike rate* for the superfloater, since for any LIBOR level below 7.5%, the coupon rate is 6%. It is referred to as the strike rate as it is nothing more than an interest rate floor. In such agreements, the buyer of the floor is guaranteed a minimum interest rate, and that minimum rate is the strike rate. Thus, the buyer of a superfloater has effectively purchased an interest rate floor. Viewed from the perspective of the buyer of the inverse superfloater, the 7.5% is effectively the strike rate on an interest rate cap sold.

The other critical LIBOR level is 9.5%. At that level, the superfloater reaches its cap (12%) and forgoes any upside potential should LIBOR rise above 9.5%. At 9.5%, the inverse superfloater reaches its floor (0%). Thus, 9.5% is also a strike rate. In this case, the buyer of the superfloater has effectively sold an interest rate cap. Viewed from the perspective of the buyer of the inverse superfloater, the 9.5% is effectively the strike rate on an interest rate floor purchased.

Between these two strike rates, the coupon rates for the superfloater and inverse superfloater change according to their respective formula. Because of the two strike rates that create a lower and upper tier for the coupon rates, this type of superfloater is referred to as a *two-tiered index bond*, or TTIB.

Exhibit 7: Coupon Rate for Superfloater (SFL) and Inverse Superfloater (ISFL) in Deal 4 at Different Levels of LIBOR

1-Month LIBOR (%)	Superfloater (%)	Inverse Superfloater (%)
1.00	6.00	10.00
2.00	6.00	10.00
3.00	6.00	10.00
4.00	6.00	10.00
5.00	6.00	10.00
6.00	6.00	10.00
7.00	6.00	10.00
7.25	5.25	11.25
7.50	6.00	10.00
7.75	6.75	8.75
8.00	7.50	7.50
8.25	8.25	6.25
8.50	9.00	5.00
8.75	9.75	3.75
9.00	10.50	2.50
9.25	11.25	1.25
9.50	12.00	0.00
11.00	12.00	0.00
12.00	12.00	0.00
13.00	12.00	0.00

Inverse Interest-Only Floater

CMO structures can be created so that a tranche can receive only the principal or only the interest. For example, consider Deal 4. Suppose that tranche B in this structure is divided into two tranches, a principal-only tranche and an interest-only tranche. We will call this structure Deal 5, described in Exhibit 8.

In the calculation of the average life for a tranche, only the principal received is considered. Since an IO does not return principal, an average life cannot be calculated. Instead, a *cash flow average life* can be computed by using cash flow in lieu of principal in the average life formula. Obviously, the cash flow is just the interest.

To illustrate other types of CMO structures including a PO or an IO, consider Deal 6 shown in Exhibit 9. This is a three-tranche structure using the $400 million, 7.5% coupon, 357 WAM collateral. Tranche F is a floater with a coupon rate of 1-month LIBOR plus 50 basis points; its par value is $300 million. There is a 10% cap on tranche F. The balance of the collateral, $100 million, is used to create the remaining two tranches. There is a principal only (PO) tranche, and there is a tranche denoted IIO, which is a bond class that receives only interest (i.e., an IO tranche) based on the outstanding balance of the PO tranche. Rather than a fixed coupon rate, the interest is based on a formula where the coupon rate changes inversely with 1-month LIBOR (i.e., it is an inverse floater). The coupon formula is the same as for Deal 4, $28.5\% - 3 \times (1\text{-month LIBOR})$. This tranche is referred to as an inverse IO (IIO).

Exhibit 8: Deal 5: A Hypothetical Six-Tranche Structure Sequential-Pay Structure with a Floater, Inverse Floater, PO, IO, and Accrual Tranches

Tranche	Par amount	Coupon rate (%)
A	$194,500,000	7.50
IO	0	*
PO	36,000,000	0
FL	72,375,000	1-month LIBOR + 0.50
IFL	24,125,000	28.50 − 3 × (1-month LIBOR)
Z (Accrual)	73,000,000	7.50
Total	$400,000,000	

* Interest equal to 7.5% times the balance outstanding for the PO tranche.

Payment rules:

1. *For payment of periodic coupon interest:* Disburse periodic coupon interest to tranches A, B, FL, and IFL on the basis of the amount of principal outstanding at the beginning of the period. Disburse periodic coupon interest to tranche IO based on the amount of principal outstanding at the beginning of the period for tranche PO. For tranche Z, accrue the interest based on the principal plus accrued interest in the previous period. The interest for tranche Z is to be paid to the earlier tranches as a principal paydown. The maximum coupon rate for FL is 10%; the minimum coupon rate for IFL is 0%.

2. *For disbursement of principal payments:* Disburse principal payments to tranche A until it is completely paid off. After tranche A is completely paid off, disburse principal payments to tranche PO until it is completely paid off. After tranche PO is completely paid off, disburse principal payments to tranches FL and IFL until they are completely paid off. The principal payments between tranches FL and IFL should be made in the following way: 75% to tranche FL and 25% to tranche IFL. After tranches FL and IFL are completely paid off, disburse principal payments to tranche Z until the original principal balance plus accrued interest is completely paid off.

Exhibit 9: Deal 6: A Three-Tranche Structure with a Floater, Inverse IO Floater, and PO

Tranche	Par amount	Coupon rate (%)
FL	$300,000,000	1-month LIBOR + 0.50
IIO	0	*
PO	100,000,000	0
Total	$400,000,000	

* Interest equal to:

$$[28.50\% - 3 \times (1\text{-month LIBOR})] \times \text{PO balance outstanding}.$$

Payment rules:

1. *For payment of periodic coupon interest:* Disburse periodic coupon interest to tranche FL determined by the specified formula and on the basis of the amount of principal outstanding at the beginning of the period. Disburse periodic coupon interest to tranche IIO using the IIO specified formula and according to the amount of principal outstanding at the beginning of the period for tranche PO. The maximum coupon rate for FL is 10%; the minimum coupon rate for IIO is 0%.

2. *For disbursement of principal payments:* Disburse principal payments to tranche FL and tranche PO on the following basis: for each principal payment of $1, distribute $0.75 to tranche FL and $0.25 to tranche PO.

The principal payment from the collateral is distributed to the floater and PO tranches on the basis of their par value relative to the total par value of the collateral, $400 million. Thus, for each $100 of principal payment from the collateral, $75 is distributed to the floater and $25 to the PO. The average life for the floater and the PO is the same as the tranche from which these two tranches were created.

Planned Amortization Class Tranches

A *planned amortization class* (PAC) bond is one in which a schedule of principal payments is set forth in the prospectus. The PAC bondholders have priority over all other bond classes in the structure with respect to the receipt of the scheduled principal payments. While there is no assurance that the principal payments will be actually realized so as to satisfy the schedule, a PAC bond is structured so that if prepayment speeds are within a certain range of prepayment speeds, the collateral will throw off sufficient principal to meet the schedule of principal payments.

The greater certainty of the cash flow for the PAC bonds comes at the expense of the non-PAC classes, called the *support* or *companion tranches*. It is these tranches that absorb the prepayment risk. Because PAC bonds have protection against both extension risk and contraction risk, they are said to provide "two-sided" prepayment protection.

To illustrate how to create a PAC bond, we will use as collateral the $400 million passthrough with a coupon rate of 7.5%, an 8.125% WAC, and a WAM of 357 months. From this collateral a PAC bond with a par value of $243.8 million will be created. The second column of Exhibit 10 shows the principal payment (regularly scheduled principal repayment plus prepayments) for selected months assuming a prepayment speed of 90 PSA, and the next column shows the principal payments for selected months assuming that the passthrough prepays at 300 PSA.

The last column of Exhibit 10 gives the minimum principal payment if the collateral speed is 90 PSA or 300 PSA for months 1 to 349. (After month 349, the outstanding principal balance will be paid off if the prepayment speed is between 90 PSA and 300 PSA.) For example, in the first month, the principal payment would be $508,169.52 if the collateral prepays at 90 PSA and $1,075,931.20 if the collateral prepays at 300 PSA. Thus, the minimum principal payment is $508,169.52, as reported in the last column of Exhibit 10. In month 103, the minimum principal payment is also the amount if the prepayment speed is 90 PSA, $1,446,761, compared to $1,458,618.04 for 300 PSA. In month 104, however, a prepayment speed of 300 PSA would produce a principal payment of $1,433,539.23, which is less than the principal payment of $1,440,825.55 assuming 90 PSA. So, $1,433,539.23 is reported in the last column of Exhibit 10. In fact, from month 104 on the minimum principal payment is the one that would result assuming a prepayment speed of 300 PSA.

Actually, if the collateral prepays at any constant speed between 90 PSA and 300 PSA, the minimum principal payment would be the amount reported in the last column of Exhibit 10. For example, if we had included principal payment figures assuming a prepayment speed of 200 PSA, the minimum principal payment would not change: from month 11 through month 103, the minimum principal payment is that generated from 90 PSA, but from month 104 on, the minimum principal payment is that generated from 300 PSA.

Exhibit 10: Monthly Principal Payment for $400 Million Par 7.5% Coupon Passthrough with an 8.125% WAC and a 357 WAM Assuming Prepayment Rates of 90 PSA and 300 PSA

Month	At 90% PSA	At 300% PSA	Minimum principal payment PAC schedule
1	$508,169.52	$1,075,931.20	$508,169.52
2	569,843.43	1,279,412.11	569,843.43
3	631,377.11	1,482,194.45	631,377.11
4	692,741.89	1,683,966.17	692,741.89
5	753,909.12	1,884,414.62	753,909.12
6	814,850.22	2,083,227.31	814,850.22
7	875,536.68	2,280,092.68	875,536.68
8	935,940.10	2,474,700.92	935,940.10
9	996,032.19	2,666,744.77	996,032.19
10	1,055,784.82	2,855,920.32	1,055,784.82
11	1,115,170.01	3,041,927.81	1,115,170.01
12	1,174,160.00	3,224,472.44	1,174,160.00
13	1,232,727.22	3,403,265.17	1,232,727.22
14	1,290,844.32	3,578,023.49	1,290,844.32
15	1,348,484.24	3,748,472.23	1,348,484.24
16	1,405,620.17	3,914,344.26	1,405,620.17
17	1,462,225.60	4,075,381.29	1,462,225.60
18	1,518,274.36	4,231,334.57	1,518,274.36
101	1,458,719.34	1,510,072.17	1,458,719.34
102	1,452,725.55	1,484,126.59	1,452,725.55
103	1,446,761.00	1,458,618.04	1,446,761.00
104	1,440,825.55	1,433,539.23	1,433,539.23
105	1,434,919.07	1,408,883.01	1,408,883.01
211	949,482.58	213,309.00	213,309.00
212	946,033.34	209,409.09	209,409.09
213	942,601.99	205,577.05	205,577.05
346	618,684.59	13,269.17	13,269.17
347	617,071.58	12,944.51	12,944.51
348	615,468.65	12,626.21	12,626.21
349	613,875.77	12,314.16	3,432.32
350	612,292.88	12,008.25	0
351	610,719.96	11,708.38	0
352	609,156.96	11,414.42	0
353	607,603.84	11,126.28	0
354	606,060.57	10,843.85	0
355	604,527.09	10,567.02	0
356	603,003.38	10,295.70	0
357	601,489.39	10,029.78	0

Exhibit 11: Deal 7: Structure with One PAC Bond and One Support Bond

Tranche	Par amount	Coupon rate (%)
P (PAC)	$243,800,000	7.5
S (Support)	156,200,000	7.5
Total	$400,000,000	

Payment rules:
1. *For payment of periodic coupon interest:* Disburse periodic coupon interest to each tranche on the basis of the amount of principal outstanding at the beginning of the period.
2. *For disbursement of principal payments:* Disburse principal payments to tranche P based on its schedule of principal repayments. Tranche P has priority with respect to current and future principal payments to satisfy the schedule. Any excess principal payments in a month over the amount necessary to satisfy the schedule for tranche P are paid to tranche S. When tranche S is completely paid off, all principal payments are to be made to tranche P regardless of the schedule.

This characteristic of the collateral allows for the creation of a PAC bond, assuming that the collateral prepays over its life at a constant speed between 90 PSA and 300 PSA. A schedule of principal repayments that the PAC bondholders are entitled to receive before any other tranche in the CMO structure is specified. The monthly schedule of principal repayments is as specified in the last column of Exhibit 10, which shows the minimum principal payment. While there is no assurance that the collateral will prepay at a constant speed between these two speeds, a PAC bond can be structured assuming that it will.

Exhibit 11 shows a CMO structure, Deal 7, created from the $400 million 7.5% coupon passthrough with a WAC of 8.125% and a WAM of 357 months. There are just two tranches in this structure: a 7.5% coupon PAC bond created assuming 90 to 300 PSA with a par value of $243.8 million, and a support bond with a par value of $156.2 million. The two speeds used to create a PAC bond are called the *initial PAC collars* (or *initial PAC bands*). For Deal 7, 90 PSA is the lower collar and 300 PSA the upper collar.

Exhibit 12 reports the average life for the PAC bond and the support bond in Deal 7 assuming various actual prepayment speeds. Notice that between 90 PSA and 300 PSA, the average life for the PAC bond is stable at 7.26 years. However, at slower or faster PSA speeds the schedule is broken and the average life changes, lengthening when the prepayment speed is less than 90 PSA and shortening when it is greater than 300 PSA. Even so, there is much greater variability for the average life of the support bond.

Most CMO PAC structures have more than one class of PAC bonds. Exhibit 12 shows six PAC bonds created from the single PAC bond in Deal 7. We will refer to this CMO structure as Deal 8. Information about this CMO structure is provided in Exhibit 12. The total par value of the six PAC bonds is equal to $243.8 million, which is the amount of the single PAC bond in Deal 7,

Exhibit 13 shows the average life for the six PAC bonds and the support bond in Deal 8 at various prepayment speeds. From a PAC bond in Deal 7 with an average life of 7.26, we have created six PAC bonds with an average life as short as 2.58 years (P-A) and as long as 16.92 years (P-F) if prepayments stay within 90 PSA and 300 PSA.

Exhibit 12: Average Life for PAC Bond and Support Bond in Deal 7 Assuming Various Prepayment Speeds

Prepayment rate (PSA)	PAC Bond (P)	Support Bond (S)
0	15.97	27.26
50	9.44	24.00
90	7.26	18.56
100	7.26	18.56
150	7.26	12.57
165	7.26	11.16
200	7.26	8.38
250	7.26	5.37
300	7.26	3.13
350	6.56	2.51
400	5.92	2.17
450	5.38	1.94
500	4.93	1.77
700	3.70	1.37

Exhibit 13: Deal 8: Structure with Six PAC Bonds and One Support Bond

Tranche	Par amount	Coupon rate (%)
P-A	$85,000,000	7.5
P-B	8,000,000	7.5
P-C	35,000,000	7.5
P-D	45,000,000	7.5
P-E	40,000,000	7.5
P-F	30,800,000	7.5
S	156,200,000	7.5
Total	$400,000,000	

Payment rules:
1. *For payment of periodic coupon interest:* Disburse periodic coupon interest to each tranche on the basis of the amount of principal outstanding at the beginning of the period.
2. *For disbursement of principal payments:* Disburse principal payments to tranches P-A to P-F based on their respective schedules of principal repayments. Tranche P-A has priority with respect to current and future principal payments to satisfy the schedule. Any excess principal payments in a month over the amount necessary to satisfy the schedule for tranche P-A are paid to tranche S. Once tranche P-A is completely paid off, tranche P-B has priority, then tranche P-C, etc. When tranche S is completely paid off, all principal payments are to be made to the remaining PAC tranches in order of priority regardless of the schedule.

Exhibit 14: Average Life for PAC Bond and Support Bond in Deal 8 Assuming Various Prepayment Speeds

Prepayment rate (PSA)	PAC Bonds					
	P-A	P-B	P-C	P-D	P-E	P-F
0	8.46	14.61	16.49	19.41	21.91	23.76
50	3.58	6.82	8.36	11.30	14.50	18.20
90	2.58	4.72	5.78	7.89	10.83	16.92
100	2.58	4.72	5.78	7.89	10.83	16.92
150	2.58	4.72	5.78	7.89	10.83	16.92
165	2.58	4.72	5.78	7.89	10.83	16.92
200	2.58	4.72	5.78	7.89	10.83	16.92
250	2.58	4.72	5.78	7.89	10.83	16.92
300	2.58	4.72	5.78	7.89	10.83	16.92
350	2.58	4.72	5.94	6.95	9.24	14.91
400	2.57	4.37	4.91	6.17	8.33	13.21
450	2.50	3.97	4.44	5.56	7.45	11.81
500	2.40	3.65	4.07	5.06	6.74	10.65
700	2.06	2.82	3.10	3.75	4.88	7.51

As expected, the average lives are stable if the prepayment speed is between 90 PSA and 300 PSA. Notice that even outside this range the average life is stable for several of the shorter PAC bonds. For example, PAC P-A is stable even if prepayment speeds are as high as 400 PSA. For the PAC P-B, the average life does not vary when prepayments are between 90 PSA and 350 PSA. Why is it that the shorter the PAC, the more protection it has against faster prepayments?

To understand why this is so, remember that there are $156.2 million in support bonds that are protecting the $85 million of PAC P-A. Thus, even if prepayments are faster than the initial upper collar, there may be sufficient support bonds to assure the satisfaction of the schedule. In fact, as can been from Exhibit 14, even if prepayments are at 400 PSA over the life of the collateral, the average life is unchanged.

Now consider PAC P-B. The support bonds are providing protection for both the $85 million of PAC P-A and $93 million of PAC P-B. As can be seen from Exhibit 15, prepayments could be 350 PSA and the average life is still unchanged. From Exhibit 15 it can be seen that the degree of protection against extension risk increases the shorter the PAC. Thus, while the initial collar may be 90 to 300 PSA, the effective collar is wider for the shorter PAC tranches.

PAC Floaters

Given a series of PAC bonds, any of the tranches can be carved up to make a floater and an inverse floater. The advantage of the PAC floater compared to a sequential-pay floater is that there is two-sided prepayment protection and therefore the uncertainty of the average life is less. The trade-off is that this greater prepayment protection is not free. All other factors constant, the margin over the same reference rate offered on a PAC floater will be less than that on a sequential-pay floater and/or the cap will be the lower.

Effective Collars and Actual Prepayments

As we have emphasized, the creation of an MBS cannot make prepayment risk disappear. This is true for both a passthrough and a CMO. Thus, the reduction in prepayment risk (both extension risk and contraction risk) that a PAC bond offers must come from somewhere.

Where does the prepayment protection come from? It comes from the support bonds. It is the support bonds that forgo principal payments if the collateral prepayments are slow; support bonds do not receive any principal until the PAC bonds receive the scheduled principal repayment. This reduces the risk that the PAC bonds will extend. Similarly, it is the support bonds that absorb any principal payments in excess of the scheduled principal payments that are made. This reduces the contraction risk of the PAC bonds. Thus, the key to the prepayment protection offered by a PAC bond is the amount of support bonds outstanding. If the support bonds are paid off quickly because of faster-than-expected prepayments, then there is no longer any protection for the PAC bonds. In fact, in Deal 8, if the support bond is paid off, the structure is effectively reduced to a sequential-pay CMO. In such cases, the schedule is unlikely to be maintained, and the structure is referred to as a *busted PAC*.

The support bonds can be thought of as bodyguards for the PAC bond-holders. When the bullets fly — i.e., prepayments occur — it is the bodyguards that get killed first. The bodyguards are there to absorb the bullets. Once all the bodyguards are killed off (i.e., the support bonds paid off with faster-than-expected prepayments), the PAC bonds must fend for themselves: they are exposed to all the bullets.

With the bodyguard metaphor for the support bonds in mind, let's consider two questions asked by CMO buyers:

1. Will the schedule of principal repayments be satisfied if prepayments are faster than the initial upper collar?
2. Will the schedule of principal repayments be satisfied as long as prepayments stay within the initial collar?

Let's address the first question. The initial upper collar for Deal 7 is 300 PSA. Suppose that actual prepayments are 500 PSA for seven consecutive months. Will this disrupt the schedule of principal repayments? The answer is: it depends! There are two pieces of information we will need to answer this question. First, when does the 500 PSA occur? Second, what has been the actual prepayment experience up to the time that prepayments are 500 PSA? For example, suppose six years from now is when the prepayments reach 500 PSA, and also suppose that for the past six years the actual prepayment speed has been 90 PSA every month. What this means is that there are more bodyguards (i.e., support bonds) around than was expected when the PAC was structured at the initial collar. In establishing the schedule of principal repayments, it was assumed that the bodyguards would be killed off at 300 PSA. But the actual prepayment experience results in them being killed off at only 90 PSA. Thus, six years from now when the 500 PSA is assumed to occur, there are more bodyguards than expected. Thus, a 500 PSA for seven consecutive months may have no effect on the ability of the schedule of principal repayments to be met.

In contrast, suppose that the actual prepayment experience for the first six years is 300 PSA (the upper collar of the initial PAC collar). In this case, there are no extra bodyguards around. As a result, any prepayment speeds faster than 300 PSA, such as 500 PSA in our example, jeopardize satisfaction of the principal repayment schedule and increase contraction risk. What this means is that the prepayment protection is reduced.

It should be clear from these observations that the initial collars are not particularly useful in assessing the prepayment protection for a seasoned PAC bond. This is most important to understand, as it is common for CMO buyers to compare prepayment protection of PACs in different CMO structures, and conclude that the greater protection is offered by the one with the wider initial collars. This approach is inadequate because it is actual prepayment experience that determines the degree of prepayment protection going forward, as well as the expected future prepayment behavior of the collateral.

The way to determine this protection is to calculate the effective collar for a PAC bond. An *effective collar* for a PAC is the lower and the upper PSA that can occur in the future and still allow maintenance of the schedule of principal repayments.

The effective collar changes every month. An extended period over which actual prepayments are below the upper range of the initial PAC collar will result in an increase in the upper range of the effective collar. This is because there will be more bodyguards around than anticipated. An extended period of prepayments slower than the lower range of the initial PAC collar will raise the lower range of the effective collar. This is because it will take faster prepayments to make up the shortfall of the scheduled principal payments not made plus the scheduled future principal payments.

It is important to understand that the PAC schedule may not be satisfied even if the actual prepayments never fall outside of the initial collar. This may seem surprising since our previous analysis indicated that the average life would not change if prepayments are at either extreme of the initial collar. However, recall that all of our previous analysis has been based on a single PSA speed for the life of the structure. If we vary the PSA speed over time rather than keep it constant over the life of the CMO, we can see what happens to the effective collar if the prepayments are at the initial upper collar for a certain number of months. For example, if one computed the average life two years from now for the PAC bond in Deal 7 assuming that prepayments are 300 PSA for the first 24 months, one would find that the average life is stable at six years if the prepayments for the following months are between 115 PSA and 300 PSA. That is, the effective PAC collar is no longer the initial collar. Instead, the lower collar has shifted upward. This means that the protection from year 2 on is for 115 PSA to 300 PSA, a narrower band than initially, even though the earlier prepayments did not exceed the initial upper collar.

Support Bonds

The support bonds are the bonds that provide prepayment protection for the PAC tranches. Consequently, support tranches expose investors to the greatest level of prepayment risk. Because of this, investors must be particularly careful in assessing the cash flow characteristics of support bonds to reduce the likelihood of adverse portfolio consequences due to prepayments.

The support bond typically is divided into different tranches. All the tranches we have discussed earlier are available, including sequential-pay support tranches, floater and inverse floater support tranches. The support bond can even be partitioned so as to create support tranches with a schedule of principal payments. That is, support tranches that are PAC bonds can be created. In a structure with a PAC bond and a support bond with a PAC schedule of principal payments, the former is called a PAC I bond or Level I PAC bond and the latter a PAC II bond or Level II PAC bond. While PAC II bonds have greater prepayment protection than the support tranches without a schedule of principal repayments, the prepayment protection is less than that provided PAC I bonds.

There is more that can be done with the PAC II bond. A series of PAC IIs can be created just as we did with the PACs in Deal 8. PAC IIs can also be used to create any other type of bond class, such as a PAC II floater and inverse floaters, for example. The support bond without a principal repayment schedule can be used to create any type of bond class. In fact, a portion of the non-PAC II support bond can be given a schedule of principal repayments. This bond class would be called a PAC III bond or a Level III PAC bond. While it provides protection against prepayments for the PAC I and PAC II bonds and is therefore subject to considerable prepayment risk, such a bond class has greater protection than the support bond class without a schedule of principal repayments.

Mega Floaters

In most cases, the underlying collateral of a CMO structure is in the form of a fixed-rate mortgage passthroughs. In general, any mortgage asset can be used as collateral for a CMO structure. Since 1992, a good number of CMO deals were created whose underlying collateral consisted of tranches from existing CMO structures. These deals are called *re-REMICs* because they use parts of previously issued REMICs to create another REMIC.

The purpose of a re-REMIC is to take advantage of pricing discrepancy by altering the existing structures of the CMO collateral. One re-REMIC structure that was popular with some floater investors was the *mega floater*. This floater, also referred to as a "kitchen sink" bond, was invented when CMO dealers had a huge inventory of CMO derivatives such as IOs, POs, inverse floaters, and support bonds. They used re-REMICs to create a floating-rate product that had better investment characteristics than the individual REMIC pieces from which they were created. The spread to the reference rate was large and the cap was high. Thus, the investor faced little cap risk. Dealers were willing to provide attractive financing for these floaters.

One of the risks associated with the mega floaters was that since the floater was created from IO and PO tranches of other deals, the interest was not guaranteed. That is, the investor knew that the principal would be returned (but not exactly when because of prepayments), but it was the IO tranches that were to generate the necessary interest to pay the interest to the holder of a mega floater. If prepayments came in too fast, the IOs underlying the deal would pay off and it was possible that there would be a shortfall in the interest payments. For example, if the mega floater had a coupon formula of 1-month LIBOR plus 300 basis points, there is a chance that less than the formula amount would be paid.

The mega floaters were commonly used in the strategy described in Chapter 1 (the "risk arbitrage" strategy). Actually, the risk of investing in a mega floater as part of the risk arbitrage strategy is not that the security will not receive the full amount of interest as specified by the coupon formula. Rather, it is the risk that the amount of the payment is less than the funding cost the dealer charged to finance the investor's purchase of the mega floater. For example, if the dealer charges a repo rate of 1-month LIBOR plus 20 basis points and the coupon formula for the mega floater is 1-month LIBOR plus 300 basis points, the investor will cover the repo finance charge unless the mega floater pays less than 1-month LIBOR plus 20 basis points.

NONAGENCY CMOS

There are CMO floaters that are created in CMO deals in which the issuer is a private entity rather than Ginnie Mae, Fannie Mae, or Freddie Mac. These securities are called *nonagency mortgage-backed securities* (referred to as nonagency securities hereafter). Other mortgage-backed products that are separately classified in the industry as asset-backed securities are home equity loan-backed securities and manufactured housing-backed securities. These products are discussed in the next section. Since all of these mortgage-related securities expose an investor to credit risk, these securities are sometimes referred to as *credit-sensitive mortgage-backed securities.*

For agency CMOs, the concern is with the redistribution or "tranching" of prepayment risk. For nonagency CMOs, the bonds issued are not guaranteed by a federally related agency or a government sponsored enterprise. Consequently, there is concern with credit risk. As a result, nonagency CMOs expose the investor to both prepayment risk and credit risk. The same types of tranches are created in nonagency CMO structures as described earlier for agency CMO structures.[1] Hence, CMO floaters are created in the same way. What is unique is the mecha-

---

[1] In the agency market we explained how cash flows for certain tranches, PACs, can be given prepayment protection. In the nonagency market, senior tranches have been structured that have relatively greater average life stability than senior sequential-pay tranches with a similar average life. These tranches are called *non-accelerating senior (NAS) tranches.* The other senior tranches in the structure are referred to as *accelerating senior tranches.*

nisms for enhancing the credit of a nonagency CMO so that an issuer can obtain any credit rating desired for a tranche in a deal. The same credit enhancement mechanisms are used for ABS structures discussed in the next chapter.

Agency CMOs are created from pools of passthrough securities. In the nonagency market, a CMO can be created from either a pool of passthroughs or unsecuritized mortgage loans. It is uncommon for nonconforming mortgage loans to be securitized as passthroughs and then the passthroughs carved up to create a CMO. Instead, in the nonagency market a CMO is carved out of mortgage loans that have not been securitized as passthroughs. Since a mortgage loan is commonly referred to as a whole loan, nonagency CMOs are commonly referred to as whole-loan CMOs.

The underlying loans for agency securities are those that conform to the underwriting standards of the agency issuing or guaranteeing the issue. That is, only conforming loans are included in pools that are collateral for an agency mortgage-backed security. The three main underwriting standards deal with (1) the maximum loan-to-value ratio, (2) the maximum payment-to-income ratio, and (3) the maximum loan amount. A nonconforming mortgage loan is one that does not conform to the underwriting standards established by any of the agencies.

Credit Enhancement Mechanisms

Typically a double A or triple A rating is sought for the most senior tranche in a nonagency CMO. The amount of credit enhancement necessary depends on rating agency requirements. There are two general types of credit enhancement mechanisms: external and internal. We describe each type below

External Credit Enhancements

External credit enhancements come in the form of third-party guarantees that provide for first protection against losses up to a specified level, for example, 10%. The most common forms of external credit enhancement are (1) a corporate guarantee, (2) a letter of credit, (3) pool insurance, and (4) bond insurance.

Pool insurance policies cover losses resulting from defaults and foreclosures. Policies are typically written for a dollar amount of coverage that continues in force throughout the life of the pool. However, some policies are written so that the dollar amount of coverage declines as the pool seasons as long as two conditions are met: (1) the credit performance is better than expected and (2) the rating agencies that rated the issue approve. Since only defaults and foreclosures are covered, additional insurance must be obtained to cover losses resulting from bankruptcy (i.e., court mandated modification of mortgage debt — "cramdown"), fraud arising in the origination process, and special hazards (i.e., losses resulting from events not covered by a standard homeowner's insurance policy).

Bond insurance provides the same function as in municipal bond structures. The major insurers are AMBAC, MBIA, FSA, and FGIC. Typically, bond insurance is not used as the primary protection but to supplement other forms of credit enhancement.

A nonagency CMO with external credit support is subject to the credit risk of the third-party guarantor. Should the third-party guarantor be downgraded, the issue itself could be subject to downgrade even if the structure is performing as expected. This is based on the "weak link" test followed by rating agencies. According to this test, when evaluating a proposed structure, credit quality of the issue is only as good as the weakest link in credit enhancement regardless of the quality of the underlying loans. This is the chief disadvantage of third-party guarantees, sometimes referred to as "event risk." Therefore, it is imperative that investors monitor the third-party guarantor as well as the collateral.

External credit enhancements do not materially alter the cash flow characteristics of a CMO structure except in the form of prepayment. In case of a default resulting in net losses within the guarantee level, investors will receive the principal amount as if a prepayment has occurred. If the net losses exceed the guarantee level, investors will realize a shortfall in the cash flows.

Internal Credit Enhancements

Internal credit enhancements come in more complicated forms than external credit enhancements and may alter the cash flow characteristics of the loans even in the absence of default. The most common forms of internal credit enhancements are reserve funds and senior/subordinated structures.

Reserve Funds *Reserve funds* come in two forms, cash reserve funds and excess servicing spread. Cash reserve funds are straight deposits of cash generated from issuance proceeds. In this case, part of the underwriting profits from the deal are deposited into a hypothecated fund which typically invests in money market instruments. Cash reserve funds are typically used in conjunction with letters of credit or other kinds of external credit enhancements.

Excess servicing spread accounts involve the allocation of excess spread or cash into a separate reserve account after paying out the net coupon, servicing fee, and all other expenses on a monthly basis. For example, suppose that the gross WAC is 7.75%, the servicing and other fees are 0.25%, and the net WAC is 7.25%. This means that there is excess servicing of 0.25%. The amount in the reserve account will gradually increase and can be used to pay for possible future losses. This form of credit enhancement relies on the assumption that defaults occur infrequently in the very early life of the loans but gradually increase in the following two to five years.

Senior/Subordinated Structure The most widely used internal credit enhancement structure is by far the *senior/subordinated structure*. Today a typical structure will have a senior tranche and several junior tranches. The junior tranches represent the *subordinated tranches* of the structure. The issuer will seek a triple A or double A rating for the senior tranche. The junior tranches will have lower ratings — investment grade and non-investment grade. Typically, the most junior tranche — called the *first loss piece* — will not be rated.

Exhibit 15: Hypothetical $200 Million Senior/Subordinated Structure

Bond	Rating	Amount ($ in millions)	Percent of deal(%)
Senior	AAA	$184.50	92.25
Junior			
X1	AA	4.00	2.00
X2	A	2.00	1.00
X3	BBB	3.00	1.50
X4	BB	4.00	2.00
X5*	Not rated	2.50	1.25

* First loss piece.

Exhibit 15 shows a hypothetical $200 million structure with a senior tranche representing 92.25% of the deal and five junior tranches representing 7.75% of the deal. Note that all that has been done in this structure is "credit tranching." The senior or any of the junior tranches can then be carved up to create other CMO tranches such as sequential pays.

The first loss piece in this hypothetical deal is tranche X5. The subordination level in this hypothetical structure is 7.75%. The junior classes will absorb all losses up to $15.5 million and the senior tranche will start to experience losses thereafter. So, if there is a $10 million loss, no loss will be realized by the senior tranche. If, instead, there is a $20 million loss, the senior tranche will experience a loss of $4.5 million ($20 million minus $15.5 million) or a 2.4% loss ($4.5/$184.5).

In the case where the loss is $10 million, the first loss piece (tranche X5), tranche X4, and tranche X3 absorb $9.5 million. These tranches will realize a loss experience of 100%. Tranche X2 will realize a loss of $0.5 million, thereby having a loss experience of 25% ($0.5/$2.0). Tranche X1 will not realize any loss. If the loss is $20 million, all junior bonds will have a loss experience of 100%.

The junior tranches obviously would require a yield premium to take on the greater credit risk exposure relative to the senior tranche. This setup is a form of self-insurance wherein investors in the senior tranche are giving up yield spread to the investors in the junior tranches. This form of credit enhancement still does not affect cash flow characteristics of the senior tranche except in the form of prepayment. To the extent that losses are within the subordination level, investors in the senior tranche will receive principal as if a prepayment has occurred.

The basic concern is that while the subordinate tranche provides a certain level of credit protection for the senior tranche at the closing of the deal, the level of protection changes over time due to prepayments and certain liquidation proceeds. The objective is to distribute these payments of principal such that the credit protection for the senior tranche does not deteriorate over time.

To accomplish this, almost all existing senior/subordinated structures incorporate a *shifting interest structure*. A shifting interest structure redirects prepayments disproportionally from the subordinated classes to the senior class according to a specified schedule. An example of such a schedule would be as follows:

Months	Percentage of prepayments directed to senior class
1-60	100%
61-72	70%
73-84	60%
85-96	40%
97-108	20%
109+	pro rata

The rationale for the shifting interest structure is to have enough insurance outstanding to cover future losses. Because of the shifting interest structure, the subordination amount may actually grow in time especially in a low default and fast prepayment environment. Using the same example of our previous $200 million deal with 7.75% initial subordination and assuming a cumulative paydown (prepayments at 165 PSA and regular repayments) of $40 million by year 3, the subordination will actually increase to 10.7% [$15.5/($184.50 − $40)] without any net losses. Even if the subordinated classes have experienced some losses, say, $1 million, the subordination will still increase to 9.3% [($15.5 − $1)/($184.50 − $40)].

While the shifting interest structure is beneficial to the senior tranche from a credit standpoint, it does alter the cash flow characteristics of the senior tranche even in the absence of defaults.

PSA Standard Default Assumption Benchmark

Because of defaults in the underlying mortgage pool of a nonagency CMO, it is necessary to project defaults and recoveries. The Public Securities Association (PSA) introduced a standardized benchmark for default rates. The PSA standard default assumption (SDA) benchmark gives the annual default rate for a mortgage pool as a function of the seasoning of the mortgages. The PSA SDA benchmark, or 100 SDA, specifies the following:

1. the default rate in month 1 is 0.02% and increases by 0.02% up to month 30 so that in month 30 the default rate is 0.60%;
2. from month 30 to month 60, the default rate remains at 0.60%;
3. from month 61 to month 120, the default rate declines from 0.60% to 0.03%;
4. from month 120 on, the default rate remains constant at 0.03%.

As with the PSA prepayment benchmark, multiples of the benchmark are found by multiplying the default rate by the assumed multiple. A 0 SDA means that no defaults are assumed.

Chapter 9

ABS Floaters

While residential mortgage loans are by far the most commonly securitized asset type, securities backed by other assets (consumer and business loans and receivables) have also been securitized. Floating-rate asset-backed securities are typically created where the underlying pool of loans or receivables pay a floating rate. The most common are securities backed by credit card receivables, home equity line of credit receivables, closed-end home equity loans with an adjustable rate, student loans, Small Business Administration loans, and trade receivables. As demonstrated in the previous chapter, fixed-rate loans also can be used to create a structure that has one or more floating-rate tranches. For example, there are closed-end home equity loans with a fixed rate that can be pooled to create a structure with floating-rate tranches.

Exhibit 1 shows the amount of asset-backed securities issued from January 1, 1998 to July 6, 1999 by major asset class. The exhibit also shows the amount and percent of each asset class that represents floating-rate bonds. Of the $269.17 billion issuance in that time period, 45% was floating-rate bonds. The major asset classes with floaters are credit card receivables, home equity loans, and student loans. While only 22.9% of auto-loan-backed securities are floaters, issuance was $13.60 billion. This was predominately auto dealer floor plans.

In this chapter we review the sectors of the asset-backed securities market where the floating-rate sector is a major component: credit card receivables, home equity loans, and student loans. Two other important floater sectors not shown in Exhibit 1 but which will be discussed in this chapter are Small Business Administration-backed loans and collateralized bond obligations.

Exhibit 1: ABS Issuance by Major Asset Class from January 1, 1998 to July 6, 1999 and Percent Floating Rate

Asset Class	Total $Bil.	Floating $Bil.	Percent Floating
Auto loans	59.50	13.60	22.9
Credit cards	56.71	35.17	62.0
Home equity loans	94.67	47.66	50.3
Manufactured housing loans	15.74	1.81	11.5
Student loans	12.28	11.52	93.8
Other	30.28	11.36	37.3
Total	269.17	121.12	45.0

Data provided by Morgan Stanley

CREDIT RISK

Asset-backed securities expose investors to credit risk. The four nationally recognized statistical rating organizations rate asset-backed securities. In analyzing credit risk, all four rating companies focus on similar areas of analysis: (1) credit quality of the collateral, (2) the quality of the seller/servicer, (3) cash flow stress and payment structure, and (4) legal structure.[1] We discuss each below.

Credit Quality of the Collateral

Analysis of the credit quality of the collateral depends on the asset type. The rating companies will look at the borrower's ability to pay and the borrower's equity in the asset. The latter has been found to be a key determinant as to whether the borrower will default or sell the asset and pay off the loan. The rating companies will look at the experience of the originators of the underlying loans and will assess whether the loans underlying a specific transaction have the same characteristics as the experience reported by the issuer.

The concentration of loans is examined. The underlying principle of asset securitization is that the large number of borrowers in a pool will reduce the credit risk via diversification. If there are a few borrowers in the pool that are significant in size relative to the entire pool balance, this diversification benefit can be lost, resulting in a higher level of default risk. This risk is called *concentration risk*. In such instances, rating companies will set concentration limits on the amount or percentage of receivables from any one borrower.

Based on its analysis of the collateral and other factors described below, a rating company will determine the amount of credit enhancement necessary for an issue to receive a particular rating. All asset-backed securities are credit enhanced. Credit enhancement is used to provide greater protection to investors against losses due to defaults by borrowers. The amount of credit enhancement is determined relative to a specific rating desired by the issuer for a security.

In the previous chapter we explained the various types of internal and external credit mechanisms for nonagency CMOs. The same credit enhancement mechanisms are used in ABS structures.

Quality of the Seller/Servicer

Underwriting standards are not established by any government agency or the rating companies. Each financial institution or loan originator establishes its own underwriting standards. In many cases the servicer is the seller or originator of the loans used as the collateral. Duff & Phelps Credit Rating Company, for example, reviews the following when evaluating servicers: (1) servicing history, (2) experience, (3) originations, (4) servicing capabilities, (5) human resources, (6)

---

[1] Suzanne Michaud, "A Rating Agency Perspective on Asset-Backed Securities," Chapter 16 in Anand K. Bhattacharya and Frank J. Fabozzi, *Asset- Backed Securities* (New Hope, PA: Frank J. Fabozzi Associates, 1997).

financial condition, and (6) growth/competition/business environment.[2] Based on its analysis, Duff & Phelps determines whether the servicer is acceptable or unacceptable. The latter are not rated.

Cash Flow Stress and Payment Structure

The cash flow of the underlying collateral of an ABS is interest and principal repayment. The cash flow payments that must be made are interest and principal to investors, servicing fees, and any other expenses for which the issuer is liable. The rating companies analyze the structure to test whether the collateral's cash flows match the payments that must be made to satisfy the issuer's obligations. This requires that the rating company make assumptions about losses and delinquencies and consider various interest rate scenarios.

There are different payment or financial structures from which an issuer can choose. By payment structure we mean payment priorities such as how the bond's principal payments should be amortized, and how any excess cash flows should be used. The structure depends on the type of collateral. As with mortgage-backed securities, there are two basic forms: passthroughs and paythroughs (i.e., multiple tranches at the same level of credit priority).

Basis Risk

An ABS is exposed to *basis risk*. This risk is defined as any mismatch between adjustments to the coupon rate paid to bondholders and the interest rate paid on the floating-rate collateral.[3] Two common sources of basis risk are index risk and reset risk. *Index risk* is a type of yield curve risk that arises because the ABS floater's coupon rate and the interest rate of the underlying collateral are usually determined at different ends of the yield curve. Specifically, the floater's coupon rate is typically spread off the short-term sector of the yield curve (e.g., U.S. Treasury) while the collateral's interest rate is spread off a longer maturity sector of the same yield curve or in some cases a different yield curve (e.g., LIBOR). This mismatch is a source of risk. For example, for home equity loan-backed securities in which the collateral is adjustable-rate loans, the reference rate for the loans may be 6-month LIBOR while the reference rate for the bonds is usually 1-month LIBOR. Both the collateral and the bonds are indexed off LIBOR, but different sectors of the Eurodollar yield curve. The reference rate for some home equity loans is a constant maturity Treasury. Thus, the collateral is based on a spread off the 1-month sector of the Eurodollar yield curve while the bonds are spread off a longer maturity sector of the Treasury yield curve. As another example, for credit cards the interest rate paid is usually a spread over the prime rate (a spread over the Treasury yield curve) while the coupon rate for the bonds is usually a spread over 1-month LIBOR (a spread over the Eurodollar yield curve).

---

[2] Duff & Phelps Credit Rating Company, *Servicer Review Policy*, undated.

[3] The definitions and examples that follow are those found in Lisa N. Wilhelm and W. Alexander Roever, "Identifying Relative Value in the ABS Market," Chapter 20 in Frank J. Fabozzi (ed.), *The Handbook of Corporate Debt Instruments* (New Hope, PA: Frank J. Fabozzi Associates, 1998), pp. 409-413.

Reset risk is the risk associated with the mismatch between the frequency of the resetting of the interest rate on the floating-rate collateral and the frequency of reset of the coupon rate on the bonds. This risk is common for ABS. For home equity loan-backed securities, for example, the underlying collateral for the adjustable-rate loans is either reset semiannually or annually. However, the coupon rate on the bonds is reset every month. For credit card-backed securities, the coupon rate for the bonds is set monthly, while the finance charges on the outstanding credit card balances are computed daily at a fixed spread over the prime rate.

Basis risk has an impact on the cap of an ABS floater. For a non-ABS floater, the coupon rate has a fixed cap (typically, for the life of the floater). In contrast, the cap for an ABS floater depends on the performance of the underlying collateral. For ABS floaters, basis risk affects the excess spread available to pay the coupon rate for the bondholders. In the case of home equity loan-backed ABS and student loan ABS, the cap on the bondholder's coupon is called the *available funds cap*. Typically, the large spread on the collateral loans compared to the spread offered on the bonds provides protection for ABS investors against basis risk.

Where there is an available funds cap, typically there is a provision for carrying any interest shortfall resulting from the cap forward to future months. So, for example, suppose that in one month the full coupon rate would be 6.5% but the available fund cap restricts the coupon rate for that month to 6.2%. The 30 basis point difference between the full coupon rate and the rate due to the available funds cap is capitalized and paid in a subsequent month (or months) when the funds are available to pay the bondholder. As a result, the presence of an available funds cap does not have the same impact on cash flow as a typical cap since such caps do not have a catch-up provision.

Legal Structure

A corporation using structured financing seeks a rating on the securities it issues that is higher than its own corporate rating. This is done by using the underlying loans as collateral for a debt instrument rather than the general credit of the issuer. Typically, however, the corporate entity (i.e., seller of the collateral) retains some interest in the collateral. For example, the corporate entity can retain a subordinated class. Because the corporate entity retains an interest, rating companies want to be assured that a bankruptcy of that corporate entity will not allow the issuer's creditors access to the collateral. That is, there is concern that a bankruptcy court could redirect the collateral's cash flows or the collateral itself from the security holders in an ABS deal to the creditors of the corporate entity if it became bankrupt.

To solve this problem, a bankruptcy-remote special purpose corporation (SPC) is formed. The issuer of the ABS is then the SPC. Legal opinion is needed stating that in the event of bankruptcy of the seller of the collateral, counsel does not believe that a bankruptcy court will consolidate the collateral sold with the assets of the seller.

The SPC is set up as a wholly-owned subsidiary of the seller of the collateral. Despite the fact that it is a wholly-owned subsidiary, it is established in such a way that it is treated as a third-party entity relative to the seller of the collateral. The collateral is sold to the SPC, which in turn, resells the collateral to the trust. The trust holds the collateral on behalf of the investors. It is the SPC that holds the interest retained by the seller of the collateral.

CASH FLOW OF ASSET-BACKED SECURITIES

The collateral for an ABS can be classified as either amortizing or non-amortizing assets. *Amortizing assets* are loans in which the borrower's periodic payment consists of scheduled principal and interest payments over the life of the loan. The schedule for the repayment of the principal is called the amortization schedule. The standard residential mortgage loan falls into this category. Auto loans and certain types of home equity loans (specifically, closed-end home equity loans discussed later in this chapter) are amortizing assets. Any excess payment over the scheduled principal payment is called a *prepayment*. Prepayments can be made to pay off the entire balance or a partial prepayment, called a *curtailment*.

In contrast to amortizing assets, *non-amortizing assets* do not have a schedule for the periodic payments that the borrower must make. Instead, a non-amortizing asset is one in which the borrower must make a minimum periodic payment. If that payment is less than the interest on the outstanding loan balance, the shortfall is added to the outstanding loan balance. If the periodic payment is greater than the interest on the outstanding loan balance, then the difference is applied to the reduction of the outstanding loan balance. There is no schedule of principal payments (i.e., no amortization schedule) for a non-amortizing asset. Consequently, the concept of a prepayment does not apply. Credit card receivables and certain types of home equity loans described later in this chapter are examples of non-amortizing assets.

For an amortizing asset, projection of the cash flows requires projecting prepayments. One factor that may affect prepayments is the prevailing level of interest rates relative to the interest rate on the loan. In projecting prepayments it is critical to estimate the extent to which borrowers are expected to take advantage of a possible decline in interest rates below the loan rate by refinancing the loan.

Modeling defaults for the collateral is critical in estimating the cash flow of an ABS. Proceeds that are recovered in the event of a default of a loan prior to the scheduled principal repayment date of an amortizing asset represent a prepayment. Projecting prepayments for amortizing assets requires an assumption of the default rate and the recovery rate. For a non-amortizing asset, while the concept of a prepayment does not exist, a projection of defaults is still necessary to project how much will be recovered and when.

CREDIT CARD RECEIVABLE-BACKED SECURITIES

Credit cards are originated by banks (e.g., Visa and MasterCard), retailers (e.g., JCPenney and Sears), and travel and entertainment companies (e.g., American Express). Deals are structured as a *master trust*. With a master trust the issuer can sell several series from the same trust. Each series issued by the master trust shares the cash flow and therefore the credit risk of one pool of credit card receivables of the issuer. For example, consider the following two deals: Sears Credit Account Master Trust II, Series 1995-4 and Standard Credit Card Master Trust I Series 1995-A.

Sears offers several open-end revolving credit plans. These plans include the SearsCharge account, the SearsCharge PLUS account, the SearsCharge Modernizing Credit Plan account, and the SearsCharge Home Improvement Plan account. From these various plans, Sears generates a portfolio of receivables. The majority of the portfolio of receivables is from the SearsCharge account. The Sears Credit Account Master Trust II, Series 1995-5 was the sixth of a series issued by Group One of Sears Credit Account Master Trust II. As of July 1995, the master trust was comprised of $4 billion of principal receivables. These receivables were randomly selected from the entire portfolio of receivables of Sears Roebuck and Co. About 38% of the accounts had credit limits of $1,999 and about 61% were seasoned at least five years. All series issued from this Master Trust II share in the pool of receivables that were randomly selected. Information about the specific accounts in the pool selected for Master Trust II was not disclosed; however, because of the random selection process, an investor might expect that the composition did not differ significantly from the entire portfolio of receivables. There were two classes of certificates that were offered to the public: Class A Master Trust Certificates and Class B Master Trust Certificates. The principal for the former was $500 million and for the latter $22.5 million.

The Standard Credit Card Master Trust I Series 1995-A is a Citibank deal. This issue is the twenty-second in a series issued by Group One of Standard Credit Card Master Trust I and is a Euro issue. The master trust as of May 22, 1995 was comprised of 20,092,662 accounts with principal receivables of approximately $24.3 billion and approximately $290.8 million of finance charge receivables. The average credit limit was $3,282 and the average principal balance of the accounts was $1,210. About 69% of the accounts were seasoned more than two years. There was only one certificate offered to the public — $300 million of Floating Rate Class A Credit Card Participation Certificates.

Cash Flow

For a pool of credit card receivables, the cash flow consists of finance charges collected, fees, interchange, and principal. Finance charges collected represent the periodic interest the credit card borrower is charged based on the unpaid balance after the grace period. Fees include late payment fees and any annual membership fees. For Visa and Mastercharge, a payment is made to originators. This payment is called *interchange* and is made to the originator for providing funding and accepting risk during the grace period. The principal is the amount of the borrowed funds repaid.

Interest to security holders is paid periodically (e.g, monthly, quarterly, or semiannually). The interest rate may be fixed or floating. As Exhibit 1 indicates, about 60% of the ABS securities issued were floaters. In the ABS market, there are both capped and uncapped floaters outstanding.

A credit card receivable-backed security is a non-amortizing security. For a specified period of time, referred to as the *lockout period* or *revolving period*, the principal payments made by credit card borrowers comprising the pool are retained by the trustee and reinvested in additional receivables. The lockout period can vary from 18 months to 10 years. So, during the lockout period, the cash flow that is paid out is based on finance charges collected and fees.

After the lockout period, the principal is no longer reinvested but paid to investors. This period is referred to as the *principal-amortization period* and the various types of structures are described later.

There are provisions in credit card receivable-backed securities that require early amortization of the principal if certain events occur. Such provisions, which are referred to as *early amortization* or *rapid amortization provisions*, are included to safeguard the credit quality of the issue. The only way that the cash flows can be altered is by the triggering of the early amortization provision. When early amortization occurs, the credit card tranches are retired sequentially (i.e., first the AAA bond, then the AA rated bond, and so on).

There are three different amortization structures that have been used in credit card receivable-backed security structures: (1) passthrough structure, (2) controlled-amortization structure, and (3) bullet-payment structure. The latter two are more common than the first structure. One source reports that 80% of the deals are bullet structures and the balance are controlled amortization structures.[4]

In a *passthrough structure*, the principal cash flows from the credit card accounts are paid to the security holders on a pro rata basis. In a *controlled-amortization structure*, a scheduled principal amount is established. The scheduled principal amount is sufficiently low so that the obligation can be satisfied even under certain stress scenarios. The investor is paid the lesser of the scheduled principal amount and the pro rata amount. In a *bullet-payment structure*, the investor receives the entire amount in one distribution. Since there is no assurance that the entire amount can be paid in one lump sum, the procedure is for the trustee to place principal monthly into an account that generates sufficient interest to make periodic interest payments and accumulate the principal to be repaid. The time period over which the principal is accumulated is called the accumulation period.

---

[4] Anthony Thompson, "MBNA Tests the Waters," *ABS Market Comment* (October 19, 1998).

Portfolio Performance

There are several concepts that must be understood in order to assess the performance of the portfolio of receivables and the ability of the issuer to meet its interest obligation and repay principal as scheduled.

We begin with the concept of *gross portfolio yield*. This yield includes finance charges collected and fees. Some issuers include interchange in the computation of portfolio yield. *Charge-offs* represent the accounts charged off as uncollectible. *Net portfolio yield* is equal to gross portfolio yield minus charge-offs. *Delinquencies* are the percentage of receivable that are past due a specified number of months.

The *monthly payment rate* (MPR) expresses the monthly payment (which includes finance charges, fees, and any principal repayment) of a credit card receivable portfolio as a percentage of debt outstanding in the previous month. For example, suppose a $500 million credit card receivable portfolio in January realized $50 million of payments in February. The MPR would then be 10% ($50 million divided by $500 million).

MPR is an important indicator for two reasons. With a low level of MPR, extension risk with respect to the principal payments may increase. Also low MPR, indicating low cash flows to satisfy principal payments, may trigger early amortization of the principal.

Credit Enhancement

Credit enhancement mechanisms for credit card receivable-backed deals have evolved over time. In the earliest credit card transactions, a AAA rating was achieved by purchasing a letter of credit (most often from a highly rated foreign bank). This structure was heavily dependent on the credit risk of the LOC provider, and consequently investors and issuers have moved away from these structures. The next structural enhancement was the use of the *cash collateral account* (CCA). A CCA is essentially a pool of cash which earns interest and can only be invested in A1/P1 rated money market investments. CCAs are funded by a loan from a third-party credit enhancer (usually a domestic or Yankee bank).

The third stage of structural development was the 2-tranche deal with two CCAs. The fourth phase of the market became popular around 1995. This was the further subordination of the structure by the creation of a C-piece. During this time period C-tranches were structured as bank loans rather than 144-A style bonds. These C-tranche loans were placed privately with Yankee banks.

The fifth and most current phase of structural development is the 144-A style bond tranches. This structure has been popular since mid-1996. The C-pieces, both structured as loans and 144-A bonds, are internally credit enhanced through the use of excess spread and reserve accounts.

Almost 90% of the senior tranches of credit card issues have been rated triple A. While there has been downgrading of issues because of a downgrading of third-party guarantors, publicly traded credit card issues have not been down-graded due to portfolio performance.[5]

CLOSED-END HOME EQUITY LOAN-BACKED SECURITIES

A *home equity loan* (HEL) is a loan backed by residential property. At one time, the loan was typically a second lien on property that has already been pledged to secure a first lien. In some cases, the lien may be a third lien. In recent years, the character of a home equity loan has changed. Today, a home equity loan is often a first lien on property where the borrower has an impaired credit history so that the loan cannot qualify as a conforming loan for Ginnie Mae, Fannie Mae, or Freddie Mac. Typically, the borrower uses a home equity loan to consolidate consumer debt using the current home as collateral rather than to obtain funds to purchase a new home.

Home equity loans can be either open end or closed end. An open-end home equity loan is discussed in the next section. A closed-end HEL is structured the same way as a fully amortizing residential mortgage loan. That is, it has a fixed maturity and the payments are structured to fully amortize the loan by the maturity date. There are both fixed-rate and variable-rate closed-end HELs. Typically, variable-rate loans have a reference rate of 6-month LIBOR and have periodic caps and lifetime caps, just as the adjustable-rate mortgages discussed in Chapter 7. The cash flow of a pool of closed-end HELs is comprised of interest, regularly scheduled principal repayments, and prepayments, just as with mortgage-backed securities. Thus, it is necessary to have a prepayment model and a default model to forecast cash flows. The prepayment speed is measured in terms of a conditional prepayment rate (CPR).

Borrowers are segmented into four general credit quality groups, A, B, C, and D. There is no standard industrywide criteria for classifying a borrower.

Cash Flow

The monthly cash flow for a security backed by closed-end HELs is the same as for mortgage-backed securities. That is, the cash flow consists of (1) net interest, (2) regularly scheduled principal payments, and (3) prepayments. The uncertainty about the cash flow arises from prepayments.

There are differences in the prepayment behavior for home equity loans and traditional residential mortgage loans. In general it is expected that prepayments due to refinancings would be less important for HELs than for traditional residential mortgage loans because typically the average loan size is less for HELs. In general it is thought that interest rates must fall considerably more for HELs than for traditional residential mortgage loans in order for a borrower to benefit from refinancing.

Wall Street firms involved in the underwriting and market making of home equity loan-backed securities have developed prepayment models for these

---

[5] Thompson, "MBNA Tests the Waters."

loans. Several firms have found that the key difference between the prepayment behavior of HELs and traditional residential mortgages is the important role played by the credit characteristics of the borrower.

Studies by several Wall Street firms strongly suggest that borrower credit quality is the most important determinant of prepayments.[6] Specifically, the lower credit quality of the borrowers, the less likely they are to refinance as interest rates decline.

Borrower characteristics must be kept in mind when trying to assess prepayments for a particular deal. In the prospectus of an offering, a base case prepayment assumption is made — the initial speed and the amount of time until the collateral is expected to season. Thus, the prepayment benchmark is issue specific and is called the *prospectus prepayment curve* or PPC.

Payment Structure

As with nonagency mortgage-backed securities discussed in the previous chapter, there are passthrough and paythrough home equity loan-backed structures. Typically, home equity loan-backed securities are securitized by both closed-end fixed-rate and adjustable-rate (or variable-rate) HELs. The securities backed by the latter are called *HEL floaters* and most are backed by non-prime HELs. The reference rate of the underlying loans is typically 6-month LIBOR. The cash flow of these loans is affected by periodic and lifetime caps on the loan rate.

To increase the attractiveness of home equity loan-backed securities to investors, the securities typically have been created in which the reference rate is 1-month LIBOR. Because of (1) the mismatch between the reference rate on the underlying loans and that of the HEL floater and (2) the periodic and lifetime caps of the underlying loans, there is a cap on the coupon rate for the HEL floater. Unlike a typical floater, which has a cap that is fixed throughout the security's life, the effective periodic and lifetime cap of a HEL floater is variable. The effective cap, referred to as the *available funds cap*, will depend on the amount of funds generated by the net coupon on the principal, less any fees.

Let's look at one issue, Advanta Mortgage Loan Trust 1995-2 issued in June 1995. At the offering, this issue had approximately $122 million closed-end HELs. There were 1,192 HELs, 727 fixed-rate loans and 465 variable-rate loans. There were five classes (A-1, A-2, A-3, A-4, and A-5) and a residual. The five classes are summarized below:

Class	Par amount ($)	Passthrough coupon rate (%)
A-1	9,229,000	7.30
A-2	30,330,000	6.60
A-3	16,455,000	6.85
A-4	9,081,000	floating rate
A-5	56,917,000	floating rate

As explained below, class A-5 had two sub-classes, A-5-I and A-5-II.

---

[6] Dale Westhoff and Mark Feldman, "Prepayment Modeling and Valuation of Home Equity Loan Securities," Chapter 16 in Frank J. Fabozzi, Chuck Ramsey, Frank Ramirez, and Michael Marz (eds.), *The Handbook of Nonagency Mortgage-Backed Securities* (New Hope, PA: Frank J. Fabozzi Associates, 1997).

The collateral is divided into group I and group II. The 727 fixed-rate loans are included in group I and support Classes A-1, A-2, A-3, and A-4. The 465 variable-rate loans are in group II and support Class A-5-I and A-5-II certificates. All classes receive monthly principal and interest (based on the passthrough coupon rate).

The initial investors in the A-5 floating-rate certificates were given a choice between two sub-classes that offered different floating rates. Sub-class A-5-I has a passthrough coupon rate equal to the lesser of (1) 12% and (2) 1-month LIBOR plus 32 basis points with a cap of 12%. Sub-class A-5-II has a passthrough coupon rate equal to the lesser of (1) the interest rate for sub-class A-5-I and (2) the group II available funds cap. The available funds cap, also called the net funds cap, is the maximum rate payable on the outstanding Class A-5 certificates. Principal balance is based on the interest due on the variable-rate loans net of fees and minus 50 basis points.

The Class A-4 certificate also has a floating rate. The rate is 7.4% subject to the net funds cap for group I. This is the rate that is paid until the outstanding aggregate loan balances in the trust have declined to 10% or less. At that time, Class A-4 will accrue interest on a payment date that depends on the average net loan rate minus 50 basis points and the net funds cap rate for group I.

Credit Enhancement

All forms of credit enhancement described earlier in this chapter and in the previous chapter have been used for home equity loan-backed securities.

OPEN-END HOME EQUITY LOAN-BACKED SECURITIES

With an open-end home equity loan (HELOC) the homeowner is given a credit line and can write checks or use a credit card for up to the amount of the credit line. The amount of the credit line depends on the amount of the equity the borrower has in the property.

The revolving period for a HELOC is the period during which the borrower can take down all or part of the line of credit. The revolving period can run from 10 to 15 years. At the end of the revolving period, the HELOC can specify either a balloon payment or an amortization schedule (of up to 10 years). Almost all HELOCs are floating-rate loans, with the interest rate paid by about 75% of HELOC borrowers resets monthly to the prime rate as reported in *The Wall Street Journal* plus a spread.[7]

The securities created in HELOC deals are floating-rate tranches. While the underlying loans are priced based on a spread over the prime rate, the securities created are based on a spread over 1-month LIBOR.

---

[7] Richard F. DeMong and John H. Lindgren, *1998 Home Equity Loan Study*, Consumer Bankers Association, 1998.

Because HELOCs are for revolving lines, the deal structures are quite different for HELOCs and closed-end HELs. As with other ABS involving revolving credit lines such as credit card deals, there is a revolving period, an amortization period, and a rapid amortization period.

STUDENT LOAN-BACKED SECURITIES

Student loans are made to cover college cost (undergraduate, graduate, and professional programs such as medical school and law school) and tuition for a wide range of vocational and trade schools. Securities backed by student loans, popularly referred to as SLABS (student loan asset-backed securities), have similar structural features as the other ABS products we discussed above.

The student loans that have been most commonly securitized are those that are made under the Federal Family Education Loan Program (FFELP). Under this program, the government makes loans to students via private lenders. The decision by private lenders to extend a loan to a student is not based on the applicant's ability to repay the loan. If a default of a loan occurs and the loan has been properly serviced, then the government will guarantee up to 98% of the principal plus accrued interest.[8] The federal government has a direct lending program — the Federal Direct Student Loan Program (FDSLP) — in which the Department of Education (DOE) makes loans directly to students; however, these loans are retained by the DOE and not securitized. Loans that are not part of a government guarantee program are called *alternative loans*. These loans are basically consumer loans and the lender's decision to extend an alternative loan will be based on the ability of the applicant to repay the loan. Alternative loans have been securitized.

As Congress did with the creation of Fannie Mae and Freddie Mac to provide liquidity in the mortgage market by allowing these entities to buy mortgage loans in the secondary market, it created the Student Loan Marketing Association ("Sallie Mae") as a government-sponsored enterprise to purchase student loans in the secondary market and to securitize pools of student loans. Its first issuance was in 1995. Sallie Mae is now the major issuer of SLABS and its issues are viewed as the benchmark issues. Other entities that issue SLABS are traditional corporate entities (e.g., the Money Store and PNC Bank) and non-profit organizations (Michigan Higher Education Loan Authority and the California Educational Facilities Authority). The SLABS of the latter are typically issued as tax-exempt securities and therefore trade in the municipal market.

Cash Flow

Let's first look at the cash flow for the student loans themselves. There are different types of student loans under the FFELP, including subsidized and unsubsidized Stafford loans, Parental Loans for Undergraduate Students (PLUS), and

---

[8] Actually, depending on the origination date, the guarantee can be up to 100%.

Supplemental Loans to Students (SLS). These loans involve three periods with respect to the borrower's payments — deferment period, grace period, and loan repayment period. Typically, student loans work as follows. While a student is in school, no payments are made by the student on the loan. This is the *deferment period*. Upon leaving school, the student is extended a grace period of usually six months when no payments on the loan need to be made. After this period, payments are made on the loan by the borrower.

Prior to July 1, 1998, the reference rate for student loans originated under the FFELP program was the 3-month Treasury bill rate plus a margin of either 250 basis points (during the deferment and grace periods) or 310 basis points (during the repayment period). Since July 1, 1998, the Higher Education Act changed the reference rate to the 10-year Treasury note. The interest rate is the 10-year Treasury note plus 100 basis points. The spread over the reference rate varies with the cycle period for the loan.

As with other ABS, the reference rate need not be the same as that of the underlying loans. For investors in non-Sallie Mae issues, there is exposure to collateral performance due to basis risk discussed earlier in this chapter. Typically, non-Sallie Mae issues have been LIBOR-based floaters. For Sallie Mae issues, there is an indirect government guarantee. Sallie Mae has typically issued SLABS indexed to the 3-month Treasury bill rate. However, late in the second quarter of 1999, Sallie Mae issued bonds in which the buyer of the 2-year tranche had the choice of receiving either LIBOR plus 8 basis points or the 3-month Treasury bill rate plus 87 basis points. There are available funds caps in ABS deals because of the different reference rates.

Prepayments typically occur due to defaults or loan consolidation. Even if there is no loss of principal faced by the investor when defaults occur, the investor is still exposed to contraction risk. This is the risk that the investor must reinvest the proceeds at a lower spread and in the case of a bond purchased at a premium, the premium will be lost. Studies have shown student loan prepayments are insensitive to the level of interest rates. Consolidations of loans occur when the students who have loans over several years combine them into a single loan. The proceeds from the consolidation are distributed to the original lender and, in turn, distributed to the bondholders.

SBA LOAN-BACKED SECURITIES

The Small Business Administration (SBA) is an agency of the federal government empowered to guarantee loans made by approved SBA lenders to qualified borrowers. The loans are backed by the full faith and credit of the U.S. government. Most SBA loans are variable-rate loans where the reference rate is the prime rate. The rate on the loan is either reset monthly on the first of the month or quarterly on the first of January, April, July, and October. SBA regulations specify the maximum coupon allowable in the secondary market. As of this writing, the maximum coupon rate is equal to the prime rate plus 1.625%. SBA loans typically do not have caps. Newly originated loans have maturities between 5 and 25 years.

The Small Business Secondary Market Improvement Act passed in 1984 permitted the pooling of SBA loans. When pooled, the underlying loans must have similar terms and features. The maturities typically used for pooling loans are 7, 10, 15, 20, and 25 years. Loans without caps are not pooled with loans that have caps.

Cash Flow

Most variable-rate SBA make monthly payments consisting of interest and principal repayment. The amount of the monthly payment for an individual loan is determined as follows. Given the coupon formula of the prime rate plus the loan's margin, the interest rate is determined. Given the interest rate, a level payment amortization schedule is determined. It is this level payment that is paid for the months until the coupon rate is reset. When variable-rate SBA loans are pooled, the amortization schedule is based on the net pool rate and the rate is recomputed either every month or every quarter.

Prepayments for SBA-backed securities are measured in terms of CPR. Voluntary prepayments can be made by the borrower without any penalty. There are several factors contributing to the prepayment speed of a pool of SBA loans. A factor affecting prepayments is the maturity date of the loan. It has been found that the fastest speeds on SBA loans and pools occur for shorter maturities.[9] The purpose of the loan also affects prepayments. There are loans for working capital purposes and loans to finance real estate construction or acquisition. It has been observed that SBA pools with maturities of 10 years or less made for working capital purposes tend to prepay at the fastest speed. In contrast, loans backed by real estate that have long maturities tend to prepay at a slow speed. All other factors constant, pools that have capped loans tend to prepay more slowly than pools of uncapped loans.

COLLATERALIZED BOND OBLIGATIONS

A *collateralized bond obligation* (CBO) is an asset-backed security backed by a diversified pool of one or more of the following types of debt obligations:

1. non-investment grade (i.e., high yield) corporate bonds
2. emerging market bonds
3. bank loans to corporate entities

When an asset-backed security has only bank loans, it is referred to as a *collateralized loan obligation* (CLO).

---

[9] Donna Faulk, "SBA Loan-Backed Securities," Chapter 10 in *Asset-Backed Securities.*

There is an asset manager responsible for managing the portfolio. There are restrictions imposed by the rating agencies as to what the asset manager may do and certain tests that must be satisfied for the tranches in the CBO to maintain their original credit rating.

The typical structure of a CBO is as follows. There is (1) a senior tranche, (2) different layers of subordinated or junior debt tranches, and (3) an equity tranche. The senior tranche is between 70% and 80% of the deal and receives a floating-rate payment — hence our interest in this ABS type for this book. The junior tranches, in contrast, receive a fixed coupon rate. So, the collateral from the diversified pool of debt obligations is going to pay the tranche holders, the majority of whom (i.e., the senior tranche investors) are being paid a floating rate. While the bank loans are typically floating rate, the other debt obligations in which the asset manager invests are typically fixed rate. Now this presents a problem — paying the majority of the tranche investors a floating rate when the majority of the debt obligations pay a fixed rate.

Because of the mismatch between the nature of the cash flows of the debt obligations in which the asset manager invests and the floating-rate liability due to the senior tranche, the asset manager uses an interest rate swap. A rating agency will require the use of swaps to eliminate this mismatch.

The junior tranches receive a fixed rate. The rate is a spread over a comparable maturity Treasury. The amount of the spread varies with market conditions and the credit rating of a junior tranche. For example, the fixed rate for a junior tranche might be the Treasury rate plus 185 basis points.

The equity tranche receives any remaining interest that is received from' the collateral but not paid to the debt tranches (i.e., the senior and junior tranches).

Phases of a CBO

There are three phases in the life of a CBO. The first phase is the *startup phase* or *ramp phase*. In this phase, which is one or two months, the asset manager assembles the portfolio with the proceeds received from the sale of the CBO tranches. Once the portfolio is assembled, the manager monitors the portfolio and is responsible for reinvesting any principal repayments due to any calls or proceeds received from any defaulted issues. This phase is called the *reinvestment phase*. This phase varies from 3 year to 5 years. Finally, principal payments to the senior and junior tranches must be made over the balance of the CBO's life. This phase is called the *pay down phase*.

Activities of the Asset Manager

The CBO structure described above is the type that is issued today. The CBO is structured to generate cash flow for the senior and junior tranches *without* the active trading of bonds. Older CBO deals were structured so that the cash flow for the structure was based on the active trading of bonds. The cash flow needed to pay principal and interest to the senior and junior tranches had to be generated from capital gains as well as coupon interest. With the difficulties encountered in the high-yield bond sector in the late 1980s and early 1990s, CBOs structured in this way lost their appeal and are no longer issued. Only those CBOs with the type of structure described above are now issued.

Because the cash flows from the structure are designed to accomplish the objective for each tranche, restrictions are imposed on the asset managers. The asset manager is not free to buy and sell bonds. The conditions for disposing of issues held are specified. Also, in assembling the portfolio during the startup phase, the asset manager must meet certain requirements set forth by the rating agency or agencies that rate the deal. These requirements have to do with constructing a diversified portfolio and minimum ratings for the issues acquired. The asset manager during the reinvestment and pay down phases must monitor the collateral to ensure that certain tests or covenants are being met.

Chapter 10

Analysis of MBS and ABS Floaters

In Chapter 4 we explained how floating-rate structures with embedded options can be valued using the binomial model. We did not address the valuation of floating-rate mortgage-backed securities and asset-backed securities. In this chapter we discuss the technique for valuing these securities, Monte Carlo simulation.

We begin the current chapter by reviewing static cash flow yield analysis and the limitations of the spread measure that is a result of that analysis — the nominal spread. We then look at a better spread measure called the zero-volatility spread, but point out its limitation as a measure of relative value. Finally, we look at the Monte Carlo simulation model. A byproduct of this model is the option-adjusted spread (OAS). This measure is superior to both the nominal spread and the zero-volatility spread because it takes into account how cash flows may change when interest rates change. That is, it recognizes the borrower's prepayment option and how it affects prepayments when interest rates change in the future. While the option-adjusted spread is far superior to the two other spread measures, it is also based on assumptions that must be understood by an investor and the sensitivity of the security's value and option-adjusted spread to changes in those assumptions must be investigated. We'll see how this is done.

STATIC CASH FLOW YIELD ANALYSIS

The yield on any financial instrument is the discount rate that makes the present value of the expected cash flow equal to its market price plus accrued interest. For MBS and ABS, the yield calculated in this manner is called a *cash flow yield*. The problem in calculating the cash flow yield of an MBS or ABS is that because of prepayments the cash flow is unknown. Consequently, to determine a cash flow yield, some assumption about the prepayment rate must be made.

The cash flow for a mortgage-backed security is typically monthly. The convention is to compare the yield on a mortgage-backed security to that of a Treasury coupon security by calculating the MBS's *bond-equivalent yield*. The bond-equivalent yield for a Treasury coupon security is found by doubling the semiannual yield. However, it is incorrect to do this for a mortgage-backed security because the investor has the opportunity to generate greater interest by reinvesting the more frequent cash flows. The market practice is to calculate a yield so as to make it comparable to the yield to maturity on a bond-equivalent yield basis. The formula for annualizing the monthly cash flow yield for a mortgage-backed security and an asset-backed security is as follows:

Bond-equivalent yield = $2[(1 + i_M)^6 - 1]$

where i_M is the monthly interest rate that will equate the present value of the projected monthly cash flow equal to the market price (plus accrued interest) of the security.

All yield measures suffer from problems that limit their use in assessing a security's potential return. The yield to maturity has two major shortcomings as a measure of a bond's potential return. To realize the stated yield to maturity, the investor must: (1) reinvest the coupon payments at a rate equal to the yield to maturity, and (2) hold the bond to the maturity date. These shortcomings are equally applicable to the cash flow yield measure: (1) the projected cash flows are assumed to be reinvested at the cash flow yield and (2) the security is assumed to be held until the final payout based on some prepayment assumption. Moreover, an additional assumption is that the projected cash flow is actually realized. If the prepayment experience is different from the prepayment rate assumed, the cash flow yield will not be realized.

Given the computed cash flow yield and the average life for a security based on some prepayment assumption, the next step is to compare the yield to the yield for a comparable Treasury security. "Comparable" is typically defined as a Treasury security with the same maturity as the average life of the security. The difference between the cash flow yield and the yield on a comparable Treasury security is called the *nominal spread.*

Unfortunately, it is the nominal spread that some investors will use as a measure of relative value. However, this spread masks the fact that a portion of the nominal spread is compensation for accepting prepayment risk. Instead of nominal spread, investors need a measure that indicates the potential compensation after adjusting for prepayment risk. This measure is the option-adjusted spread that was introduced in Chapter 4. Before discussing this measure, we describe another spread measure commonly quoted for mortgage-backed and asset-backed securities called the *zero-volatility spread.*

ZERO-VOLATILITY SPREAD

The proper procedure to compare an MBS or ABS to a Treasury is to compare it to a portfolio of Treasury securities that have the same cash flow. The value of the MBS or ABS is then equal to the present value of all of the cash flows. The security's value, assuming the cash flows are default-free, will equal the present value of the replicating portfolio of Treasury securities. In turn, these cash flows are valued using the appropriate Treasury spot rates.

The zero-volatility spread is a measure of the spread that the investor would realize over the entire Treasury spot rate curve if the security is held to maturity. It is not a spread off one point on the Treasury yield curve, as is the nominal spread. The zero-volatility spread (also called the *Z-spread* and the *static spread*) is the spread that will make the present value of the cash flows from the security when discounted at the Treasury spot rate plus the spread equal to the price of the security. A trial-and-error procedure (or search algorithm) is required to determine the zero-volatility spread.

In general, the shorter the average life of the MBS or ABS, the less the zero-volatility spread will differ from the nominal spread. The magnitude of the difference between the nominal spread and the zero-volatility spread also depends on the shape of the yield curve. The steeper (flatter) the yield curve, the greater (smaller) the difference.

MONTE CARLO SIMULATION FOR VALUING MBS FLOATERS[1]

In fixed income valuation modeling, there are two methodologies commonly used to value securities with embedded options — the binomial model and the Monte Carlo model. The latter model involves simulating a sufficiently large number of potential interest rate paths in order to assess the value of a security along these different paths. This model is the most flexible of the two valuation methodologies for valuing interest rate sensitive instruments where the history of interest rates is important. Mortgage-backed securities are commonly valued using this model. As explained in Chapter 4, a byproduct of a valuation model is the OAS.

The binomial model is used to value callable agency debentures and corporate bonds. This valuation model accommodates securities in which the decision to exercise a call option is not dependent on how interest rates evolved over time. That is, the decision of an issuer to call a bond will depend on the level of the rate at which the issue can be refunded relative to the issue's coupon rate, and not the path interest rates took to get to that rate. In contrast, there are fixed income securities for which the periodic cash flows are *interest rate path-dependent*. This means that the cash flow received in one period is determined not only by the current interest rate level, but also by the path that interest rates took to get to the current level.

In the case of passthrough securities, prepayments are interest rate path-dependent because this month's prepayment rate depends on whether there have been prior opportunities to refinance since the underlying mortgages were originated — a phenomenon referred to as *prepayment burnout*. Pools of passthroughs are used as collateral for the creation of CMOs. Consequently, there are typically two sources of path dependency in a CMO tranche's cash flows. First, the collateral prepayments are path-dependent as discussed above. Second, the cash flows

---

[1] Portions of the material in this section and the one to follow are adapted from Frank J. Fabozzi, Scott F. Richard, and David S. Horowitz, "Valuation of CMOs," Chapter 6 in Frank J. Fabozzi (ed.), *Advances in the Valuation and Management of Mortgage-Backed Securities* (New Hope, PA: Frank J. Fabozzi Associates, 1998).

to be received in the current month by a CMO tranche depend on the outstanding balances of the other tranches in the deal. Thus, we need the history of prepayments to calculate these balances.

In the case of ARMs, there is another element of path dependency caused by the periodic cap and floor for an ARM. That is, suppose that the coupon rate at a reset date is 6% and there is a 2% periodic cap. Also assume that the cap resets every year and the 6% was set for year 1. Then year 2's coupon rate is dependent on year 1's coupon rate. Specifically, for the 12 months in year 2, the coupon rate cannot exceed 8% (the 6% in year 1 plus the 2% periodic cap). Moreover, the coupon rate depends on the life time cap.

Monte Carlo Methodology

Conceptually, the valuation of passthroughs using the Monte Carlo model is simple. In practice, however, it is very complex. The simulation involves generating a set of cash flows based on simulated future mortgage refinancing rates, which in turn imply simulated prepayment rates.

Valuation modeling for agency CMOs is similar to valuation modeling for passthroughs, although the difficulties are amplified because the issuer has sliced and diced both the prepayment risk and the interest rate risk into tranches. The sensitivity of the passthroughs comprising the collateral to these two risks is not transmitted equally to every tranche. Some of the tranches wind up more sensitive to prepayment risk and interest rate risk than the collateral, while some of them are much less sensitive.

The objective is to figure out how the value of the collateral gets transmitted to the CMO tranches. More specifically, the objective is to find out where the value goes and where the risk goes so that one can identify the tranches with low risk and high value: the tranches an investor wants to consider for purchase. The good news is that this combination usually exists in every deal. The bad news is that in every deal there are usually tranches with low value and high risk that managers want to avoid purchasing.

A valuation model for nonagency CMOs requires another input, a default model. A default model is used to determine monthly defaults on each interest rate path and then to adjust the cash flows accordingly.

Generating Interest Rate Paths

The typical model that Wall Street firms and commercial vendors use to generate these random interest rate paths takes as inputs today's term structure of interest rates and a volatility assumption. The term structure of interest rates is the theoretical spot rate (or zero coupon) curve implied by today's prices of Treasury securities. The simulations should be calibrated so that the average simulated price of a zero-coupon Treasury bond equals today's actual price.

Some models use the on-the-run Treasury issues in the calibration process. Other dealers, such as Lehman Brothers, use off-the-run Treasury issues.

The argument for using off-the-run Treasury issues is that the price/yield of on-the-run Treasury issues will not reflect their true economic value because the market price reflects their value for financing purposes (i.e., an issue may be on special in the repo market). Some dealers and vendors of analytical systems use the LIBOR curve instead of the Treasury curve — or give the user a choice to use the LIBOR curve. The reason is that some investors are interested in spreads that they can earn relative to their funding costs and LIBOR for many investors is a better proxy for that cost than Treasury rates.

Each model has its own model of the evolution of future interest rates and its own volatility assumptions. Typically, there are no significant differences in the interest rate models of dealer firms and vendors, although their volatility assumptions can be significantly different.

The volatility assumption determines the dispersion of future interest rates in the simulation. Today, many vendors do not use one volatility number for the yield of all maturities of the yield curve. Instead, they use either a short/long yield volatility or a term structure of yield volatility. A short/long yield volatility means that volatility is specified for maturities up to a certain number of years (short yield volatility) and a different yield volatility for greater maturities (long yield volatility). The short yield volatility is assumed to be greater than the long yield volatility. A term structure of yield volatilities means that a yield volatility is assumed for each maturity.

The random paths of interest rates should be generated from an arbitrage-free model of the future term structure of interest rates. By arbitrage-free it is meant that the model replicates today's term structure of interest rates, an input of the model, and that for all future dates there is no possible arbitrage within the model.

The simulation works by generating many scenarios of future interest rate paths. In each month of the scenario (i.e., path), a monthly interest rate and a mortgage refinancing rate are generated. The monthly interest rates are used to discount the projected cash flows in the scenario. The mortgage refinancing rate is needed to determine the cash flows because it represents the opportunity cost the mortgagor is facing at that time.

If the refinancing rates are high relative to the mortgagor's original coupon rate (i.e., the rate on the mortgagor's loan), the mortgagor will have less incentive to refinance, or even a positive disincentive (i.e., the homeowner will avoid moving in order to avoid refinancing). If the refinancing rate is low relative to the mortgagor's original coupon rate, the mortgagor has an incentive to refinance.

Prepayments are projected by feeding the refinancing rate and loan characteristics into a prepayment model. Given the projected prepayments, the cash flows along an interest rate path can be determined.

To make this process more concrete, consider a newly issued mortgage passthrough security with a maturity of 360 months. Exhibit 1 shows N simulated interest rate path scenarios. Each scenario consists of a path of 360 simulated 1-month future interest rates. (The number of paths generated is based on a well known principle in simulation which will be discussed later.) So, our first assumption that we make to get Exhibit 1 is the volatility of interest rates.

Exhibit 2 shows the paths of simulated mortgage refinancing rates corresponding to the scenarios shown in Exhibit 1. In going from Exhibit 1 to Exhibit 2 an assumption must be made about the relationship between the Treasury rates and refinancing rates. The assumption is that there is a constant spread relationship between the mortgage-refinancing rate and the 10-year Treasury yield.

Given the mortgage refinancing rates, the cash flows on each interest rate path can be generated. This requires a prepayment model. So our next assumption is that the prepayment model used to generate prepayments, and therefore the cash flows, is correct. The resulting cash flows are depicted in Exhibit 3.

Exhibit 1: Simulated Paths of 1-Month Future Interest Rates

	Interest Rate Path Number						
Month	1	2	3	...	n	...	N
1	$f_1(1)$	$f_1(2)$	$f_1(3)$	...	$f_1(n)$	...	$f_1(N)$
2	$f_2(1)$	$f_2(2)$	$f_2(3)$	...	$f_2(n)$	...	$f_2(N)$
3	$f_3(1)$	$f_3(2)$	$f_3(3)$	...	$f_3(n)$	...	$f_3(N)$
...	...	...	...	...	...	...	...
t	$f_t(1)$	$f_t(2)$	$f_t(3)$	...	$f_t(n)$	...	$f_t(N)$
...	...	...	...	...	...	...	...
358	$f_{358}(1)$	$f_{358}(2)$	$f_{358}(3)$	...	$f_{358}(n)$	...	$f_{358}(N)$
359	$f_{359}(1)$	$f_{359}(2)$	$f_{359}(3)$	...	$f_{359}(n)$	...	$f_{359}(N)$
360	$f_{360}(1)$	$f_{360}(2)$	$f_{360}(3)$	...	$f_{360}(n)$	...	$f_{360}(N)$

Notation:

$f_t(n)$ = 1-month future interest rate for month t on path n
N = total number of interest rate paths

Exhibit 2: Simulated Paths of Mortgage Refinancing Rates

	Interest Rate Path Number						
Month	1	2	3	...	n	...	N
1	$r_1(1)$	$r_1(2)$	$r_1(3)$	...	$r_1(n)$	...	$r_1(N)$
2	$r_2(1)$	$r_2(2)$	$r_2(3)$	...	$r_2(n)$	...	$r_2(N)$
3	$r_3(1)$	$r_3(2)$	$r_3(3)$	...	$r_3(n)$	...	$r_3(N)$
...	...	...	...	...	...	...	...
t	$r_t(1)$	$r_t(2)$	$r_t(3)$	...	$r_t(n)$	...	$r_t(N)$
...	...	...	...	...	...	...	...
358	$r_{358}(1)$	$r_{358}(2)$	$r_{358}(3)$	...	$r_{358}(n)$	...	$r_{358}(N)$
359	$r_{359}(1)$	$r_{359}(2)$	$r_{359}(3)$	...	$r_{359}(n)$	...	$r_{359}(N)$
360	$r_{360}(1)$	$r_{360}(2)$	$r_{360}(3)$	...	$r_{360}(n)$	...	$r_{360}(N)$

Notation:

$r_t(n)$ = mortgage refinancing rate for month t on path n
N = total number of interest rate paths

Exhibit 3: Simulated Cash Flows on Each of the Interest Rate Paths

Month	Interest Rate Path Number						
	1	2	3	...	n	...	N
1	$C_1(1)$	$C_1(2)$	$C_1(3)$	...	$C_1(n)$	...	$C_1(N)$
2	$C_2(1)$	$C_2(2)$	$C_2(3)$	...	$C_2(n)$	...	$C_2(N)$
3	$C_3(1)$	$C_3(2)$	$C_3(3)$	...	$C_3(n)$	...	$C_3(N)$
...	...	...	...	...	...	...	...
t	$C_t(1)$	$C_t(2)$	$C_t(3)$	...	$C_t(n)$	...	$C_t(N)$
...	...	...	...	...	...	...	...
358	$C_{358}(1)$	$C_{358}(2)$	$C_{358}(3)$	...	$C_{358}(n)$	...	$C_{358}(N)$
359	$C_{359}(1)$	$C_{359}(2)$	$C_{359}(3)$	...	$C_{359}(n)$	...	$C_{359}(N)$
360	$C_{360}(1)$	$C_{360}(2)$	$C_{360}(3)$	...	$C_{360}(n)$	...	$C_{360}(N)$

Notation:

$C_t(n)$ = cash flow for month t on path n

N = total number of interest rate paths

Calculating the Present Value for a Scenario Interest Rate Path

Given the cash flows on an interest rate path, the path's present value can be calculated. The discount rate for determining the present value is the simulated spot rate for each month on the interest rate path plus an appropriate spread. The spot rate on a path can be determined from the simulated future monthly rates. The relationship that holds between the simulated spot rate for month T on path n and the simulated future 1-month rates is:

$$z_T(n) = \{[1 + f_1(n)][1 + f_2(n)]...[1 + f_T(n)]\}^{1/T} - 1$$

where

$z_T(n)$ = simulated spot rate for month T on path n

$f_j(n)$ = simulated future 1-month rate for month j on path n

Consequently, the interest rate path for the simulated future 1-month rates can be converted to the interest rate path for the simulated monthly spot rates as shown in Exhibit 4. Therefore, the present value of the cash flows for month T on interest rate path n discounted at the simulated spot rate for month T plus some spread is:

$$PV[C_T(n)] = \frac{C_T(n)}{[1 + z_T(n) + K]^T}$$

where

$PV[C_T(n)]$ = present value of cash flows for month T on path n

$C_T(n)$ = cash flow for month T on path n

$z_T(n)$ = spot rate for month T on path n

K = spread

Exhibit 4: Simulated Paths of Monthly Spot Rates

Month	Interest Rate Path Number						
	1	2	3	...	n	...	N
1	$z_1(1)$	$z_1(2)$	$z_1(3)$	...	$z_1(n)$	...	$z_1(N)$
2	$z_2(1)$	$z_2(2)$	$z_2(3)$	...	$z_2(n)$	...	$z_2(N)$
3	$z_3(1)$	$z_3(2)$	$z_3(3)$	...	$z_3(n)$	...	$z_3(N)$
...	...	...	...	...	...	...	...
t	$z_t(1)$	$z_t(2)$	$z_t(3)$	...	$z_t(n)$	...	$z_t(N)$
...	...	...	...	...	...	...	...
358	$z_{358}(1)$	$z_{358}(2)$	$z_{358}(3)$	...	$z_{358}(n)$	...	$z_{358}(N)$
359	$z_{359}(1)$	$z_{359}(2)$	$z_{359}(3)$	...	$z_{359}(n)$	...	$z_{359}(N)$
360	$z_{360}(1)$	$z_{360}(2)$	$z_{360}(3)$	...	$z_{360}(n)$	...	$z_{360}(N)$

Notation:

$z_t(n)$ = spot rate for month t on path n

N = total number of interest rate paths

The present value for path n is the sum of the present value of the cash flows for each month on path n. That is,

$$PV[\text{Path}(n)] = PV[C_1(n)] + PV[C_2(n)] + ... + PV[C_{360}(n)]$$

where $PV[\text{Path}(n)]$ is the present value of interest rate path n.

Determining the Theoretical Value

The present value of a given interest rate path can be thought of as the theoretical value of a passthrough if that path was actually realized. The theoretical value of the passthrough can be determined by calculating the average of the theoretical values of all the interest rate paths. That is, the theoretical value is equal to

$$\text{Theoretical value} = \frac{PV[\text{Path}(1)] + PV[\text{Path}(2)] + ... + PV[\text{Path}(N)]}{N}$$

where N is the number of interest rate paths.

This procedure for valuing a passthrough is also followed for a CMO tranche. The cash flow for each month on each interest rate path is found according to the principal repayment and interest distribution rules of the deal. In order to do this for a CMO, a structuring model is needed.

Option-Adjusted Spread

In the Monte Carlo model, the *option-adjusted spread* (OAS) is the spread K that when added to all the spot rates on all interest rate paths will make the average present value of the paths equal to the observed market price (plus accrued interest). Mathematically, OAS is the spread that will satisfy the following condition:

$$\text{Market price} = \frac{\text{PV}[\text{Path}(1)] + \text{PV}[\text{Path}(2)] + \ldots + \text{PV}[\text{Path}(N)]}{N}$$

where N is the number of interest rate paths.

The procedure for determining the OAS is straightforward, although time consuming. The next question, then, is how to interpret the OAS. Basically, the OAS is used to reconcile value with market price. On the left-hand side of the previous equation is the market's statement: the price of a mortgage-backed security. The average present value over all the paths on the right-hand side of the equation is the model's output, which we refer to as value.

What an investor seeks to do is to buy securities where value is greater than price. By using a valuation model such as the Monte Carlo model, an investor could estimate the value of a security, which at this point would be sufficient in determining whether to buy a security. That is, the investor can say that this bond is 1 point cheap or 2 points cheap, and so on. The model does not stop here. Instead, it converts the divergence between price and value into some type of spread measure since most market participants find it more convenient to think about spreads than price differences.

The OAS was developed as a measure of the spread that can be used to convert dollar differences between value and price. But what is it a "spread" over? In describing the model above, we can see that the OAS is measuring the average spread over the Treasury spot rate curve, not the Treasury yield curve. It is an average spread since the OAS is found by averaging over the interest rate paths for the possible Treasury spot rate curves. Of course, if the LIBOR curve is used, the OAS is the spread over that curve.

This spread measure is superior to the nominal spread which gives no recognition to the prepayment risk. The OAS is "option adjusted" because the cash flows on the interest rate paths are adjusted for the option of the borrowers to prepay.

Option Cost

The implied cost of the option embedded in an MBS can be obtained by calculating the difference between the option-adjusted spread at the assumed volatility of interest rates and the zero-volatility spread. That is,

Option cost = Zero-volatility spread – Option-adjusted spread

The option cost measures the prepayment (or option) risk embedded in the MBS. Note that the cost of the option is a byproduct of the option-adjusted spread analysis and is not valued explicitly with some option pricing model.

Simulated Average Life

The average life of a mortgage-backed security is the weighted average time to receipt of principal payments (scheduled payments and projected prepayments). The average life reported in a Monte Carlo model is the average of the average lives along the interest rate paths. That is, for each interest rate path, there is an average life. The average of these average lives across paths is the average life reported by the model.

Selecting the Number of Interest Rate Paths

Let's now address the question of the number of scenario paths, N, needed to value an MBS. A typical analysis might be for 256 to 1,024 interest rate paths. The scenarios generated using the Monte Carlo model look very realistic, and furthermore reproduce today's Treasury curve. By employing this technique, one is effectively saying that Treasuries are fairly priced today and that the objective is to determine whether a security is rich or cheap relative to Treasuries.[2]

The number of interest rate paths determines how "good" the estimate is, not relative to the truth but relative to the model used. The more paths, the more average spread tends to settle down. It is a statistical sampling problem.

Most models employ some form of *variance reduction* to cut down on the number of sample paths necessary to get a good statistical sample. A variance reduction technique allows one to obtain price estimates within a tick. By this we mean that if the model is used to generate more scenarios, price estimates from the model will not change by more than a tick. So, for example, if 1,024 paths are used to obtain the estimated price for a CMO tranche, there is little additional information to be had from the model by generating more than that number of paths. (For some very sensitive CMO tranches, more paths may be needed to estimate prices within one tick.)

Several vendor firms have developed computational procedures that reduce the number of paths required but still provide the accuracy of a full Monte Carlo analysis. The procedure is to use statistical techniques to reduce the number of interest rate paths to similar sets of paths. These paths are called *representative paths*. For example, suppose that 2,000 sample paths are generated. Using a statistical technique, these 2,000 sample paths can be collapsed to, say, 16 representative paths. The security is then valued on each of these 16 representative paths. The theoretical value of the security is then the weighted average of the 16 representative paths. The weight for a path is the percentage of that representative path relative to the total sample paths.

Illustrations

Let's illustrate how the Monte Carlo model/OAS analysis can be applied to the valuation of an ARM and a floating-rate CMO.

Valuing ARMs[3]

As explained in Chapter 7, the basic structure and attributes of an adjustable-rate mortgage security (ARM) are the teaser rate, teaser period, index, margin, reset

---

[2] In other words, Treasury prices are taken as given and the Monte Carlo model is silent as to whether or not Treasuries are correctly priced.

[3] This illustration is from Frank J. Fabozzi and David Yuen, *Managing MBS Portfolios* (New Hope, PA: Frank J. Fabozzi Associates), pp. 186-188.

frequency, periodic cap, and lifetime cap. For example, a 5.5% 1-year CMT + 2.25% ARM with 2/12 caps means the security has a 5.5% net coupon for the first year. It will reset the second year coupon to the then 1-year CMT index rate plus 2.25% on the anniversary date subject to the 2% periodic cap and 12% lifetime cap constraints. Due to all these features, an ARM has other embedded options such as periodic caps and lifetime caps in addition to the normal prepayment option on a mortgage. The value of an ARM is also interest rate path dependent and it has to be valued using a Monte Carlo simulation/OAS framework.[4]

To illustrate how this framework is used to value ARMs, consider the two almost identical ARMs shown in Exhibit 5. One ARM has tight periodic and life caps and the other has higher caps. The market would obviously trade the high cap ARM at a higher price because of the better periodic and life caps. The question is how much higher; how much are the caps worth?

One simple way to approach it is to calculate the effective margin as explained in Chapter 5. The convention in the ARM market is to trade ARMs based on effective margin or BEEM (bond equivalent effective margin). This method uses the current index level to project the future coupon resets based on the periodic and life cap constraints. The future cash flows would then be discounted to obtain a bond equivalent yield and the spread above the current index level is the BEEM. Due to the tight periodic cap of 1% on the low cap ARM, the projected coupon on the next reset may not be fully indexed, therefore generating less coupon cash flows than the high cap ARM. The BEEM calculation would factor that in and price the low cap ARM at a lower price.

Exhibit 5: Two Hypothetical ARMs

	Low Cap	High Cap
Teaser Rate	5.5%	5.5%
Index	1yearCMT	1yearCMT
Net Margin	2.25%	2.25%
Gross Margin	3.0%	3.0%
Age	2 months	2 months
WAM	30 years	30 years
Reset Frequency	Annual	Annual
Periodic Cap	1%	2%
Life Cap	11%	12%
Next Reset	10 months	10 months
Stated Delay	45 days	45 days
Look Back	45 days	45 days

---

[4] In fact, option-adjusted spread was first developed to deal with ARMs by Michael Waldman and Stephen Modzelewski then at Salomon Brothers in the early 1980s. They referred to the OAS as the option-adjusted margin (OAM). See, Michael Waldman and Stephen Modzelewski, "A Framework for Evaluating Treasury-Based Adjustable Rate Mortgages," Chapter 12 in Frank J. Fabozzi (ed.) *The Handbook of Mortgage-Backed Securities* (Chicago, IL: Probus Publishing, 1985).

Exhibit 6: Summary of Analysis of Two Hypothetical ARMs

		Low Cap Based on Price Equal to	
	High Cap	BEEM of High Cap	OAS of High Cap
Price (% of Par)	99.72	99.17	98.72
BEEM (bps)	150	150	164
OAS (bps)	134	118	134
Average Life (years)	3.1	3.6	3.6
Effective Duration	1.28	2.16	2.15
Effective Convexity	−0.59	−0.69	−0.67

Values obtained using *Derivative Solutions Fixed Income System.*

For example, if we were to price both ARM securities at 1.5% BEEM, the price of the low cap ARM would be 99.17 and the price of the high cap ARM would be 99.72. However, this methodology assumes the current CMT index to be static, and ignores the optionality of the periodic and life caps due to the volatility of the CMT index, the changes in the shape of the yield curve, and the interest rate paths. In fact, the OASs obtained from a 300-path Monte Carlo simulation using those equal BEEM prices are 118 basis points versus 134 basis points on the low cap ARM and high cap ARM, respectively.

To price both ARM securities at an equal OAS (134 basis points), the price of the low cap ARM has to be lowered to 98.72, a point lower than that of the high cap ARM. In addition, the effective duration of the low cap ARM is 2.15 compared to the 1.28 duration of the high cap ARM. The results are summarized in Exhibit 6.

CMO Application

Now let's look at how to apply the Monte Carlo/OAS methodology to a CMO structure, FHLMC Series 1706. The collateral for this structure is Freddie Mac 7s. A summary of the deal is provided in Exhibit 7. A diagram of the principal allocation is given in Exhibit 8.

There are 19 classes in this structure: ten PAC bonds (including one PAC IO bond), three scheduled bonds (also called PAC IIs), two TAC support bonds, a floating-rate support bond, an inverse floating-rate support bond, and two residual bonds. The tranche of interest to us is the CMO floating-rate support tranche, PF. Recall from Chapter 8 that the role of a support tranche is to absorb the prepayment risk

The top panel of Exhibit 9 shows the base case OAS and the option cost for the collateral (i.e., the passthroughs from which the CMO deal was created) and tranche PF. The collateral OAS is 60 basis points, and the option cost is 44 basis points. The static spread of the collateral to the Treasury spot curve is 104 basis points.

The 60 basis points of OAS does not get equally distributed among the tranches. As can be seen in the top panel, tranche PF has an OAS of 17 basis points. To assess whether or not that OAS is fair, an investor must compare it to other CMO floaters with an effective duration of 1.5 years (the effective duration of the tranche PF).

Exhibit 7: Summary of Federal Home Loan Mortgage Corporation — Multiclass Mortgage Participation Certificates (Guaranteed), Series 1706

Total Issue:	$300,000,000	Original Settlement Date:	3/30/94	
Issue Date:	2/18/94	Days Delay:	30	
Structure Type:	REMIC CMO	Payment Frequency:	Monthly;	
Issuer Class:	Agency		15th day of month	
Dated Date:	3/1/94			

Tranche	Original Balance ($)	Coupon (%)	Stated Maturity	Original Issue Pricing (225% PSA Assumed) Average Life (yrs)	Expected Maturity
A (PAC Bond)	24,600,000	4.50	10/15/06	1.3	6/15/96
B (PAC Bond)	11,100,000	5.00	9/15/09	2.5	1/15/97
C (PAC Bond)	25,500,000	5.25	4/15/14	3.5	6/15/98
D (PAC Bond)	9,150,000	5.65	8/15/15	4.5	1/15/99
E (PAC Bond)	31,650,000	6.00	1/15/19	5.8	1/15/01
G (PAC Bond)	30,750,000	6.25	8/15/21	7.9	5/15/03
H (PAC Bond)	27,450,000	6.50	6/15/23	10.9	10/15/07
J (PAC Bond)	5,220,000	6.50	10/15/23	14.4	9/15/09
K (PAC Bond)	7,612,000	7.00	3/15/24	18.8	5/15/19
LA (SCH Bond)	26,673,000	7.00	11/15/21	3.5	3/15/02
LB (SCH Bond)	36,087,000	7.00	6/15/23	3.5	9/15/02
M (SCH Bond)	18,738,000	7.00	3/15/24	11.2	10/15/08
O (TAC Bond)	13,348,000	7.00	2/15/24	2.5	1/15/08
OA (TAC Bond)	3,600,000	7.00	3/15/24	7.2	4/15/09
IA (IO, PAC Bond)	30,246,000	7.00	10/15/23	7.1	9/15/09
PF (FLTR, Support Bond)	21,016,000	6.75	3/15/24	17.5	5/15/19
PS (INV FLTR, Support Bond)	7,506,000	7.70	3/15/24	17.5	5/15/19
R (Residual)	—	0.00	3/15/24		
RS (Residual)	—	0.00	3/15/24		

Structural Features

Prepayment Guarantee: None

Assumed Reinvestment Rate: 0%

Cash Flow Allocation: Excess cash flow is not anticipated; in the event that there are proceeds remaining after the payment of the bonds, however, the Class R and RS Bonds will receive them. Commencing on the first principal payment date of the Class A Bonds, principal equal to the amount specified in the Prospectus will be applied to the Class A, B, C, D, E, G, H, J, K, LA, LB, M, O, OA, PF, and PS Bonds. After all other Classes have been retired, any remaining principal will be used to retire the Class O, OA, LA, LB, M, A, B, C, D, E, G, H, J, and K Bonds. The Notional Class IA Bond will have its notional principal amount retired along with the PAC Bonds.

Redemption Provisions: Nuisance provision for all Classes: Issuer may redeem the Bonds, in whole but not in part, on any Payment Date when the outstanding principal balance declines to less than 1% of the original amount.

Other: The PAC Range is 95% to 300% PSA for the A - K Bonds, 190% to 250% PSA for the LA, LB, and M Bonds, and 225% PSA for the O and OA Bonds.

Exhibit 8: Diagram of Principal Allocation Structure of FHLMC 1706 (as of 3/10/98)

Low	Tranches R and RS							
	Tranche LB				Tranche	Tranches	Tranches
	Tranche LA				M	O and OA	PF and PS
High	Tranche C	Tranche D	Tranche E	Tranche G	Tranche H	Tranche J	Tranche K

Structural
Priority   Time

Exhibit 9: OAS Analysis of FHLMC 1706 (As of 3/10/98)
Base Case (assumes 13% interest rate volatility)

	OAS (in basis points)	Option Cost (in basis points)	Effective Duration (in years)
Collateral	60	44	2.6
PF (Support Fltr)	17	58	1.5

Prepayments at 80% and 120% of Prepayment Model
(assumes 13% interest rate volatility)

	Base Case OAS	New OAS (in basis points)		Change in Price per $100 par (holding OAS constant)		Effective Duration (in years)	
		80%	120%	80%	120%	80%	120%
Collateral Class	60	63	57	$0.17	−$0.11	3.0	2.4
PF (Support Fltr)	17	26	7	0.75	−0.69	1.8	1.3

Interest Rate Volatility of 9% and 17%

	Base Case OAS	New OAS (in basis points)		Change in Price per $100 par (holding OAS constant)		Effective Duration (in years)	
		9%	17%	9%	17%	9%	17%
Collateral	60	81	35	$0.96	−$0.94	2.9	2.5
PF (Support Fltr)	17	51	−27	3.11	−2.92	1.0	2.1

The next two panels in Exhibit 9 show the sensitivity of the OAS and the price (holding OAS constant at the base case) to changes in the prepayment speed (80% and 120% of the base case) and to changes in volatility (9% and 17%). This analysis shows that the change in the prepayment speed does not affect the collateral significantly, while the change in the OAS (holding the price constant) and price (holding OAS constant) for the tranches can be significant. In the case of tranche PF, a slow down to 80% of the base case prepayments increases the OAS to 26 basis points from the base case of 17 basis points. In contrast, a speeding up of prepayments by 120% of the base case reduces the OAS to 7 basis points.

Note also what happens to the value of the tranche if prepayments are different from the base case. The second panel shows that if the OAS is unchanged from the base case but the prepayments are 80% slower, then the value of the floater would increase by $0.75 per $100 of par value. If, instead, the prepayments are 120% of the base case and the OAS is constant, then the value of the floater would decrease by $0.69 per $100 of par value.

The sensitivity of the collateral and the tranches to changes in volatility are shown in the third panel of Exhibit 9. A lower volatility increases the value of the collateral, while a higher volatility reduces its value. Similarly, but in a more pronounced fashion, lower volatility increases the value of tranche PF, and higher volatility decreases its value. At a 9% volatility, the OAS increases to 51 basis points, but at 17% the OAS becomes negative. Again, looking at the effect on value holding OAS constant from the base case, the value would be $3.11 higher at a 9% volatility but $2.92 less if volatility is 17%.

Also shown in Exhibit 9 is how the effective durations would change if the prepayment rates and volatility are changed.

APPROACHES TO ABS VALUATION

In the preceding sections, we discussed three valuation approaches. The first approach is to value a security by discounting the expected cash flows by the issuer's on-the-run spot rates. If some type of spread measure is sought, the zero-volatility spread is calculated. This is the spread that must be added to either the on-the-run Treasury spot rates or the on-the-run spot rate for the issuer to obtain the market price (plus accrued interest). The zero-volatility spread differs from the nominal spread if (1) the yield curve is steep and/or (2) the security is an amortizing asset (i.e., principal is repaid periodically). Because most ABS are amortizing assets, the zero-volatility approach is superior to the nominal spread.

When there is an embedded option in a security, then either the binomial model or Monte Carlo simulation model can be used. When an ABS has an embedded option it is in the form of a call or prepayment option. Whether the binomial or Monte Carlo model should be used depends on whether or not the cash flows are interest rate path-independent or interest rate path-dependent. In the former case, at any point on an interest rate path or node of an interest rate tree, how the interest rate evolved to get to that point is unimportant and will not affect the cash flow at that point. In such cases, the binomial model is employed. This is why the binomial model is used to value agency, corporate, and municipal bonds. In contrast, because of prepayment burnout, the prepayments at a given point on an interest rate path will depend on how the interest rate evolved to get to that point. For interest rate path-dependent securities, the Monte Carlo model is employed. This is why this model is used to value mortgage-backed securities. With either model, an option-adjusted spread (OAS) can be calculated.

The decision of which valuation model to employ is diagramed in Exhibit 10. Which model should be used for ABS? The answer depends on the particular type of ABS. Specifically, while an ABS that has a prepayment or call option whose exercise will depend on the prevailing level of interest rates versus the loan rate paid by the borrower, whether or not in practice that option will be exercised must be assessed empirically. As explained in Chapter 9, there are types where borrowers have a prepayment option but borrowers have not demonstrated that they take advantage of refinancing when market rates decline below the rate on their loan. Thus, the approach of discounting at the spot rate for the on-the-run issuer or Treasury is employed to obtain the value of the ABS and the zero-volatility spread is used as the spread measure. When there is a prepayment option that borrowers appear to exercise when the prevailing borrowing rate declines below the loan rate, typically the cash flows are interest rate path-dependent. Thus, the Monte Carlo model is used and OAS is used as a spread measure.

Exhibit 10: Selecting a Model for the Valuation of Asset-Backed Securities

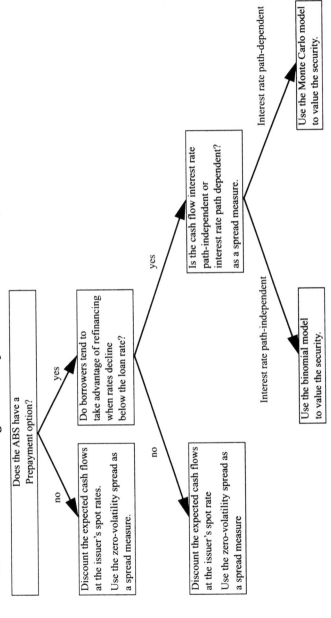

Chapter 11
Inverse Floaters

An inverse floating-rate security, or simply, *inverse floater*, possesses a coupon rate that changes in the direction opposite to that of some reference rate or market rate. Inverse floaters exist in the corporate bond market, the municipal bond market, and the collateralized mortgage obligations market. In this chapter, we will see how an inverse floater is created, how it is valued, and how to determine its duration.

CREATION OF AN INVERSE FLOATER

An inverse floater is created in one of the following three transactions:

Transaction 1: A dealer buys a fixed-rate bond in the secondary market and places the bond in a trust. Subsequently, the trust issues a floating-rate security and an inverse floating-rate security.

Transaction 2: A new fixed-rate issue is underwritten by an investment banking firm and placed in a trust. The trust then issues a floating-rate security and an inverse floating-rate security.

Transaction 3: An investment banking firm underwrites a long-term fixed-rate bond and simultaneously enters into an interest rate swap with a tenor generally less than the bond's term to maturity. The investor owns an inverse floater for the swap's tenor which then converts to a fixed-rate bond (the underlying) when the swap contract expires.

Note that in the first two transactions, both a floater and an inverse floater are created. In the third transaction, only an inverse floater is created owing to the presence of the interest rate swap and this security eventually converts into a fixed-rate security.

Inverse Floaters Created from Secondary Bonds or New Issues

Exhibit 1 shows how an inverse floater is created in the first or second transaction The security from which the inverse floater is created is called the *collateral*. From the collateral two bonds, or tranches, are created: a floater and an inverse floater.

The dealer determines the ratio of floaters to inverse floaters. For example, a dealer firm may purchase $200 million of the underlying bond in the secondary market and issue $100 million of floaters and $100 million of inverse floaters. The dealer may opt for a 60/40 or any other split. As explained later, the split of the floaters/inverse floaters determines the leverage of the inverse floaters and thus affects the inverse floater's price volatility (duration) when interest rates change.

Conditions that Must Be Satisfied

The two tranches are created such that

1. The total coupon interest paid to the two tranches in each period is less than or equal to the collateral's coupon interest in each period.

and

2. The total principal paid in any period to the two tranches is less than or equal to the collateral's total principal in each period.

Equivalently, the floater and inverse floater are structured so that the cash flow from the collateral in each period will be sufficient to satisfy the obligation of the two tranches.

For example, consider a 10-year 7.5% coupon semiannual-pay bond. Suppose $100 million par value of the bond is used as collateral to create a floater with a principal of $50 million and an inverse floater with a principal of $50 million. Suppose the reference rate is 6-month LIBOR (denoted by simply LIBOR below) and that the coupon rate for the floater and the inverse floater are reset every six months based on the following formula:

Floater coupon: LIBOR + 1%
Inverse floater coupon: 14% − LIBOR

Notice that the total principal of the floater and inverse floater equals the principal of the collateral, $100 million. The weighted average of the coupon rate of the combination of the two tranches is:

0.5(LIBOR + 1%) + 0.5(14% − LIBOR) = 7.5%

Thus, the combined coupon rate for the two tranches is the coupon rate of the collateral (i.e., 7.5%) regardless of LIBOR's level.

Exhibit 1: Creation of an Inverse Floater

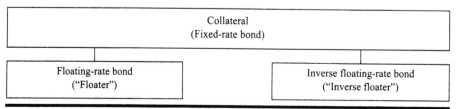

There is one disturbing element with the coupon formulas presented above. Suppose that LIBOR exceeds 14%. If this occurs, the inverse floater's coupon rate will be negative. Most investors would find this unappealing. To prevent this from occurring a restriction or floor is placed on the coupon rate for the inverse floater. Typically, the floor is set at zero. Since both the floater and inverse floater are derived from the same fixed-rate collateral, whenever a restriction is placed on the coupon rate of one tranche, an offsetting restriction must be placed on the other tranche. Because of the floor, the floater's coupon rate must be restricted so that the coupon interest paid to the two tranches does not exceed the collateral's coupon interest. In our hypothetical structure, the maximum coupon rate that must be imposed on the floater is 15%. Accordingly, when a floater and an inverse floater are created from the collateral, a floor is imposed on the inverse floater and a cap is imposed on the floater.

General Formula for Inverse Floater Coupon

In general, a wide range of allocations of the collateral's principal are possible, permitting countless possibilities for the formula for the inverse floater. The general formula for the inverse floater is:

$$K - (L \times R)$$

where R is the reference rate, and K and L are values selected by the creator of the floater and the inverse floater.

Let's define and interpret the two parameters K and L. K is the maximum coupon rate that inverse floater can realize; that is, it is the inverse cap. The maximum coupon attainable by an inverse floater occurs when the reference rate is zero. L is the coupon leverage, or simply, leverage. The value for L indicates the multiple by which the coupon rate will change for a 100 basis point change in the reference rate. For example, if L is 4, this means that the inverse floater's coupon rate will change 400 basis points for each 100 basis point change in the reference rate (subject to any restrictions imposed on the coupon). Thus, the general formula for the coupon rate of an inverse floater can be expressed as follows:

inverse cap − leverage × reference rate

Any cap and/or floor imposed on the coupon rate for the floater/inverse floater must be selected so as to maintain the integrity of the combined coupon rate. Put simply, the combined coupon rate must be less than or equal to the collateral's coupon rate. The relationship among the parameters for collateral, floater, and inverse floater are shown in Exhibit 2.

Naturally, the amount of leverage is not determined arbitrarily by creators of inverse floater. The market is the final arbiter. Specifically, the amount of coupon leverage is dictated by client inquiries and/or market demand for recently created issues.

Exhibit 2: Relationships for Principal and Coupon for Creation of Floater and Inverse Floater Tranches*

Parameters for collateral:
Collateral principal
Collateral coupon rate

Parameters for floater tranche:
Floater spread
Floater cap
Floater floor
Current value of reference rate

Parameters for inverse floater tranche:
Coupon leverage
Inverse floater cap
Inverse floater floor

Relationships:
Floater coupon = Current value fo refernce rate + Floater spread

$$\text{Floater principal} = \frac{\text{Coupon leverage} \times \text{Collateral principal}}{(1 + \text{Coupon leverage})}$$

Inverse principal = Collateral principal − Floater principal

Inverse interest = (Collateral principal × Collateral coupon rate) − (Floater principal × Floater coupon rate)

$$\text{Floater cap} = \frac{\text{Collateral coupon}}{\text{Floater principal}}$$

$$\text{Inverse floor} = \frac{\text{Inverse interest when floater coupon at cap}}{\text{Inverse principal}}$$

$$\text{Inverse cap} = \frac{\text{Inverse interest when floater coupon at floor}}{\text{Inverse principal}}$$

* Assumes that all of the collateral principal and interest will be distributed to the floater and inverse floater.

Inverse Floaters Created via the Swap Market

An inverse floater can also be created when an investment banking firm underwrites a fixed-rate bond (corporates, agencies, and municipalities) and simultaneously enters into an interest rate swap for a time that is generally less than the swap's tenor. The investor owns an inverse floater for the swap's tenor, which then converts to a fixed-rate bond (the underlying collateral) when the swap contract expires. An inverse floater creating using a swap is called an *indexed inverse floater.*

To see how this can be accomplished, let's assume the following. An issuer wants to issue $200 million on a fixed-rate basis for 20 years. An investment bank suggests two simultaneous transactions.

Transaction 1: Issue $200 million of a 20-year bond in which the coupon rate is determined by the following rules for a specific reference rate:

For years 1 through 5: 14% – reference rate
For years 6 through 10: 5%

Transaction 2: Enter into a 5-year interest rate swap with the investment bank with a notional principal amount of $200 million in which semiannual payments are exchanged as follows using the same reference rate:

Issuer pays the reference rate
Issuer receives 6%

Note that for the first five years, the investor owns an inverse floater because as the reference rate increases (decreases) the coupon rate decreases (increases). However, even though the security issued pays an inverse floating rate, the combination of the two transactions results in fixed-rate financing for the issuer:

Rate issuer receives
From the investment bank via the swap: 6%

Rate issuer pays
To security holders: 14% – reference rate
To the investment bank via the swap: reference rate

Net payments
(14% – reference rate) + reference rate – 6% = 8%

MAJOR ISSUERS OF INVERSE FLOATERS

In this section, we describe the major issuers/issuances of inverse floaters. Inverse floaters are issued in the mortgage, municipal, and corporate sectors. As we will see, all inverse floaters possess the same basic characteristic (i.e., the coupon rate is inversely related to the level of the reference rate). However, there are some important differences between the inverse floaters issued in these sectors.

CMO Inverse Floater Tranches

The largest issuance of inverse floaters has been in the CMO market. In describing CMO inverse floaters we must modify our terminology for ease of exposition. In our earlier discussion, we referred to the fixed-rate bond from which the floater and inverse floater are created as "the collateral." We referred to the floater and inverse floater as tranches. To participants in the CMO market, the term collateral refers to the mortgage-related product (e.g., passthroughs or whole loans) from which CMOs are created. The cash flows from the collateral are redirected according to a set of specified rules to create various tranches. From any fixed-rate tranche, a floater and an inverse floater can be created.

The term "collateral" for the floater and the inverse floater can be misleading in the CMO market. It could mean the collateral for the CMO deal or it could mean the fixed-rate tranche which is carved up to create the floater and inverse floater. To allay potential confusion, one should refer to the collateral for the entire CMO deal as the "CMO collateral" and the fixed-rate tranche from which the floater and inverse floater are created as the "tranche collateral."

In Chapter 8, we showed how a CMO inverse is created from tranche collateral. Just as individual tranches of a sequential CMO can serve as tranche collateral for floaters/inverse floaters, PAC tranches can also to be divided into a floater/inverse floater combination. The inverse floaters are referred to an PAC inverse floaters. The difference between an inverse floaters created from a collateral tranche that is a PAC tranche and those described heretofore is simply the prepayment protection offered by the PAC structure.

Tranche collateral can also used to create a floater/inverse interest-only (IO) floater combination. Like inverse floaters, the coupon rate of inverse IO floaters rises (falls) as the reference rate falls (rises). Like IOs, slower prepayments represent more cash flow for inverse IOs than faster prepayments since only interest and no principal is received by the holder of this security. At first glance, it appears that inverse IOs have the potential for offsetting risks — higher (lower) interest rates mean lower (higher) coupon rates for a longer (shorter) periods of time. Unfortunately, this is largely an illusion. The relationship between the reference rates embedded in inverse IO floater's coupon formula and mortgage rates (upon which prepayments depend) is unstable.

As explained in Chapter 8, a variant of a floater/inverse floater is a superfloater/inverse floater combination. A superfloater is called a two-tiered index bond (TTIB). In this structure, the corresponding inverse floater has a coupon rate that varies as follows: (1) when the reference rate is above a designated rate, the coupon rate is capped at the designated rate, (2) when the reference rate is below a designated rate, a floor is set for the coupon rate at the designated rate, and (3) when the reference rate is between the cap and the floor, the coupon rate has the standard formula for an inverse floater. An illustration of a TTIB is shown in Exhibit 7 in Chapter 8.

Municipal Inverse Floaters

Inverse floaters are created in the municipal bond market using all three types of transactions described at the outset of this chapter. The most popular split of floaters and inverse floaters in the municipal market in the first two types of transactions used to create an inverse floater has been 50/50.

Suppose that interest rates are rising and an investor wishes to close out an inverse floater position. In the municipal market, the investor in the municipal inverse floater can purchase the corresponding floater at auction and combine the two positions to effectively own the underlying fixed-rate bond. This combination represents an easy way to convert a position into a synthetic fixed-rate municipal bond. This bond can then be hedged, if desired, by conventional methods. Subsequently, the investor can elect to split the issue again and retain the inverse floater. This flexibility represents a valuable option for investors. As a result, the yield on this bond is generally less than the yield on a comparable fixed-rate bond that does not possess this option.

Several dealer firms active in the municipal bond market have developed proprietary floater/inverse products. Merrill Lynch's institutional floaters are called FLOATS and its inverse floaters are called RITES (Residual Interest Tax Exempt Securities). Goldman Sachs' proprietary floater products are called PARS (Periodic Auction Reset Securities) and its inverse floaters are called INFLOS. Finally, Lehman Brothers' proprietary products are called RIBS (Residual Interest Bonds) and SAVRS (Select Auction Variable Rate Securities).

Creating an inverse floater using the swap market (i.e., the third type of transaction described earlier in this chapter for creating an inverse floater) eliminates the need for selling the floaters through a Dutch auction. The investor has the option of converting the inverse floater — called an indexed inverse floater — to a fixed-rate bond before the swap contract expires by unwinding the swap. The cost of conversion is satisfied either up-front or is satisfied by adjusting the fixed rate the investor was to begin receiving at the end of initial swap tenor. The fixed rate would be adjusted down if the short-term interest rates have risen. An upward adjustment would be made if the investor converts the security when short-term interest rates have declined.[1]

Indexed inverse floater proprietary products are sold by investment banking firms. Merrill Lynch sells these instruments as institutional Short RITES. Merrill's retail inverse floating-rate product is called TEEMS (Tax Exempt Enhanced Municipal Securities). Goldman Sachs markets their indexed inverse floaters under the name Indexed INFLOS. J. P. Morgan calls these securities Residual Adjustable Yield Securities. Lehman also markets a variation called Bulls and Bears.

In the municipal market, dealer firms employing subtle complications on the structures described above have created variations of the floater/inverse floater instruments. Several of these variations are described below.

An investment bank may create putable floating-rate securities with inverse floaters. This type of security is an example of a senior/subordinated class structure. The overall design is the same as with a floater and an inverse floater created by purchasing bonds in the secondary market. However, if the remarketing agent fails to sell out the floaters or the underlying bonds fall below a minimum collateral value and investors in the inverse floaters do not purchase the corresponding floaters, the trustee terminates the trust and liquidates the bonds. The proceeds of the liquidation are used first to pay the par value of the floater

---

[1] See Lynn Stevens Hume, "Indexed Inverse Floater Deals Allow Investors to Convext to Fixed Term if Market Turns," *The Bond Buyer* (October 21, 1992).

and any accrued interest. The inverse floater investor receives the residual. Merrill Lynch markets these products as *Putable Floats/RITES*.

A variation on the putable floater structure gives the owner of the floater a senior lien on only the interest portion of the issue. The investor has a parity lien with the inverse floater investor on the underlying bond principal.

Another type of security that has been created is the opposite of an inverse floater created via an interest rate swap. In this case, the investor in the first phase of the issue effectively owns a floating-rate bond.[2] When the swap contract expires, the bond converts to the fixed-rate underlying bond. Merrill Lynch markets these bonds as *Reverse Short RITES*.

Synthetic floating-rate securities have been created from the cash flows of coupon paying bonds. They are called Tender Option Bonds (TOBs). In this case, the investment bank creating the securities deposits fixed-rate bonds in a trust. Custodial receipts for floating-rate securities (which depend on the interest on the underlying fixed-rate bond) are sold that offer the investor the ability to tender the custodial receipt for par value to the investment bank with seven days notice. The investor has the option to own the underlying fixed-rate bond by paying an opt-out fee to the investment bank. This *opt-out fee* is determined by the relationship between the fixed-rate bond market and the level of interest rates in the swap market.

Corporate Inverse Floaters

Virtually all corporate inverse floaters are issued as structured notes which means they are issued along with an underlying swap transaction. Moreover, as of this writing, the vast majority of inverse floaters have cash flows denominated in currencies other than U.S. dollars. Some notable exceptions are the inverse floaters issued by U.S. government sponsored enterprises (GSEs). For example, the Federal Home Loan Bank issued two leveraged inverse floating-rate notes in early 1999. The first, issued in March 1999 and due in January 2005, delivers quarterly cash flows with a coupon formula of 17.45% − (2.0 × 3-month LIBOR). The coupon floor is 4%. The second, issued in April 1999 and due in April 2002, also delivers quarterly cash flows with a coupon formula of 18% − (2.5 × 3-month LIBOR). The coupon floor is 3%.

Many inverse floating-rate notes deliver cash flows in currencies other than U. S. dollars. Some prominent issuers include supranational institutions (e.g., World Bank, European Bank for Reconstruction and Development, Inter-American Development Bank) and large non-U.S. financial institutions (e.g., Banque Paribas, Deutsche Bank, DG Bank, National Westminster Bank). Exhibits 3 and 4 present Bloomberg DES (description) screens for two inverse floating-rate notes with cash flows denominated in Japanese yen. Exhibit 3 describes an inverse floater issued by Salomon Smith Barney with a reference rate of 6-month ¥ LIBOR. Exhibit 4 describes an inverse floater issued by Toyota Motor Credit with a reference rate of 3-month ¥ LIBOR.

---

[2] The term of the first phase is the tenor of the underlying swap.

Exhibit 3: Bloomberg Description Screen for a Salomon Smith Barney Inverse Floater

```
1                                                    DG36 Corp   DES

STRUCTURED NOTE DESCRIPTION Page 1/ 3        ████████
SALOMON INC    C Float 12/06/99      N O T   P R I C E D
┌─────────────────────────────┬─────────────────────────┬──────────────────────┐
│ ISSUER INFORMATION          │ IDENTIFIERS             │ 1) Additional Sec Info│
│ Name SALOMON SMITH BARNEY HLD│ BB number    SNB029977 │ 2) Floating Rates     │
│ Type Finance-Invest Bnkr/Brkr│                        │ 3) Identifiers        │
│ Market of Issue EURO MTN    │                         │ 4) Ratings            │
│ SECURITY INFORMATION        │ RATINGS                 │ 5) Prospectus         │
│ Country US      Currency JPY│ Moody's        Aa3      │ 6) Custom Notes       │
│ Collateral Type NOTES       │ S&P            A        │ 7) Issuer Information  │
│ Calc Typ (303)INVERSE FLOATER│ DCR           A+       │ 8) ALLQ               │
│ Maturity  12/ 6/1999 Series EMTN│ ISSUE SIZE          │ 9) Pricing Sources    │
│ NORMAL                      │ Amt Issued              │ 10) Prospectus Request│
│ Coupon 3.4%      FLOATING S/A│ JPY 300,000.00   (M)  │                        │
│ S/A    3.6 -JY00       30/360│ Amt Outstanding        │                        │
│ Announcement Dt 12/ 6/95    │ JPY 300,000.00   (M)   │                        │
│ Int. Accrual Dt 12/ 6/95    │ Min Piece/Increment     │                        │
│ 1st Settle Date 12/ 6/95    │ 100000000/ 100000000    │                        │
│ 1st Coupon Date  6/ 6/96    │ Par Amount  100000000   │                        │
│ Iss Pr 100.0000             │ BOOK RUNNER/EXCHANGE    │                        │
│                             │ SALOMON BROTHERS        │ 65) Old DES           │
│ HAVE PROSPECTUS             │                         │ 66) Send as Attachment│
└─────────────────────────────┴─────────────────────────┴──────────────────────┘
CPN RATE=3.6% - 6MO ¥LIBOR. MIN CPN=0%. INVERSE 6MO ¥LIBOR-INDEXED BONDS. SERIES
D.
Copyright 1999 BLOOMBERG L.P.   Frankfurt:69-920410  Hong Kong:2-977-6000  London:171-330-7500  New York:212-318-2000
Princeton:609-279-3000    Singapore:226-3000   Sydney:2-9777-8686    Tokyo:3-3201-8900    Sao Paulo:11-3048-4500
                                                                    1464-169-0 19-Nov-99 17:33:27
```

Source: Bloomberg Financial Markets

Exhibit 4: Bloomberg Description Screen for a Toyota Motor Credit Inverse Floater

```
1                                                    DG36 Corp   DES

STRUCTURED NOTE DESCRIPTION No Calculations  ████████
TOYOTA MTR CRED  TOYOTA3 ½ 10/07     N O T   P R I C E D
┌─────────────────────────────┬─────────────────────────┬──────────────────────┐
│ ISSUER INFORMATION          │ IDENTIFIERS             │ 1) Additional Sec Info│
│ Name TOYOTA MOTOR CREDIT CORP│ Common    008056269    │ 2) Floating Rates     │
│ Type Finance-Auto Loans     │ ISIN      XS0080562696  │ 3) Call Schedule      │
│ Market of Issue EURO MTN    │ BB number  MM1302916   │ 4) Identifiers        │
│ SECURITY INFORMATION        │ RATINGS                 │ 5) Ratings            │
│ Country US      Currency JPY│ Moody's        Aa1      │ 6) Involved Parties   │
│ Collateral Type NOTES       │ S&P            AAA      │ 7) Custom Notes       │
│ Calc Typ (521)ACCRUED ONLY FLOAT│ Composite  AA1      │ 8) Issuer Information  │
│ Maturity  10/16/2007 Series EMTN│ ISSUE SIZE          │ 9) ALLQ               │
│ CALLABLE  CALL 11/29/99@ 100.00│ Amt Issued           │ 10) Pricing Sources   │
│ Coupon           VARIABLE S/A│ JPY  8,400,000   (M)  │                        │
│ S/A    N/A          ISMA-30/360│ Amt Outstanding      │                        │
│ Announcement Dt 9/18/97     │ JPY  8,400,000   (M)   │                        │
│ Int. Accrual Dt 10/16/97    │ Min Piece/Increment     │                        │
│ 1st Settle Date 10/16/97    │ 10,000,000/10,000,000   │                        │
│ 1st Coupon Date  4/16/98    │ Par Amount 10,000,000   │                        │
│ Iss Pr 100.0000             │ BOOK RUNNER/EXCHANGE    │                        │
│                             │ DB-sole                 │ 65) Old DES           │
│ NO PROSPECTUS               │ NOT LISTED              │ 66) Send as Attachment│
└─────────────────────────────┴─────────────────────────┴──────────────────────┘
CPN RATE=3.5% TO 10/98 S/A (30/360); THEN 3.8% -3MO ¥LIBOR QTRLY (ACT/360); BASE
RESET ANNLY @4.2%,4.6%,5%,5.4%,5.8%,6.2%,7.2%,8.2%.MIN CPN=0%.CALL W/10 BUS DAYS
Copyright 1999 BLOOMBERG L.P.   Frankfurt:69-920410  Hong Kong:2-977-6000  London:171-330-7500  New York:212-318-2000
Princeton:609-279-3000    Singapore:226-3000   Sydney:2-9777-8686    Tokyo:3-3201-8900    Sao Paulo:11-3048-4500
                                                                    1464-169-0 19-Nov-99 17:37:44
```

Source: Bloomberg Financial Markets

VALUING AN INVERSE FLOATER

The starting point of any discussion of valuation – as emphasized throughout this book -- is the value of any financial asset is the present value of its expected cash flows. Applying this principle to the valuation of inverse floaters is problematic owing to uncertainty about future values for the reference rate. Fortunately, the valuation of an inverse floater is not complex, as we shall see.

Fundamental Principle

We can express the relationships among the collateral, the floater, and the inverse floater as follows:

collateral = floater + inverse floater

This relationship applies to cash flows as well as valuation. In other words, the sum of the value of the floater and the value of the inverse floater must be equal to the value of the collateral from which they are created. If this relationship does not hold, opportunities for arbitrage arise.

An alternative way to express the relationship is:

value of an inverse floater = value of collateral – value of floater

This expression states that the value of an inverse floater can be found by valuing the collateral and valuing the floater, and then calculating the difference between these two values. In this case, the value of an inverse floater is not found directly, but is instead derived from the value of the collateral and the value of the floater. We have discussed how to value the floater in previous chapters.

Given that the floater created from the collateral is a capped floater, the value of an inverse floater can be expressed as:

value of an inverse floater = value of collateral – value of a capped floater

The factors that affect the value of an inverse floater are the same factors that affect the collateral's value and the capped floater's value.

Leverage and Valuation

Additional intuition about the valuation of inverse floaters can be garnered by looking at the importance of the security's coupon leverage. Suppose that the creator of the floater and inverse floater divides the collateral into 100 bonds, 20 inverse floater bonds and 80 floater bonds.[3] Accordingly, the leverage in this structure is 4:1 of floater bonds to inverse floater bonds. Then, the following relationship must hold:

100(collateral price) = 20(inverse price) + 80(floater price)

---

[3] The principles here were first expressed in William R. Leach, "A Portfolio Manager's Perspective of Inverses and Inverse IOs," Chapter 10 in Frank J. Fabozzi (ed.), *CMO Portfolio Management* (Summit, NJ: Frank J. Fabozzi Associates, 1994).

This relationship can also be expressed as:

20(1+4)(collateral price) = 20(inverse price) + 20(4)(floater price)

Dividing both sides by 20, we get:

(1+4)(collateral price) = (inverse price) + 4(floater price)

This relationship can generalized for any leverage L as follows:

(1+L)(collateral price) = (inverse price) + L(floater price)

Solving for the inverse price we obtain:

inverse price = (1+L)(collateral price) − L(floater price)

This price relationship contains two important implications. First, typically it is not difficult to price the floater. The greater difficulty may be in determining the collateral's price. Notice the implication of mispricing the collateral. *The greater the leverage, the greater the impact of mispricing of the inverse floater resulting from mispricing the collateral.* Specifically, every one point mispricing of the collateral results in a 1+L point mispricing of the inverse floater. So with a leverage of 3, a 4 point mispricing of the inverse results for each one point mispricing of the collateral.

The second implication is that the price of the inverse floater is not related to the level of the reference rate as long as the floater cap is not affected. The factors that drive the price performance of an inverse floater are explored in the next section.

Using Interest Rate Swaps to Value Inverse Floaters

In Chapter 6 we described and illustrated the fixed-equivalent coupon calculation. Suppose an investor is analyzing a CMO inverse floater. We could use the swap market to convert an inverse floater into a fixed-rate bond using an amortizing swap. Recall, amortizing swaps are swaps in which the notional principal is reduced at one or more dates during a swap's life.[4] The amortizing swap is created, in effect, by using Eurodollar futures to convert the LIBOR portion of each cash flow of the inverse floater into a fixed-rate cash flow on a notional principal that declines over time consistent with an assumed prepayment speed. Once again, future forward LIBOR rates at each of the inverse floater's coupon reset dates are taken as given and the security's cash flow is determined under that assumption. To replicate the cash flows for a CMO inverse floater, this process is repeated for different prepayment speeds.

We will illustrate this calculation using a CMO inverse floater (FNR 93-183 S) issued by Fannie Mae that matures on October 25, 2023 assumed to be trading at a price of 53.[5] The security delivers coupon payments monthly with a cou-

---

[4] There are also swaps that allow for the amortization of the notional principal in a manner that is consistent with the amortization of a mortgage pool called mortgage-indexed or CMO swaps.

pon formula of 22.8931% − (3.27044% × 1-month LIBOR). The cap or maximum coupon rate on this inverse floater is 22.893131% and this will occur if 1-month LIBOR falls to zero. Correspondingly, the floor or minimum coupon rate is 0% and will occur if 1-month LIBOR is greater than or equal to 7%. Finally, the coupon leverage is 3.27044 which means that a 100-basis point change in 1-month LIBOR will change the coupon rate on the inverse floater by approximately 327 basis points (subject to any restrictions on the coupon rate). An inverse floater with a coupon leverage between 2.1 and 4.5 is considered medium leverage.

The calculation proceeds as follows. First, we use a strip of Eurodollar CD futures contracts to establish a set of forward 1-month LIBOR rates for each of the monthly coupon reset dates. Second, determine the security's cash flows based on these forward LIBOR rates. For example, suppose forward 1-month LIBOR in a particular month is 5.5%, the security's coupon rate is 4.91%. Accordingly, the inverse floater's monthly cash flow is 4.91% multiplied by the tranche's projected outstanding principal amount for this particular prepayment speed divided by 12. Note the projected cash flows will change each period because the forward 1-month LIBOR rate changes and the principal amount changes. Third, fixed-equivalent coupon is the rate (appropriately annualized) that discounts these cash flows back to the security's market price.

The end product of this analysis is presented in Exhibit 5. The first row presents fixed-equivalent coupon for FNR 93-183 S for various prepayment (PSA) speeds. The second row is yield-to-current-LIBOR which is calculated in a similar manner except the projected cash flows are based on the current value of 1-month LIBOR, 4.5% (assumed to remain constant until maturity).[6] The last row is the security's average life in years for each prepayment speed. The fixed-equivalent coupon is lower than yield-to-current-LIBOR for all prepayment speeds. This is true because the fixed-equivalent coupon reflects an upward sloping yield curve and rising implied forward rates which in turn portend lower coupon payments for inverse floaters. The yields increase considerably for faster prepayment speeds because the inverse floater is trading at a substantial discount to par (Price = 53).

Exhibit 5: Yield-to-Forward-LIBOR of FNR 93-183 S

	Prepayment rate (PSA)					
	100	105	120	130	145	225
Yield to Forward LIBOR	4.29	4.54	6.64	12.30	30.79	32.14
Yield to Current LIBOR	16.95	17.11	19.47	25.93	42.01	43.10
Average Life	17.29	16.36	11.81	7.35	2.90	2.72

Source: *PaineWebber MortgageStrategist* (August 8, 1994) by Laurie Goodman, Linda Lowell, Jeff Ho, and Diana Rich.

[5] This example is adapted from analysis presented in *PaineWebber Mortgage Strategist* (August 8, 1994) by Laurie Goodman, Linda Lowell, Jeff Ho, and Diana Rich.
[6] Recall from Chapter 6, fixed-equivalent coupon is also known as *yield-to-forward LIBOR* since we use implied forward rates for determining future floating-rate payments. Yield-to-current LIBOR assumes the reference rate (i.e., LIBOR) remains at its current level.

Limitations of Fixed-Equivalent Coupon Analysis

The intent of fixed-equivalent coupon analysis is to use a swap (in effect) to transform the cash flows of a floater (inverse floater) into a fixed-rate security whose yield can then be compared to other fixed-rate bonds. There are of course limits to this comparison. First, in the inverse floater example presented above, the amortizing swap that we effectively created does not reflect the uncertainty in the security's cash flows due to faster/slower prepayments. This uncertainty will be priced. Thus, other things equal, the yield on a CMO inverse floater should be higher than a fixed-rate bond.

Second, fixed-equivalent coupon analysis ignores any embedded option in the floater/inverse floater. For example, the coupon formula for the inverse floater is 22.8931% − (3.27044% × 1-month LIBOR). As noted in the security's description, this inverse floater has a cap and a floor. For any value of LIBOR below 7% (called the strike rate), the coupon rate is determined by the formula. However, for any value of 1-month LIBOR greater than or equal to 7%, the coupon rate is 0% i.e., the inverse floater has a 0% coupon floor.

Inverse floater investors are in essence long 3.27044 caps with a strike rate of 7%. To this see, recall that the companion floater (with a cap) and the inverse floater are created from the same fixed-rate collateral. Thus the following relationship is true:

Long a fixed-rate collateral = Long a capped floater + Long an inverse floater

Rearranging this relationship in terms of the inverse floater, we can write

Long an inverse floater = Long a fixed-rate collateral + Short a capped floater

Thus, a long position in an inverse floater is equivalent to purchasing fixed-rate collateral by borrowing funds at a floating interest rate equal to the reference rate plus the spread. A floater's cap can be viewed as a cap on an inverse floater investor's borrowing rate. This cap on the borrowing rate is owned by the inverse floater investor and written by the companion capped floater investor. These valuable options are not priced in the fixed-equivalent coupon analysis. Since these options are ignored, the fixed-equivalent coupon should be lower than an otherwise identical fixed-rate bond.

Valuing an Inverse Floater with Embedded Options

An alternative swap-based approach for evaluating floaters/inverse floaters is to effectively strip off the embedded caps (thereby allowing us to value them) and then calculate the floater/inverse floater's yield without the caps. This yield is compared to the yield on a synthetic floater/inverse floater with the same cash flow characteristics. The synthetic security can be constructed with Treasuries and interest rate swaps.

To illustrate this approach, we will continue to use the same CMO inverse floater described above.[7] A synthetic inverse floater with the same average life (i.e., 7.35 years) in the base case prepayment speed (PSA 130) can be created in the following manner. Suppose a US Treasury security is available that has a remaining maturity of 7.35 years. This Treasury carries a coupon rate of 7.5% and is yielding 6.92%. We will take a long position in this Treasury while simultaneously taking a short position in 3.27044 interest rate swaps in which we will pay 1-month LIBOR and receive a fixed rate of 7.12%. Given the current value of 1-month LIBOR is say 4.5%, we can determine the yield on the synthetic inverse floater. We receive 6.92% from the Treasury and 23.28% (3.27044 × 7.12) from the interest rate swaps and pay 14.72% (3.72044% × 1-month LIBOR which is 4.5%) which results in a net yield of 15.48%.

The final step in making the inverse floater's yield comparable to the synthetic inverse floater's yield is to adjust for the presence of the 3.27044 caps. We do this by adjusting the yield upward to reflect the fact that the inverse floater investor has in effect a long position in the 3.27044 caps.[8] Each cap is worth 5.92 (per $100 of par value) assuming a 7% strike rate, a 7.35 years average life and an 18% volatility. Accordingly, the 3.27044 caps are worth 19.36 (per $100 of par value). The cap-adjusted price of the inverse floater is the inverse floater's price (53) less the value of the 3.27044 caps (19.36) which is 33.64. Given this price, the cap-adjusted yield is 47.97% which is considerably larger than the yield on the synthetic inverse floater of 15.49%. This analysis suggests that the inverse floater is cheap relative to its synthetic counterpart. We should hasten to add that this analysis does not reflect the uncertainty in mortgage cash flows so this method will overstate the value of the inverse floater.

PERFORMANCE OF AN INVERSE FLOATER

A common misperception is that the value of an inverse floater should change in a direction opposite from the change in the reference rate. Thus, if the reference rate falls (rises), the value of an inverse floater should rise (fall). This view is incorrect because, as we just explained, the value of an inverse floater is not solely dependent on the level of the reference rate. The reference rate affects the value of the inverse floater only through its effect on the value of the cap of the capped floater, and does not take into consideration the other factors that we have noted will affect the value of an inverse floater.

To understand the importance of these relationships for the value of an inverse floater and to make the analysis simple, let's assume that an inverse

---

[7] This example is adapted from analysis in *PaineWebber Mortgage Strategist* (August 8, 1994) by Laurie Goodman, Linda Lowell, Jeff Ho and Diana Rich.

[8] The investor in the floater created from the same collateral has effectively written 3.27044 caps. Accordingly, the floater's yield would be adjusted downward.

floater and floater are created from the on-the-run 10-year Treasury issue. While the creation of such securities is being not performed at the time of this writing, this example illustrates the basic principles and can be extended to more complicated collateral such as corporate bonds, municipal bonds, and collateralized mortgage obligations. The assumptions for the illustration are:

- The reference rate for the floater and inverse floater is the 6-month Treasury bill rate which is currently 6%. (Thus, the reference rate is a short-term rate.)
- The coupon rate for the floater is the 6-month Treasury bill rate flat (i.e., the spread is zero).
- The cap for the floater is 5%.
- The yield on the 10-year Treasury is 9.5% and the yield on a 9-year Treasury is 9.3%.

Now consider three scenarios one year from now. For each scenario, we make an assumption about

1. the reference rate one year from now
2. the expected volatility of the reference rate one year from now
3. the yield on a 9-year Treasury

We will look at the effect one year from now on the value of the collateral (the original 10-year Treasury) and the value of the capped floater. The difference between these two values is the value of the inverse floater.

Scenario 1: In this scenario, it is assumed that one year from now:

1. the reference rate declines to 4%
2. expected volatility of the 6-month Treasury bill rate declines
3. the yield on a 9-year Treasury increases from its current rate of 9.3% to 11%.

Thus, in Scenario 1, one year from now it is assumed that short-term Treasury rates have declined and intermediate-term rates have increased. This means that the Treasury yield curve has steepened in the short- to intermediate-term maturity sectors.

Given this scenario, the value of the capped floater will increase for two reasons. First, today the coupon rate on the floater would be 6% in the absence of the floater cap. Because of the floater cap, the coupon rate is 5%. One year from now, the capped floater's value increases because the coupon rate falls below the cap (the new coupon rate is 4%), thereby reducing the cap's value. Second, expected volatility of the reference rate decreases. On the other hand, the collateral's value declines because the 9-year Treasury yield rises.

Let's determine the net effect on the inverse floater's value. Recall, the inverse floater's value is the difference in the collateral's value and the capped floater's value. The collateral's value has decreased and the inverse floater's value has increased. Accordingly, the inverse floater's value has declined. *Notice that the inverse floater declined in value even though the reference rate is assumed to decline in this scenario.*

Scenario 2: In this scenario, it is assumed that one year from now:

1. the reference rate rise to 7%
2. expected volatility of the 6-month Treasury bill rate increases
3. the 9-year Treasury yield declines from its current rate of 9.3% to 7.6%

In this scenario, it is assumed that short-term rates rise and intermediate-term rates fall. This means that the Treasury yield curve has flattened in the short- to intermediate-term maturity sector.

As before, two factors are at work. In this instance, the combined effect of these two factors causes the floater's value to decrease because the value of the cap increases. First, the reference rate has risen above the cap rate so one year from now the coupon rate is even further below the market rate. Second, the expected volatility has increased.

As for the collateral, its value will increase due to the drop in the 9-year Treasury yield. To summarize, the collateral's value increases and the capped floater's value decreases so the net effect is an increase the inverse floater's value. Notice that the inverse floater increases in value even though the reference rate for the inverse floater has increased.

Scenario 3: In this last scenario, the following is assumed one year from now:

1. the reference rate declines to 4% (as in Scenario 1)
2. expected volatility of the reference rate decreases (as in Scenario 1)
3. the yield on a 9-year Treasury declines from its current rate of 9.3% to 7.6% (as in Scenario 2)

Under this scenario, the collateral's value will rise. The inverse floater's value can either rise or fall since the collateral has risen in value and the capped floater has risen in value. The net effect depends on the relative change of the collateral and the capped floater.

These illustrations make it clear that the change in the yield curve's shape is the key factor driving the performance of an inverse floater.[9] Moreover, when valuing an inverse floater created from non-Treasury collateral (rather than our hypothetical inverse floater created from a Treasury issue), two additional

---

[9] This is why inverse floaters are called "yield curve enhanced notes" by Lehman Brothers.

factors become relevant. Specifically, the following will affect how non-Treasury collateral and the floater created will affect the inverse floater's value: (1) how the spread of the floater changes and (2) the option-adjusted spread at which the collateral trades.

Typically, dealers analyze inverse floaters for a potential buyer by modeling the performance under various scenarios. For example, performance assumptions could cover a rise or decline of up to 300 basis points. Such analysis can be misleading for several reasons. First, there is no such thing as an "interest rate." Rather, there is a structure of interest rates as depicted by the yield curve and, as demonstrated above, changes in the yield curve's shape affect the inverse floater's value. Simply assuming that "interest rates" rise or fall by a particular number of basis points means all interest rates along the Treasury yield curve change by the same amount (i.e., a parallel shift in the yield curve). Our discussion clearly demonstrates this approach is naive. The value of an inverse floater requires a more in-depth analysis than a simple assumption of parallel shifts in the yield curve. Specifically, the valuation model must simulate changes in the yield curve's shape and slope.

INTERPRETATION OF AN INVERSE FLOATER POSITION

Since the capped floater and inverse floater are created from the fixed-rate collateral, the following relationship holds:

long a fixed-rate collateral = long a capped floater + long an inverse floater

Recasting this relationship in terms of an inverse floater (i.e. put the inverse floater on the left-hand side of the equation), we can write

long an inverse floater = long a fixed-rate collateral − long a capped floater.

This relationship can be equivalently expressed as

long an inverse floater = long a fixed-rate collateral + short a capped floater

Thus, the owner of an inverse floater has effectively purchased fixed-rate collateral and sold a capped floater (i.e., shorted a capped floater). Shorting a floater is equivalent to borrowing funds at an uncertain rate. Therefore, shorting a floater is equivalent to borrowing at the reference rate plus the spread. Consequently, the owner of an inverse floater has effectively purchased a fixed-rate asset with borrowed funds (i.e., a levered long position.)

Given this interpretation, an interest rate swap and an inverse floater possess similar characteristics. As described in Chapter 6, an interest rate swap is a contract between two counterparties who agree to exchange periodic interest payments based on some notional principal. One party — the fixed-rate payer — agrees to pay the other party fixed interest rate payments at designated dates for the contract's tenor. The other party — the floating-rate payer — agrees to make interest rate payments that float with some reference rate. An interest rate swap can be interpreted as a package of cash market instruments. The fixed-rate payer has a cash market position that is equivalent to a long position in a floating-rate and a short position in a fixed-rate bond — the short position being the equivalent of borrowing by issuing a fixed-rate bond. Conversely, the floating-rate payer's position is equivalent to purchasing a fixed-rate bond and financing that purchase at a floating-rate, where the floating rate is the swap's reference rate. In other words, the position of a floating-rate payer is equivalent to a long position in a fixed-rate bond and a short position in a floating-rate bond. With the exception of the cap on the floater, the owner of an inverse floater receives fixed and pays floating. Thus, it should not be surprising that the swap market has also been used to value inverse floaters.

DURATION OF AN INVERSE FLOATER

Duration is a measure of a security's price sensitivity to a change in required yield. Because valuations are additive (i.e., the value of collateral is the sum of the floater and inverse floater values), durations (properly weighted) are additive as well. Accordingly, the duration of the inverse floater is related in a particular fashion to the duration of the collateral and the duration of the floater.

The duration of an inverse floater will be a multiple of the duration of the collateral from which it is created. To understand this, suppose that a 30-year fixed-rate bond with a market value of $100 million is split into a floater and an inverse floater with market values of $80 million and $20 million, respectively. Assume also that the duration of the collateral (i.e, the 30-year fixed-rate bond) is 8. Given this information, we know that for a 100 basis point change in required yield that the collateral's value will change by approximately 8% or $8 million (8% times $100 million). Since the floater and inverse floater are created from the underlying collateral, the combined change in value of the floater and the inverse floater must be $8 million given a 100 basis point change in required yield. The question becomes how do we partition the change in value between the floater and inverse floater. If the duration of the floater is small as explained in Chapter 5, then the inverse floater must experience the full force of the $8 million change in value. For this to occur, the duration of the inverse floater must be approximately 40. A duration of 40 will mean a 40% change in the inverse floater's value for a 100 basis point change in required yield and a change in value of approximately $8 million (40% times $20 million).

Notice from our illustration that the duration of an inverse floater is greater the collateral's term to maturity. For those individuals who interpret duration in terms of years (i.e., Macaulay duration) this presents something of a puzzle. After all, how can a security can have a duration greater than the collateral from which it is created? Of course, there is no puzzle. The confusion is the residue from continuing to think about duration in the context in which it was developed by Frederick Macaulay in 1938 — as a measure of the average time taken by a security, on a discounted basis, to return the original investment. The significance and interpretation of Macaulay duration lie in its link to bond price volatility.

In general, assuming that the duration of the floater is close to zero, it can be shown that the duration of an inverse floater is:

$$\text{duration of inverse floater} = (1+L)(\text{duration of collateral}) \times \frac{\text{collateral price}}{\text{inverse price}}$$

where L = leverage of inverse floater.

Index